Y0-BEB-131

Do-It-Yourself Marketing Research

George Edward Breen

Do-It-Yourself Marketing Research

Illustrated by Howard Munce

McGRAW-HILL BOOK COMPANY
New York St. Louis San Francisco Auckland Bogotá Düsseldorf Johannesburg London Madrid Mexico Montreal New Delhi Panama Paris São Paulo Singapore Sydney Tokyo Toronto

Library of Congress Cataloging in Publication Data

Breen, George Edward, 1911—
Do-it-yourself marketing research.

Includes index.
1. Marketing research. I. Title.
HF5415.2.B67 658.8′34 76-43066
ISBN 0-07-007445-3

34567890 KPKP 78654321098

The editors for this book were W. Hodson Mogan and Lester Strong, the designer was Naomi Auerbach, and the production supervisor was Teresa F. Leaden. It was set in Souvenir by University Graphics, Inc.

Printed and bound by The Kingsport Press.

Contents

Preface

The thesis of this book is simple. In many decisions that have to be made by middle and top management in all kinds of companies, more marketing research *can* and *should* be done. And good marketing research can be carried out by nonprofessional people now on the staff.

Marketing research, as described in this book, consists of simple procedures to check, in advance, the correctness of marketing, sales, and product decisions. If errors are made in such decisions, either from lack of judgment or lack of knowledge, resulting losses can easily be too great for a modern company of any size to bear comfortably.

This book, therefore, is a practical guide that shows the nonprofessional how to do *enough* marketing research—and how to do it in a semiprofessional and unbiased manner. It is not written for the professional researcher, or for a college course. It does not assume knowledge of statistics, computers, or anything except the ordinary mathematics common to all of us. In a sense, it is not meant to be "read" like an ordinary book except for the first several chapters. It is to be kept handy for use when a problem arises that can be solved most readily and simply with techniques of marketing research.

Good do-it-yourself marketing research techniques will be found here for middle and top management people in manufacturing, distributing, and retailing. Also, for those engaged in the service trades.

We do not say that problems that involve very large sums of money should be tackled in a do-it-yourself manner by nonprofessionals. Especially where the difference between "go and no-go" is hazy and difficult to see.

But for the host of lesser problems that beset business people, this book shows the nonprofessional how to do marketing research simply and inexpensively. Performed correctly, a little marketing research *is* better than none at all. Very often, indeed, a little marketing research is entirely sufficient. For example, when unexpected insurmountable problems suddenly show up in early research. A new product or a new marketing idea can often be killed early in the game, under these circumstances, before substantial amounts of development money have been spent by a manufacturer.

As I said, none of the activities described in this book requires large sums of money. For the kind of questions that are being addressed here, market studies can frequently be completed for a few hundred dollars. For many managers, in many situations, it is not so much a matter of money as it is using available information, or spending a little personal time. Certainly this is reasonable enough if it means stopping an action that could bring financially troublesome results.

Or, looking at the matter in a more positive way, a little marketing research is good when it can keep a viable idea alive although many people are lukewarm about it, or actively negative.

It is hard to argue with the person who can prove a case with sound marketing research—even of the do-it-yourself variety.

Before ending this preface I want to extend my most sincere appreciation to people who have been of invaluable assistance to me in preparing the book. First, John Sears, Manager of Marketing Research, The Stanley Works. John and I worked closely together for some years in the Marketing Research Department of that company, and I think he had almost a sixth sense of just how he could help me in gathering materials.

Other people whose help I most gratefully acknowledge include: Mr. John Barry and Mrs. Janice A. Parkins, Southam Marketing Research, Don Mills, Ontario; Mr. Charles L. Hoffman, of Charles L. Hoffman Associates, Weatogue, Connecticut; Mr. Richard C. Kilbourn, Director, and Mr. John J. Cabitor, Trade Specialist, Hartford District Office, U.S. Department of Commerce; Mr. Daniel Peters, Vice President, Ducker Research, Inc., of Birmingham, Michigan; Mr. Hubert J. Sebastian, of Trendex, Inc., Westport, Connecticut; all the members of my former staff at The Stanley Works (too numerous over the years to mention singly); Mrs. Joseph Korzeniecky, member of the department and my chief and accurate "looker-upper"; and, finally, Mrs. Carlo A. Berardinelli, my former secretary, typist of this book, friend, and chief helper in all major problems and daily frustrations such as, "What did I do with that paper?" and "I've got a blank in my mind—does accurate have two r's?"

Anyone who attempts a book like this must acknowledge that hundreds of people have taught him many things over many years. I wish I could thank every one of them. Whatever wisdom I may have obtained has come from the people mentioned above and all these others. Finally, special gratitude must go to my wife, who has contributed so much from her knowledge of people and experience in dealing with people. She has been a good teacher.

Here and there throughout the book, I have used the generic term "he" to make the writing flow more smoothly. However, anyone in marketing research knows the increasingly important part being played by women at all levels of the profession. The word "he," therefore, must be understood to mean both men and women.

GEORGE EDWARD BREEN
Farmington, Connecticut

Do-It-Yourself Marketing Research

ONE

What Is Do-It-Yourself Marketing Research?

You can use simple research techniques to help solve your marketing problems. With a do-it-yourself approach you can find better solutions to these problems and make fewer mistakes in judgment.

The whole purpose of this book is to help you to help yourself. It is true, whether you are in manufacturing, or at some point in the distribution channel, or in retailing, that many questions can be answered more wisely and more correctly if a little do-it-yourself marketing research is used.

All of us in business have problems. Some are big, and involve matters of policy. But most of the time we are faced with a constant flow of relatively small questions that must be answered in one way or another. We can guess, we can ask our spouses and friends, or we can do a little semiscientific marketing research. Reliable methods for doing small, quick, and inexpensive studies will be clearly outlined in this book.

To be quite specific, let me give some examples. Does the package of a new product reach out and "grab" the browsing customer? Do the instructions, which seem so simple to the company engineers, come across at all to the final buyer? Is that corner site in a shopping center really right for the kind of customers you want, the price levels and margins you will have to maintain? None of these should be the subject of guesswork. All can be researched.

No business these days, large or small, can afford to make many errors. Or proceed very far with inadequate knowledge of the facts. Far too much money is still being wasted through incorrect decisions made at all levels of marketing.

Consider, for example, in almost every town and city, the number of shopping centers that are only partially successful, because something went wrong in site selection. Or consider the stores filled with slow-moving, unprofitable merchandise. Or the consumers who feel, and *are,* stuck with goods that are unsatisfactory or useless for their needs. This is all a tremendous waste that has been discussed ad infinitum—but goes on and on.

One or two errors in judgment will not put most manufacturers out of business. But a succession of such errors can hurt. And only one mistake in site selection can ruin the life of a store or shopping center. If a marketing decision is to be made, and if that decision can be financially painful when incorrect, then it is wise to consider some marketing research along the lines to be explained in these chapters.

This book is designed, as I said, to help *you* make better market, sales, and product decisions. Better decisions can only help you in your firm. If you own the company, you will make more profit. If you work for a company, and

Most of the time, we're faced with a constant flow of small questions.

A brighter future as top management develops greater faith in your wisdom . . .

perhaps consider yourself as middle or lower management, your own future can become brighter as top management develops greater faith in your wisdom.

Although marketing research may seem beyond your scope and ability, I assure you that it is not. Some studies require the knowledge of professional specialists. Most do not. Every problem, every day, cannot be subjected to marketing research procedures. But many can be, and *should* be.

A Little Introduction to the "Science" of Marketing Research

Marketing research is any *planned* and *organized* effort to gather new facts and new knowledge to help make better market decisions.

Without calling it by name, sales and marketing people have always done informal marketing research. Any salesperson understands that a great deal must be known about customers, their attitudes, and their buying habits. The process of achieving this knowledge may come close to true marketing research.

Much business knowledge gathering can be done more systematically, however. Organizing the search for facts, writing up clear and definite objectives, giving consideration to how the facts can be gathered completely and without bias, and putting these facts together in a way that will bring the most profitable course of action make at least a semiscience of an activity that has previously been haphazard.

Over the years, a number of formal techniques for gathering market knowledge have been developed. These are nothing more than "tools" to help business people do a better job. Some of the highly technical tools are outside of the typical business person's present ability. Nevertheless, the major part of the marketing research tool inventory is quite within his grasp.

It is these techniques that are the subject matter of this book. They are not exotic or esoteric. With a little effort, in most situations, any business person can use them. There are a few rules of the game, to be covered in later chapters when we get down to the *how* of marketing research. Even the word "rules" is too strong, since fresh approaches to a problem often yield surprising results. Nevertheless, many, many people have had a great amount of experience in marketing research over the past half-century. You can benefit from their failures and successes, from knowledge that they gained painfully and expensively.

As we said, American business is approaching a time when it cannot afford to do without proper marketing research. And for most companies, for most marketing problems, this will have to mean a do-it-yourself approach. No one else will be available to do the job.

Why Marketing Research Is So Often Neglected

If marketing research is so necessary, you may ask why it has not been used more for the everyday kinds of questions that business faces. It is good to consider some prevalent attitudes among many management persons, and even among many marketing people themselves. Recognizing these, you may take steps to avoid them.

- There is often fear of a "science" which appears to be mathematical, involved, and mysterious. The fact that many of the techniques are simple is not recognized. Reading some of the professional journals in marketing research is enough to frighten anyone. I hope that this book will help to allay this fear. Of course, larger studies conducted by professionals may be quite mathematical and involved. But the average study need not be so. The trouble is that as the specialists have introduced new theoretical mathematics, many of the simplicities of former years have been forgotten. Because of this fear of the specialist, many smaller problems that *could* and *should* have been researched have not been researched.
- Among middle and lower management there is often real fear of seeming to waste time on research. The fear is not irrational if management does not understand what marketing research can do. Management people may show real impatience; a course of action may look so obviously *right* that they cannot understand further delay. Perhaps they think a market must be "hit" right now, while it is hot. In fact, a competitor may be doing little more than "filling the pipelines" with his new product. Nevertheless there is fear that he will get such a large market share that no one will ever be able to catch up. Hence the need for speed, and hence the well-stocked shelves of wholesalers and retailers, all of whom may later regret this hurry. In all truth, how often must *any* company rush so much that it cannot spare a few weeks to "make sure"? This is as true for the retailer as for the manufacturer.
- Often, as we have said, there is a lack of understanding by management of marketing research in its role of insurance. Even though a proposed course of action may be quite correct, it will be reassuring if a little marketing research shows that management was right all along. It is very likely, in many cases, that marketing research will also point to things that were not known. Small and beneficial changes in product design, some alteration of a color scheme, and themes to use in future advertising can be the result for a manufacturer. Similar extra benefits can come to a wholesaler or retailer. For the retailer, research can tell him what kinds of customers he is getting, where they are coming from, what they think of him as a primary supply source, where he should advertise, and what he should say. This is very basic knowledge that is worth the little effort required to get it.

Professional journals in marketing research are enough to frighten anyone.

▪ And finally, there is a lack of understanding by almost everyone that most marketing research studies can be done quite adequately in a "cheap and dirty" manner. By no means does every study have to involve months of time. Long, costly studies are and *should* be the exception.

A real disservice to American industry has been done if marketing research is made to look so complex that only specialists can perform it. There is need for specialists, but certainly not in every case. You can do most of the investigating work yourself.

What Kind of Problems Lend Themselves to Do-It-Yourself Marketing Research?

In this book I am trying to address myself to all the kinds of business that must market their goods and services. Perhaps I may lean a little strongly toward manufacturing in my illustrations, but the methods can be used by everyone.

It may seem unnecessary to define a problem, but perhaps a few examples will set you to thinking about your own situation, and what you can do:

Confirmation is needed to avoid hearing "I told you so," if something goes wrong with a decision.

1. You have a new product in the design stage. Its sales will not be large, but it can be profitable if costs are kept down. What combination of product features, colors, and design will appeal to the most customers at the lowest cost? Forecast sales will not allow a large and expensive market study, but you would feel more comfortable if you were a little more sure of the information being given to the product design engineers. It is possible that they want to provide even more features and better quality than the typical customer needs or wants.

2. You have to make a decision, but two strong "sides" have made their appearance. Confirmation is needed so that you will not be hearing "I told you so," if something goes wrong. It would be nice to be able to say, "My research shows. . . ." Thus, even if things should turn out badly, you can demonstrate that you truly tried. But—much more likely—the research will point to the proper road to take.

3. You may own, or manage, a retail store in a deteriorating neighborhood. Relocation is desirable, but where? Much local information may already be available, as you will see in a later chapter.

4. Whether you are a manufacturer or retailer, the return on advertising investment is often questioned (and questionable). This can be an extremely difficult kind of research, but you still can do enough, particularly if you are in retailing or are a small manufacturer, to get some idea of what, if anything, advertising is bringing you.

5. You feel the need for more knowledge about your share of market. It may be that you are not doing as well as you think you are. A little more effort

could bring extra and profitable business. Complacency about share of market can be a deadly killer. While studying your market share, there are all sorts of other information that you can easily find. What do customers *really* think about your company, your product, your service, your pricing? It is possible, even *probable,* that you are continuing to do some of the very things that hurt you the most. Like the golfer who practices his swing without the help of a "pro." Sometimes the practicer is merely hardening and increasing the things he was doing wrong in the first place.

Retailers like to know the geographic and economic sources of their customers.

The rest of this book could be taken up with lists of typical questions and problems in the marketing area. A retailer would like to know from what geographic and economic areas he is drawing his customers, so that he can merchandise for this group, or try to broaden his base. A wholesaler would like to know if he is considered a secondary source for many customers, and why—and what he can do about it. A manufacturer wonders if an older product with decreasing sales is really on the way out, or if his salespeople are tired of it and spending too much time on newer and more stimulating products. This could result in some change of emphasis in sales direction and in sales incentives. But the manufacturer has to *know* first.

The problem situations that lend themselves best to the methodologies to be described in this book are the relatively simple, straightforward matters, where easily obtainable facts, opinions, and knowledge can be organized in such a way that proper actions become obvious.

For most active marketing people, at any level of distribution, time is not available for studies that demand weeks or months of effort. Regular work must go forward. So, in this book, we are talking about part-time methods that can easily be justified to yourself and to management.

For anything beyond this scale, the company's own marketing research department should be used, if one exists. Or an outside consultant should be hired.

But thousands of situations cannot economically stand such outside efforts. And it is safe to say that marketing people, at any level of management or distribution, will be stronger in their jobs if they do some marketing research on their own. At every point in distribution, it is always wise for the decision makers to "get out in the market" frequently. For a retailer, this includes some time on the floor. Do-it-yourself marketing research can be a *planned* way of learning about the market, and can be the most instructive of all.

It's always wise for decision makers to "get out in the market" frequently.

Begin Putting the Problem on Paper

At this point it seems to be a reasonable recommendation that you begin listing those questions and problems for which you would like to have more

First, list areas in which you may make a weak and doubtful decision for want of facts.

information, and where you have almost an instinctive feeling that you could make a wiser decision if you just had more knowledge.

You are not ready yet to think about how you will *do* the job of getting the information. All you are going to do is to list those areas where you feel that you may make a weak and doubtful decision for want of facts.

A quick inspection of your list will point to those situations which clearly require the services of a consultant. You do not have the time or the money to do them yourself.

Other questions will be removed from your list because, in your own good judgment, they probably cannot be done at all. You would like to know something about your competitor's plans, for example. But short of industrial espionage (illegal) this will be impossible.

But after all these eliminations you will probably be left with a list of questions where a little organized effort on your part can develop answers.

Summary

I have tried to lead you to the belief that there is much marketing research that can be done without employing a professional, either from your company or from outside.

If you have followed along on this preliminary discussion, you probably realize that you, too, have some decisions to make—decisions that can be more soundly made with more facts.

Remember that there are three things that are much too easy for all of us:

1. It is too easy to say no to a new product or a new idea. An action that is never taken cannot fail. It might have been profitable, but no one will ever know.

2. It is too easy to take the simple road in reaching a decision. To talk to a few customers, to your wife, or to a few people at a cocktail party, and then make a decision. This is not marketing research; often it is no more than a "cop-out."

3. And, finally, it is too easy to say that there is no time for good marketing research. This is one of the most frequent situations. Having ruminated on an idea for weeks and months, suddenly everyone wants action *now*. Rarely, as a matter of fact, is this sudden speed really necessary. Moving rapidly ahead, saying "damn the torpedoes," can sink the ship.

The next chapter will begin an explanation of *how* a problem can be identified and how work can be started on getting necessary facts to solve the problem.

TWO

Evaluation of a Problem

The facts and knowledge that you need are more easily obtainable, in most cases, than you probably realize. This information will come either from secondary, published sources, or through some form of communication with people who know the answers. In later chapters we will cover all the standard ways of communication: the mail questionnaire, telephone interviewing, group sessions, and others. Many times all that is necessary, to borrow an old expression, is a little "gumption" to get started. And a little time and money.

Before you get started, it is extremely important that you have a very clear and accurate definition of the problem that needs studying. Even the smallest problem—if it warrants studying at all—should be defined carefully, and agreed upon by all those who are now or *will be* concerned with the findings.

If those who will be required to act upon the results are not convinced of the need for the study in the first place, nothing at all will happen. All marketing research people have had this experience. You will, too, if you do not lay the groundwork carefully. To ignore human relations—you may call it "company politics"—is to invite disaster.

The most important first step of any research, be it large or small, is to "sell" both superiors and subordinates on the necessity of doing the study at all. Higher management can neglect the findings; subordinates can nullify them. It is almost impossible to convince any person, high or low on the business ladder, to do what he does not want to do or thinks is wrong. Presidents of corporations have discovered this fact. With all legal authority granted by corporate charter, they still must persuade their immediate subordinates, or often nothing happens.

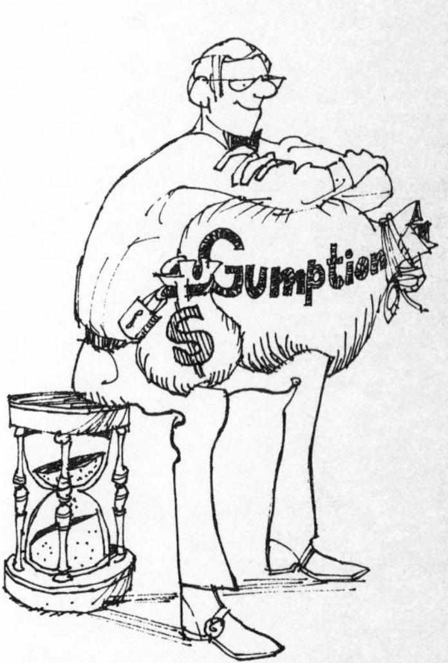

All you need is time, money, and gumption.

Statement of Why a Particular Problem Is Worth Studying

As part of your selling job, and also as a means of getting the precise problem into writing, there are some preliminary and very important steps that should be taken.

These steps require no more than a few hours, or a day or two, depending upon the circumstances and how many people must be consulted. My only hesitation in writing this chapter is that this preliminary work will sound too formidable and tedious, when actually it is neither. The final study will be much more readily accepted, and much more likely to be acted upon, if you do these things.

First, ask yourself some preliminary questions (I'll assume that you have chosen one problem by now that you would like to work on):

Are you leaning in one direction, or are there alternative actions?

1. What are the probable alternative actions that can be taken, depending upon the findings of a research project? If there are *no* alternatives, as sometimes happens, then a study is useless.

2. If there are alternative actions, is there already some disagreement about them? Who is on each side? How important would their opposition or support be? In general, how thorough must your study be to convince some of the people involved?

3. In your own opinion, do the several alternative actions have equal merit? Or are you leaning in one direction yourself? You must "know thyself" very well if you are to do unbiased research.

4. What can go *wrong* if a bad decision is made? It is time to begin getting a numerical handle on the importance of this problem. This will determine how much can be spent for research.

5. What can go *right?* This is the opposite of question 4 above, but requires separate thought. What can you do for your company by helping the right decision to be made?

6. Is the decision one that can really be made more wisely through research? A question can be very important, but not lend itself to research at all. It would be almost impossible, for example, if you are in manufacturing or wholesaling, to prove through research that your salespeople would sell more goods if they drove comfortable, middle-size cars instead of small ones. It can be presumed that comfortable salespeople will do a better job. But even comparing one year of small cars with another year of larger cars would introduce so many variables that the results would be valueless. The same thing would be true with other methods of sampling.

7. At this point—even though there is no final "go or no-go" in the particular study you have selected—it should begin to be more clear whether a do-it-yourself marketing research project will be feasible. You may have a feeling by now that too much time will be required, and management will probably decide to use older decision-making processes. But I urge courage. If the proposition is worthwhile, and can ensure greater safety of investment and profit, management will often surprise you by saying yes. *But only if you have done your homework.*

The above points are preliminary. The matters below are for your own consideration before any formal proposal is made. It would be good to get even these into writing—questions and answers both—even though no other person will see them in this form.

It's good sense to get as much advice from others as possible.

Getting Opinions of Others

It is good sense to get as much advice from others as possible. If you are going to propose some do-it-yourself marketing research, it is doubly important to do so, especially if the whole field is new to your company. If other people are to act upon your findings, their prior agreement to purposes, methods, and procedures is essential.

Let me take an illustration from manufacturing. The same human actions and reactions could be expected in any type of business. Product ideas do not originate from nowhere. Someone, either in product engineering, marketing, sales, or some sort of development group, first gets the notion. In the manner of all human beings, having had the idea in the first place, he is "stuck" with it. No longer can he ever be completely unbiased. Now, unless the idea is foolish, a group of other people, at various levels, will begin to lend their support.

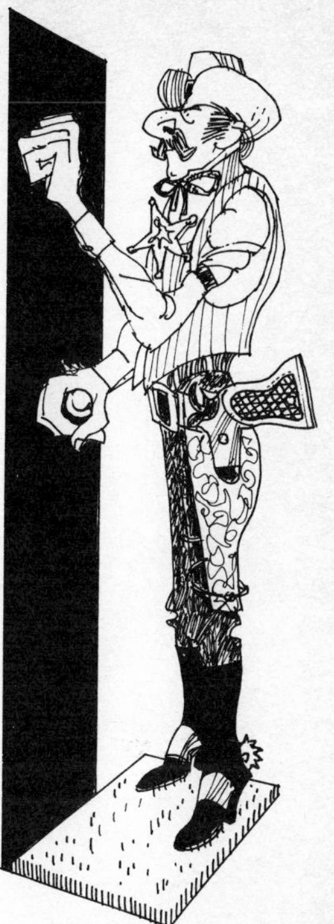

If every new idea is killed off for safety's sake and conservatism, the sheriff can be expected at the door.

Again, in the normal human way, an opposition group will spring up. The idea is good, they will say, but it will not sell. It was tried once during the 1940s, and completely flopped. A competitor tried a version of it, and *he* failed.

It is certainly healthy for the company that these pro and con groups exist. If everyone was "for" everything, the company would be bankrupt in short order. But if every new idea is killed off for the sake of safety and conservatism, the sheriff can also be expected at the door.

Marketing research, even the smallest of do-it-yourself kinds, will give everyone a say. Who should be studied? What geographical areas should be covered? What research methods are most likely to uncover the "real truth"? What particular topics absolutely have to be included? Each contending team has its time at bat. The research will be the better for it, and the results will be much less likely to be questioned.

Depending on the study itself and the kind of business you are in, such groups as in the following list should be consulted. If you are going to do a small study, the consultation will be once-over-lightly, since few people will care a great deal, or get very excited over the matter. But even with a small study, you may regret it later on if you miss seeing someone who can later have a knife out for your findings.

- *Product design, product engineering.* These persons are very likely to be highly biased in favor of their own ideas.
- *The sales department* (if sales and marketing are separate). At all levels of distribution, the sales department can quickly *prove* that a product will not sell—by not selling it. Usually, this is not conscious sabotage, but is just as effective.
- *Advertising, packaging.* These departments can tell you in advance some matters they would like to know to help them do a better job later on.
- *Manufacturing people.* As with the advertising and packaging departments, your research can help the factory do a better job. They want to know exactly what colors, materials, configurations, and so on are acceptable. There are many opportunities for cost cutting here.

Banks are possible sources of data.

- *Upper management.* The upper management people are sometimes hard to catch, and obviously they should not be bothered with every small job. But if your supervisor, and *your supervisor's* supervisor, is interested in your do-it-yourself study, it is more likely to "fly."
- *A few good customers.* Manufacturers and wholesalers usually have a few very good customers that can advise on a proposed study. It would be foolish not to use them.
- *Subordinates.* In all areas of distribution, including retailing, your subordinates are very likely to have sound suggestions to make your study more useful and realistic. Use these people.
- *Noncompetitive business.* Particularly in retailing, it is always possible that some sort of cooperative research can be arranged, spreading the cost around. This might be a combined study of the customers of a shopping area, for example.
- *Newspapers.* Even large manufacturers can get unexpected help from local newspapers. Local retailers would be foolish not to use this source.
- *Your banker.* This applies to every business from small retailer to large manufacturer. Many banks now have on hand, or have access to, certain information, some of which may be useful in any specific study, and thus are possible sources of data.

Much more on source material will be covered in a later chapter. I only mention newspapers and the banks here, since in some cases they can be helpful in the planning stage of a study.

What is likely to be the short- and long-term cost of a wrong decision?

Financial Importance of the Problem

Very early in this planning stage (to be covered in the next chapter), it is necessary to decide on the amount of time and money that can be spent. You should have already given some thought to this matter.

It is one of the unhappy facts of life for a dedicated marketing researcher that there has to be a limit. It would be nice to study and study and study, or to get greater and greater accuracy. But this is obviously impossible, even for the situations that involve the greatest risk.

Before starting specific plans, therefore, you must arrive at some maximum figure that this particular research can stand. To help you think about this (even at the risk of repeating a little), consider these two questions:

1. *What is very likely to be the short- and long-term cost of a wrong decision?* No management will approve much money for research if risks of loss are very low, even if the very worst happens. If we *do* produce the widget, fill the pipelines, do a little advertising, and then find that we have "laid an egg"—if only a few thousand dollars can be lost under these very worst conditions, a thousand-dollar study is clearly not called for.

2. *What is very likely to be the short- and long-term profit from a correct decision?* Even here there are real limitations on research costs. What percentage of the greatest possible future profit can be spent to "make sure"? As an example, consider a retailer who would like to devote some selling area to recreation goods. National figures may be available for average sales per square foot for this type of merchandise. The total size of this particular store will allow only a few hundred square feet to be made available for these new goods. With the greatest success, therefore, we can still predict that sales and profits will be modest. How much is research worth in this situation? Probably the store management will decide that it cannot spend very much.

Summary up to Now

If you have followed through with me in these first two chapters, here is where we now stand:

- You would not be reading this book if you were not interested in the possibility of doing some marketing research yourself.
- You have listed a few problems where you would like more knowledge and facts.
- You have decided on one problem where you would like to start.
- You have talked over the problem and its possible solution with a number of people who have direct or indirect interest in its solution.
- You have made a preliminary decision about the amount of money that you believe should be spent on this particular study.

Still to be decided is *how* the research is to be done. The remainder of the book concerns itself with this how.

But first a few words of caution and painfully learned wisdom. Marketing research is wholly useless unless something is *done* with the results. Not only should there be a clear purpose for the research, but there should be a clear understanding *in advance* about how the findings will be used for the advantage of the company. Knowledge for knowledge's sake can be precious to a scientist; it can be a waste of time and money for the commercial profit-making organization. Not one bit of information should be collected that cannot be used, either now or in the near future.

There will always be surprises!

This does not mean that there never are any surprises. Research may reveal a completely different marketing world than we had thought. But this is clearly a useful finding.

To make a point, let me be a little ridiculous. If we should find that our product is used slightly more by blue-eyed people than brown-eyed people, this would be interesting to a sociologist. It *might* indicate that we should change our finish a bit. But the likelihood is that nothing can or will be done.

Advertising cannot be directed only to blue-eyed people, or to brown-eyed people, and so on. We would have a case of fascinating futility.

The next chapter will show you how to write a research proposal for management. A clear, well-thought-out proposal is just as important in many ways as the completed study. You cannot have one without the other. A badly written proposal may kill off a much-needed study before it starts. Or it may lead to a study that is not done thoroughly.

The very worst minute in the life of a marketing research person comes when he has presented a study; there is a moment of silence, and then some important officer of the company says, "but you have not said a word about the West"—or about retailer reaction, or whatever. Somehow, in planning the study, an important phase has inadvertently been overlooked. That is why these first three chapters are being devoted to planning and preparation. A good research study cannot skip any important matter that will later affect sales and profits.

THREE

How to Plan a Study

Get It into Writing

If you are now convinced that there are marketing questions which you could answer better with do-it-yourself research (and there *must* be), then it is important to get the problem and the plan of attack into writing. A small study that requires only a small amount of time and money will require only a short write-up. Larger, important studies should be done more extensively.

In either case, there is something about writing that forces precise thinking. Aspects of the question at hand are not overlooked. Portions of the study that are really not vital show themselves and can be discarded.

Moreover (a point that needs reemphasizing), a written plan is more likely to send you to others for guidance and help. I really cannot overstate the need for getting the "team" lined up in advance. This does not mean that everyone thinks alike at the start—or that complete agreement will be reached when the study is over. But it can mean that everyone important sees the need for research, approves the method by which it will be accomplished, and has at least implied that he will abide by the results when the facts and recommendations are presented. Needless to say, this is half of the battle.

A fad word of the business world at the moment is "involved." Corporations advertise that they want to be "involved" (without being very clear about what they mean), but the psychological principle is sound. The more people who become involved in one way or another, the better the study will be and the more likely it is to be acted upon.

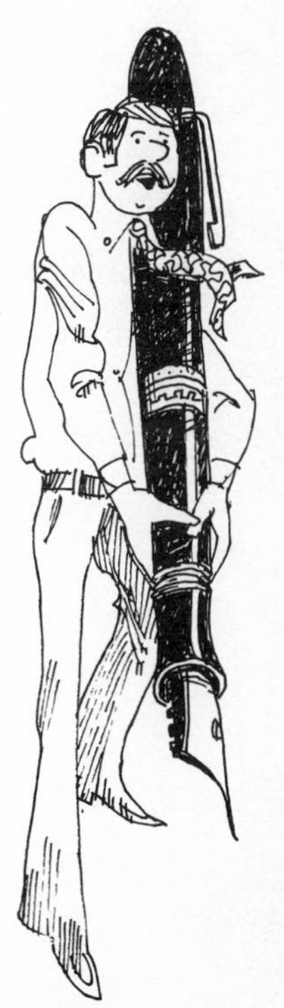

Get the problem and plan of attack into writing.

Statement of Why the Study Needs Doing

The first portion of your plan should clearly outline the specific reasons why time and money should be devoted to this study:

1. What is the specific nature of the step that we want to take? A new product, a new store location, or whatever?
2. What specific information do we lack? What facts, knowledge, or opinions will enable us to make a wiser decision?
3. What are the alternative actions that can be taken, either with research or without it? Exactly *how* will the information that we propose to get help us choose among these alternatives?

For the most part, just from your preliminary work discussed in Chapter 2, you are ready to write this section of your plan.

Spend as little as possible, so long as good research is done.

Statement of Money That Can Be Spent

Again, from your own preliminary thinking, and from your discussions with other people, you have a pretty good idea of what this marketing research is really worth. You know the costs involved in a wrong decision. You have a fair notion of the profits that will develop if a "go" signal is given by research.

What, then, is this marketing research worth? Perhaps there is a decision that can bring an extra $100,000 in profits during the first three years. Can you afford just 1 percent of this to be sure you are right? Or 2 percent? Perhaps less than 1 percent? It is impossible to be definite here, since management attitudes vary greatly. If marketing research has never before been attempted by your company, it will be wise to spend as little as possible, so long as good research is done.

It will also be wise to have alternative plans ready. For $500 you can do this. For $1,000 you can do this much more. The lower-cost study will take so many weeks; the higher-cost study will take longer, but produce more. Management (if you need permission of a supervisor) can then decide how much is enough, and what degree of risk it is willing to take for the sake of saving money and time.

It is probably unnecessary to say that the better and more complete the plan, the better the chance you will have of doing a thorough study. The plan, in other words, is a selling instrument to management and to yourself. You are selling what you know is a good product, one that you believe in. Others must be made to believe in it, too. Important marketing benefits at a low cost make a pretty good selling argument.

Somewhere in that great big world are your sources of knowledge.

Sources of Information for Plan

You now have reached the most interesting part of planning. You have a question that needs answering, you have a decision to make, and you want more facts. Somewhere out there in that great big world are your sources of knowledge. There are people who know how to help you. There are printed sources, if you only know where they are.

If you had hundreds of thousands of dollars to spend, you could throw out a huge study, like a big net to catch a small fish. But you do not have that much money. Nor, in fact, do you have the time, even if you do have the money.

The trick is, of course, to know how to go to the right printed, secondary sources. And to know how to communicate directly with those people in the field who have the knowledge that you want.

Broadly, your sources will be divided into two groups: *secondary* material already available from the government, from associations, etc., and *primary* material which you will have to develop yourself through one or another marketing research technique.

For secondary sources, you may refer to some that are listed in Chapter 4 of this book. Or you may know of sources in your own industry. More often than can be imagined, companies which have belonged to their own trade associations for years have failed to use the facts that almost every association collects. More on that later.

For primary sources, you must now decide which of the information-gathering methods, to be described in later chapters, will be appropriate for this study. There should first be a very specific description of those people whom it is necessary to contact, such as buyers and sales managers of wholesale houses, people who use pavement breakers and the purchasing agents that buy them, and households which appear close enough to use your shopping center. By carefully listing these people you will free yourself to eliminate respondents who might have interesting viewpoints, but who are not vital to the problem at hand.

Don't disregard the weight of other work bearing down on you.

The way you approach these primary sources must be your own decision, based upon the amount of money you have to spend, the type of information you need, the attitude of your management, and the time you can spare to do the work. However, usually the information needed and the primary sources where the information is available will dictate the kind of research you will use. These research methods are described in detail later in the book; usually the decision between methods is not at all difficult to make.

Not to be disregarded, however, is the weight of other work bearing down upon you. Before deciding on how to approach the primary sources, you must also give some consideration to the time it will take to tabulate and analyze mail questionnaires, for example. I do not want to frighten you; most of the work will not be overly time-consuming. For the most part we are talking about hours, rather than days, whether you are analyzing mail questionnaires, or a few group interviews, or the result of a telephone study.

Read the chapters on *how* to do various kinds of marketing research, and then be very realistic about what can be done in your own particular circumstances.

Nevertheless, your plan must list both secondary and primary sources, and show how, in general, you intend to use them.

Where the Information Is

You are now well on your way to a good plan for research. You have clearly stated your purpose. You have made an estimate of cost. You have some idea of primary and secondary sources. You have made a decision about which method or methods you will recommend to reach both primary and secondary sources.

Various sections of the country hold fast to different life-styles.

Now you must make a judgment about *where* you are going to go. It would be good if you could complete a "national survey" by visiting a few people just around the corner. Unfortunately, more is usually required, in spite of the old joke that it only takes one man sitting on a tack to find that it hurts. Whether your business is in a national market, or a local market around a shopping center, there must be a good reason not to take your sample of opinions and facts from every part of your territory.

Once again, time and money enter the picture, and a judgment must be made. Would an Eastern manufacturer of can openers really have to sample West Coast opinion? Or vice versa? Are can openers used in different fashion in the several parts of the country?

The first guess would be no. Yet it would be wise to check a few sources. In a surprising number of ways, various sections of the country hold fast to different life-styles. In the West, for example, the outdoors life is well known to anyone who has worked in that area. But other things are less obvious. Houses look different and are decorated differently. Even the tools used for construction tend to differ. Customs and taste, in such things as coffee brewing, vary markedly from coast to coast.

Radio and television have, fortunately, not completely destroyed the individuality of North, South, East, and West. Up until a few years ago, for example (and I dare say it is still true), one could walk across the bridge from Cincinnati into Kentucky and feel in a different world. To some real extent, all these differences affect the purchase and sale of a great many products.

But you still must use judgment. Most manufacturers cannot produce models for East, West, North, and South. Shopping centers cannot have a different set of stock and fixtures for separate sections of their areas. And many studies can still be done fairly close at hand, with reasonable certainty that the results in other areas would not be materially different.

Importance of Women

It should not be necessary to point to the growing importance of women in the marketplace, for both consumer and nonconsumer goods. But for the few male chauvinists left around, you must be sure that your study—if it pertains to persons of both sexes—contains an adequate representation of each. As women attain higher positions in industry, this will have to be reckoned with in the design of a sample. The relative weight of women in consumer purchasing decisions appears to vary among products. But even in the choice of an automobile brand, formerly considered (by men) a masculine prerogative, women have had an increasing voice. It would be a mistake to assume offhand that women have little to do with industrial purchasing. Within a decade or two it is probable that women will have equal positions with men right up the executive ladder. And, interestingly enough, many home decisions that used to be made almost entirely by women are being shared with husbands and children. All these things must be remembered in planning a study.

Deadline for Completing the Study

There is nothing worse for anyone conducting marketing research than to discover that the final decision was made before the study had been completed. Silly as this may sound, it has nevertheless happened to a great many fact finders who were too slow about their work.

A great many fact finders are too slow about their work.

Do not take this point too lightly. What may happen will follow a scenario like this:

1. You see the need for studying a question before some marketing decision is made. You are told to go ahead. Meanwhile, of course, you have done all the consulting, planning, and preparing recommended in these first three chapters.
2. But meanwhile (we will assume you are in manufacturing, even though a similar story could be told about other distribution levels) product engineering says that it might as well go ahead on preliminary work of design, or redesign. What they are doing "can always be stopped, or changed in direction." "Why," they say, "waste this time just waiting for a study?"
3. Likewise, the sales department makes preliminary plans. The agency is brought in for early thought sessions. And so on. All sorts of people are busy on this new product before the study has even been completed.
4. By the time the study is well under way, a great momentum has been built up. It can all be stopped, but the stopping becomes increasingly difficult every passing day. A "little preliminary work" by each of a number of departments amounts to a lot of time and money. People are caught up in the moving tide, and the poor individual doing marketing research may come to feel like a little Dutch boy with his finger in the dike.

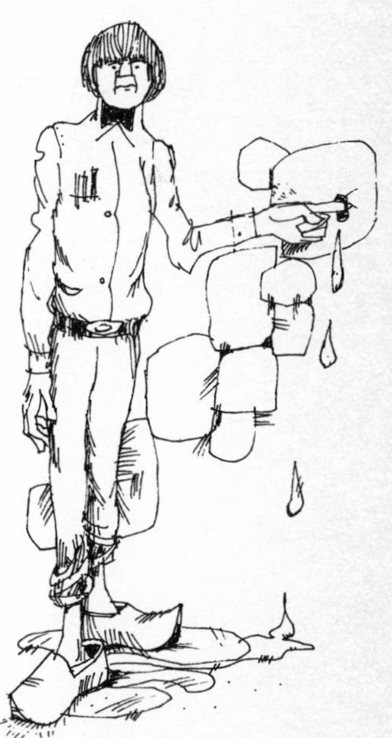

The poor researcher may come to feel like the Dutch boy with his finger in the dike.

I have no magic way of alleviating this type of situation. A record of success in marketing decisions will help. Speed in completing a study can be a very important element. And, to help the speed, if young people from several departments are actually used in part of the study itself, a very good psychological atmosphere is created. Any department will be more willing to listen to its own people; and their communication with that department will be more constant than yours. The best thing of all, if people are getting edgy, is to get the study *done.* That is why it is often wise to be satisfied with less than academic perfection in sampling the market.

A study that is produced in time to be useful is certainly far better than a professionally ideal study that *follows* a decision rather than leading it.

Outline of Final Report

Now it is possible and advisable to write an outline of the final report, to show what it will be like. This can be included with the plan and is all that many executives may want to read. The outline could take somewhat the shape of the following:

1. Purpose of study. Short statement of questions that need research and why.
2. Possible actions as a result of findings.
3. Secondary sources covered.
4. Primary sources covered, and how.
5. Extent of coverage.
6. Findings and recommendations. Show possible alternatives.
7. Actions that should be taken in the case of each of the possible sets of findings.

It's often good to let someone else have the credit for a good study.

In a sense this effort is simply a version of your plan. But it is written as an outline of the final report and will make the writing easier when that time comes. It gives the prospective user a last chance to find a weakness, or an area missed.

These first three chapters have tried again and again to show the value of communication and cooperation. It is often good, especially for a young marketing person, to let someone else have the "credit" for a good study and resulting profitable action. Giving up a little credit in the early days of marketing research will build a solid foundation for later, larger, and more important studies. When the company has reached the point at which someone regularly says, "Let's do a little research and get the facts," then you have accomplished something very good.

Now you are ready to begin actual work on a study. From here on, this book will concentrate on sources of knowledge and how to tap them.

FOUR

How to Use Secondary Sources

You must use the work previously done by other people if it is at all relative to your problem. Otherwise you could very likely be wasting your time and the company's money. An almost unlimited amount of material is available from hundreds of sources. You cannot make an exhaustive study of all these publications, but there are some that are easily obtainable and can be quite useful in the solution of your problem.

These published sources, depending upon their nature, can be used in several ways in your work:

1. To help in the *planning* of your study. For example, in choosing areas for most productive field work.
2. To give background information that will "fill out" what you find. Your own research can become more valuable for your company if it shows the "whole picture," i.e., your research in a setting of the *complete* market. You may find information against which you can measure your own findings and experience.
3. Or you may find, if you are lucky, that the study you want to do has already been completed and published by someone else. Then you must make a judgment about how complete and accurate this other study is, and whether it really answers your *own specific needs.*
4. Statistical series that are published on a regular basis can give you benchmarks to measure how you are doing in comparison with the market.

In the rest of this chapter I will cover some of the most readily available materials. The kinds of offices and people that are ready to help you will also be discussed.

You may start with the sources listed here, but undoubtedly you will find other sources for any particular study. Just for the sake of having some organization of this chapter, I intend to list sources under several headings, such as federal government, state government, local government, associations, and so on.

Secondary sources of information are listed under several headings—federal government, state government, associations, etc.

Federal Government

Department of Commerce The first place that you should go for statistics, if at all possible, is the local field office of the U.S. Department of Commerce. If you cannot go there personally, you can send a letter, explaining what you need to know, and asking for whatever publications they think will help. You may have to buy these materials through the Government Printing Office, Washington, D.C., but the advice can be obtained locally. At present there are field offices in over forty cities in the fifty states and Puerto Rico.

Table P-1. General Characteristics of the Population: 1970—Continued

[For minimum base for derived figures (percent, median, etc.) and meaning of symbols, see text]

Census Tracts	Hartford—Con.														
	Tract 5008	Tract 5009	Tract 5010	Tract 5011	Tract 5012	Tract 5013	Tract 5014	Tract 5015	Tract 5016	Tract 5017	Tract 5018	Tract 5019	Tract 5020	Tract 5021	Tract 5022
RACE															
All persons	**1 703**	**3 621**	**4 376**	**1 296**	**2 935**	**3 651**	**4 518**	**5 737**	**1 170**	**2 739**	**5 938**	**1 118**	**966**	**811**	**1 158**
White	979	631	481	145	135	597	399	543	972	1 191	1 704	1 101	930	772	1 078
Negro	645	2 922	3 799	1 141	2 779	3 030	4 044	5 152	181	1 486	3 891	16	17	30	61
Percent Negro	37.9	80.7	86.8	88.0	94.7	83.0	89.5	89.8	15.5	54.3	65.5	1.4	1.8	3.7	5.3
AGE BY SEX															
Male, all ages	**844**	**1 692**	**1 979**	**659**	**1 358**	**1 720**	**2 081**	**2 748**	**809**	**1 449**	**3 091**	**555**	**604**	**428**	**529**
Under 5 years	108	267	317	46	219	280	321	359	43	162	413	45	27	1	33
3 and 4 years	40	124	152	19	75	117	130	134	18	62	161	17	11	–	9
5 to 9 years	95	281	455	58	203	309	250	370	35	202	424	35	17	–	12
5 years	13	75	94	11	42	52	60	86	10	30	85	7	4	–	1
6 years	20	56	100	10	54	71	61	71	4	38	70	8	3	–	3
10 to 14 years	105	245	337	84	148	223	191	319	33	155	339	44	24	2	13
14 years	17	52	54	16	30	44	33	52	3	21	63	8	7	–	1
15 to 19 years	81	165	176	77	118	176	155	220	41	140	232	40	11	4	14
15 years	21	43	41	16	35	44	30	53	6	29	30	9	1	–	1
16 years	14	39	54	12	17	35	36	49	10	33	52	6	1	–	–
17 years	8	39	35	26	21	48	25	43	6	29	45	7	1	1	1
18 years	17	23	26	13	22	23	31	49	13	29	54	8	4	1	4
19 years	21	21	20	10	23	26	33	26	6	20	51	10	4	2	8
20 to 24 years	76	119	90	44	91	113	226	252	39	76	301	48	35	23	72
20 years	15	22	23	16	12	23	49	48	3	12	63	8	–	2	9
21 years	16	29	20	10	24	17	45	52	1	15	51	9	7	2	10
25 to 34 years	106	173	228	64	210	221	374	412	82	212	492	76	46	128	106
35 to 44 years	106	142	117	83	143	174	231	285	136	160	324	62	87	103	59
45 to 54 years	70	122	156	87	95	108	185	275	223	129	267	86	115	73	70
55 to 59 years	29	59	40	45	46	28	51	75	86	80	101	42	41	27	31
60 to 64 years	22	40	16	28	36	19	29	55	51	53	63	20	46	35	31
65 to 74 years	43	56	32	38	35	59	37	86	33	57	103	28	79	26	62
75 years and over	3	23	15	5	14	10	31	40	7	23	32	29	76	6	26
Female, all ages	**859**	**1 929**	**2 397**	**637**	**1 577**	**1 931**	**2 437**	**2 989**	**361**	**1 290**	**2 847**	**563**	**362**	**383**	**629**
Under 5 years	143	264	316	34	236	307	313	330	56	157	402	48	9	–	30
3 and 4 years	54	112	150	18	92	115	124	133	19	62	165	14	4	–	5
5 to 9 years	107	258	397	56	174	260	265	343	36	169	366	27	14	–	11
5 years	25	53	72	9	39	55	62	75	7	34	85		[illegible]		3
6 years	[illegible]	[illegible]	99	10	34	52	69	72	10						
10 to 14 years															

FIG. 1 Example of the type of information available in census tracts, 1970 *Census of Population and Housing*, U.S. Department of Commerce, Bureau of the Census, issued May 1972.

Of particular interest are:

CENSUS OF POPULATION Too familiar to all of us to require much description here. Very detailed information on the population, its social and economic makeup.[1]

THE ECONOMIC CENSUSES These are truly said by the Department to be the "primary source of facts" about the structure and functioning of the economy and, therefore, provide information essential for government business. There is widespread use of the economic censuses by manufacturers and distributors who need to establish measures of their potential markets in terms of areas, kinds of business, and kinds of products; and by management in various industries and trades which need facts for purposes of economic or sales forecasting, allocation of advertising budgets, and location of plants, warehouses, and stores.[2]

The censuses make facts available on a national basis and also for each state. States are further broken down where possible into Standard Metropolitan Statistical Areas (the larger cities and their suburbs; henceforth to be called SMSAs), counties, and single large cities.

The economic censuses include: Manufacturers, Retail Trade, Selected Service Industries, Wholesale Trade, Construction Industries, Transportation, Minority-Owned Business Enterprises, and Statistics for Outlying Areas (Puerto Rico, Virgin Islands, and Guam).[3]

CENSUS OF HOUSING Occupancy, tenure, color or ethnic group of occupants, persons, rooms, persons per room, status and other housing characteristics on a comprehensive basis.[4] Figures available on a national basis, divisions, states, urban, rural areas, counties, city blocks, and census tracts.

Census figures are available on a national basis.

COUNTY BUSINESS PATTERNS Provides information by state, and by county within the state on: agriculture, mining, contract construction, major types of manufacturing, transportation, wholesale trade, retail trade, financial, insurance, and real estate establishments. Gives number of employees in total, taxable payrolls, total units, and number of units by various employment size classes. Also has a similar breakdown for SMSAs.[5]

CENSUS TRACT REPORTS Provides information from the census of Population and the Census of Housing about "tracts" within SMSAs. There are 241 reports available on metro areas. Reports cover general population characteristics, social characteristics, income breakdowns, employment information, housing characteristics, and many other matters. In Hartford, Connecticut, for example, there are over 150 tracts for the city and county and adjacent areas. This fine breakdown is useful for many studies.

[1]U.S. Bureau of the Census, Social and Economic Statistics Administration, *Census of Population: 1970.*

[2]U.S. Department of Commerce, *Selected Publications to Aid Business and Industry.*

[3]U.S. Bureau of the Census, Social and Economic Statistics Administration, *Economic Census.*

[4]U.S. Bureau of the Census, Social and Economic Statistics Administration, *Census of Housing.*

[5]U.S. Bureau of the Census, *County Business Patterns.*

7-16 CONNECTICUT 1972 CENSUS OF MANUFACTURES

TABLE 6. **General Statistics by Industry for Standard Metropolitan Statistical Areas: 1972 and 1967**—Continued

Ind. code	Standard metropolitan statistical area and industry	1972 Establishments: Total (number)	1972 Establishments: With 20 employees or more (number)	1972 All employees: Number (1,000)	1972 All employees: Payroll (million dollars)	1972 Production workers: Number (1,000)	1972 Production workers: Man-hours (millions)	1972 Production workers: Wages (million dollars)	1972 Value added by manufacture (million dollars)	1972 Cost of materials (million dollars)	1972 Value of shipments (million dollars)	1972 Capital expenditures, new (million dollars)	1967 All employees (1,000)	1967 Value added by manufacture (million dollars)
	HARTFORD[1]													
	ALL INDUSTRIES, TOTAL.	1 192	437	86.0	891.0	51.0	104.0	432.3	1 389.5	1 194.8	2 540.4	58.0	110.6	1 432.2
20	FOOD AND KINDRED PRODUCTS. . E1	62	21	2.2	20.0	1.5	2.7	11.4	89.5	107.2	196.2	3.9	3.0	70.9
202	DAIRY PRODUCTS	16	7	.9	7.5	.6	.9	3.7	14.2	46.7	60.4	1.0	1.2	22.2
205	BAKERY PRODUCTS.	12	4	.6	5.5	.4	.8	3.4	12.9	14.4	27.3	.6	.9	10.8
2051	BREAD, CAKE, AND RELATED PRODUCTS. .	12	4	.6	5.5	.4	.8	3.4	12.9	14.4	27.3	.6	.9	10.8
208	BEVERAGES. E1	11	3	.3	3.9	.3	.5	2.4	49.5	25.4	74.9	1.5	.6	28.4
22	TEXTILE MILL PRODUCTS.	21	15	2.5	17.3	2.1	4.4	12.8	30.0	19.2	48.1	3.6	2.2	21.3
226	TEXTILE FINISHING, EXCEPT WOOL . .	4	4	1.0	7.4	.8	1.6	5.4	12.9	4.1	16.8	2.4	(NA)	(NA)
2262	FINISH. PLTS, MANMADE FIBER, SILK. .	4	4	1.0	7.4	.8	1.6	5.4	12.9	4.1	16.8	2.4	(NA)	(NA)
23	APPAREL, OTHER TEXTILE PRODS . .	28	18	1.4	8.6	1.1	1.7	5.2	19.4	11.4	30.7	.1	1.2	10.8
233	WOMEN'S AND MISSES' OUTERWEAR. . .	14	13	1.1	6.0	.9	1.3	4.0	13.8	9.0	22.8	.1	.9	7.7
2337	WOMEN'S, MISSES' SUITS AND COATS . .	5	5	.6	3.6	.5	.7	2.2	6.7	6.8	13.4	(Z)	(NA)	(NA)
24	LUMBER AND WOOD PRODUCTS	38	8	.6	4.6	.5	1.0	3.3	7.8	9.5	17.3	.2	(NA)	(NA)
25	FURNITURE AND FIXTURES . . . E1	26	11	.9	7.5	.7	1.4	4.6	13.5	11.9	25.2	.4	.7	8.2
251	HOUSEHOLD FURNITURE. E2	11	5	.4	2.5	.3	.6	1.5	5.2	5.5	10.7	.1	(NA)	(NA)
254	PARTITIONS AND FIXTURES.	8	5	.4	4.2	.3	.6	2.6	7.0	5.6	12.4	.3	(NA)	(NA)
26	PAPER AND ALLIED PRODUCTS. . . .	22	14	1.7	17.3	1.3	2.7	11.4	37.3	34.5	71.6	1.9	1.5	24.9
265	PAPERBOARD CONTAINERS AND BOXES. .	8	6	.4	3.9	.3	.7	2.6	7.1	7.2	14.2	.3	(NA)	(NA)
27	PRINTING AND PUBLISHING.	159	45	4.4	37.6	2.6	5.1	21.1	67.0	36.3	103.0	4.7	3.9	47.7
2711	NEWSPAPERS	17	8	1.8	14.6	.7	1.2	6.0	27.3	12.7	40.0	2.1	1.7	19.3
275	COMMERCIAL PRINTING. E1	99	26	1.9	16.9	1.4	2.8	10.9	30.6	19.0	49.4	1.7	(NA)	(NA)
2751	COMMERCIAL PRINTING, LETTERPRESS E2	42	5	.4	3.6	.3	.6	2.1	7.8	6.7	14.5	.5	(NA)	(NA)
2752	COMMERCIAL PRINTING, LITHOGRAPHIC E1	52	19	1.3	12.4	1.0	2.1	8.2	21.2	11.9	32.9	1.1	(NA)	(NA)
279	PRINTING TRADE SERVICES.				[illegible]	.2	.5	2.3	4.5	.5	5.0	.2	(NA)	(NA)
28	CHEMICALS AND ALLIED [illegible]						1.0	3.9	27.1	16.5				
	[illegible]							2.2	17.0					

FIG. 2 From 1972 *Census of Manufactures, Area Series, Connecticut,* U.S. Department of Commerce, Bureau of the Census, issued April 1975. All other states, of course, are available.

36-20 OHIO — 1972 CENSUS OF MANUFACTURES

TABLE 6. **General Statistics by Industry for Standard Metropolitan Statistical Areas: 1972 and 1967**—Continued

Ind. code	Standard metropolitan statistical area and industry	1972											1967	
		Establishments		All employees		Production workers			Value added by manufacture	Cost of materials	Value of shipments	Capital expenditures, new	All employees	Value added by manufacture
		Total (number)	With 20 employees or more (number)	Number (1,000)	Payroll (million dollars)	Number (1,000)	Man-hours (millions)	Wages (million dollars)	(million dollars)	(million dollars)	(million dollars)	(million dollars)	(1,000)	(million dollars)
	CINCINNATI--CONTINUED													
29	PETROLEUM AND COAL PRODUCTS. . .	14	4	1.3	15.1	1.1	2.5	12.0	45.9	91.5	136.8	1.5	(NA)	(NA)
30	RUBBER, MISC. PLASTICS PROD. . .	72	31	4.5	39.1	3.7	7.5	28.2	90.4	62.9	151.3	6.9	(NA)	(NA)
3079	MISCELLANEOUS PLASTICS PRODUCTS. . .	60	27	4.1	35.6	3.4	7.0	26.3	82.0	58.1	138.2	6.4	(NA)	(NA)
31	LEATHER AND LEATHER PRODUCTS . .	14	5	1.3	8.0	1.1	2.1	6.1	13.9	10.1	23.7	.1	1.8	11.3
314	FOOTWEAR, EXCEPT RUBBER.	4	3	1.1	6.9	1.0	1.9	5.3	11.9	8.3	20.0	.1	1.6	9.6
3144	WOMEN'S FOOTWEAR, EXCEPT ATHLETIC. .	4	3	1.1	6.9	1.0	1.9	5.3	11.9	8.3	20.0	.1	(NA)	(NA)
32	STONE, CLAY, GLASS PRODUCTS. . .	104	28	2.3	20.7	1.8	3.5	14.1	48.4	40.1	88.0	5.1	2.9	39.9
327	CONCRETE, GYPSUM, PLASTER PRODS. .	64	15	.9	8.8	.6	1.3	5.6	18.5	19.0	37.6	3.7	1.1	15.7
3272	CONCRETE PRODUCTS, NEC	19	6	.3	2.6	.2	.5	1.9	5.8	3.2	9.0	.4	.3	4.5
3273	READY-MIXED CONCRETE	34	8	.5	5.4	.3	.6	3.3	11.1	13.8	24.9	3.2	.6	9.8
329	MISC. NONMETALLIC MINERAL PRODS. .	20	6	.6	5.2	.4	.8	3.2	15.1	9.0	24.2	.4	(NA)	(NA)
33	PRIMARY METAL INDUSTRIES	58	35	4.9	47.7	4.0	8.3	36.4	83.9	84.6	171.0	3.8	4.0	56.7
332	IRON AND STEEL FOUNDRIES	8	8	.9	6.8	.7	1.4	4.8	9.6	4.9	14.2	.4	1.1	10.9
336	NONFERROUS FOUNDRIES	24	12	.9	7.9	.7	1.4	6.1	13.0	13.3	26.9	.4	.8	10.0
339	MISC. PRIMARY METAL PRODUCTS . E1	12	7	.4	3.8	.4	.7	2.8	5.6	2.2	7.4	(D)	(NA)	(NA)
34	FABRICATED METAL PRODUCTS. . . .	228	118	14.4	131.6	10.7	22.1	87.4	230.0	247.4	477.0	11.3	(NA)	(NA)
341	METAL CANS, SHIPPING CONTAINERS. .	5	5	1.2	13.1	1.0	2.2	9.4	26.4	46.5	72.9	1.2	(NA)	(NA)
344	FABRICATED STRUC. METAL PRODS. . .	77	45	5.2	49.0	3.8	8.2	31.9	79.8	106.3	184.8	3.8	4.1	52.5
3441	FABRICATED STRUCTURAL METAL.	17	8	.5	5.3	.4	.8	3.1	9.7	14.2	23.5	.3	.4	5.3
3443	FABRICATED PLATEWORK, BOILER SHOP. .	14	9	.8	7.9	.6	1.2	5.1	12.2	9.7	21.9	.5	.8	11.6
3444	SHEET METALWORK.	25	18	1.8	17.7	1.4	2.8	12.2	27.7	34.5	62.1	.7	1.8	22.3
345	SCREW MACHINE PROD., BOLTS, ETC. .	15	8	.4	3.6	.3	.6	2.4	7.9	6.3	14.3	.4	.5	6.5
346	METAL FORGINGS AND STAMPINGS . . .	32	21	1.7	14.8	1.3	2.6	9.7	23.8	23.4	47.1	1.1	(NA)	(NA)
3469	METAL STAMPINGS, NEC	28	18	1.6	13.7	1.2	2.4	8.9	22.1	21.4	43.3	1.1	(NA)	(NA)
347	METAL SERVICES, NEC. E1	45	10	.9	6.6	.7	1.5	5.0	10.6	9.5	20.0	.9	1.0	10.1
3471	PLATING AND POLISHING. E1	33	7	.6	4.7	.6	1.1	3.6	7.2	6.6	13.8	.6	.5	5.3
349	MISC. FABRICATED METAL PRODUCTS. .	39	23	4.4	40.3	3.2	6.3	26.1	76.3	49.0	124.1	3.8	(NA)	(NA)
3494	VALVES AND PIPE FITTINGS	7	6	3.0	28.1	2.2	4.2	18.6	61.9	36.8	96.0	1.9	3.2	47.0
3495	WIRE SPRINGS	6	4	.4	2.9	.4	.7	2.4	4.8	4.9	9.4	.9	(NA)	(NA)
3499	FABRICATED METAL PRODUCTS, NEC . . .	19	11	.9	8.6	.6	1.2	4.7	8.8	6.4	17.0	[illegible]	[illegible]	[illegible]
35	MACHINERY [illegible]	[illegible]	[illegible]	[illegible]	[illegible]	10.7	21.4	93.0	314.2	[illegible]	[illegible]	[illegible]	[illegible]	[illegible]

FIG. 3 Another example of types of information available from 1972 *Census of Manufactures,* U.S. Department of Commerce, Bureau of the Census, issued April 1975.

7-18 CONNECTICUT — WHOLESALE TRADE—AREA STATISTICS

TABLE 6. Standard Metropolitan Statistical Areas, by Kind of Business Based on 1967 Standard Industrial Classification: 1972

1967 SIC code	Standard metropolitan statistical area and kind of business	Total: Estab-lish-ments (number)	Total: Sales ($1,000)	Total: Inventories, end of year 1972 ($1,000)	Total: Payroll, entire year ($1,000)	Total: Payroll, first quarter 1972 ($1,000)	Total: Paid employees for week including March 12 (number)	Merchant wholesalers: Estab-lish-ments (number)	Merchant wholesalers: Sales ($1,000)	Other operating types[1]: Estab-lish-ments (number)	Other operating types[1]: Sales ($1,000)
	BRIDGEPORT SMSA										
	WHOLESALE TRADE, TOTAL	567	856 774	64 525	68 235	16 984	7 111	463	498 149	104	358 625
501	MOTOR VEHICLES AND AUTOMOTIVE EQUIPMENT. . . .	63	40 875	5 626	4 788	1 263	600	61	(D)	2	(D)
502	DRUGS, CHEMICALS, AND ALLIED PRODUCTS.	15	33 019	6 631	1 356	336	182	9	23 386	6	9 633
503	PIECE GOODS, NOTIONS, AND APPAREL.	14	55 090	5 675	4 942	1 460	418	13	(D)	1	(D)
504	GROCERIES AND RELATED PRODUCTS	62	(D)	(D)	(D)	(D)	(D)	53	(D)	9	(D)
505	FARM PRODUCTS--RAW MATERIALS	2	(D)	(D)	(D)	(D)	(D)	-	-	2	(D)
506	ELECTRICAL GOODS	53	48 584	6 035	4 353	1 077	459	35	(D)	18	(D)
507	HARDWARE, PLUMBING, HEATING EQUIPMENT,SUPPLIES	36	21 992	4 215	2 924	682	359	32	19 814	4	2 178
508	MACHINERY, EQUIPMENT, AND SUPPLIES	142	100 512	8 853	15 761	3 742	1 505	108	51 918	34	48 594
5091	METALS AND MINERALS.	21	125 482	7 899	4 176	1 036	374	18	(D)	3	(D)
5092	PETROLEUM AND PETROLEUM PRODUCTS	11	118 880	1 332	4 569	1 290	449	4	(D)	7	(D)
5093	SCRAP AND WASTE MATERIALS.	20	(D)	(D)	(D)	(D)	(D)	20	(D)	-	-
5094	TOBACCO AND ITS PRODUCTS	5	31 236	889	668	148	74	5	31 236	-	-
5095	BEER, ALE, AND DISTILLED ALCOHOLIC BEVERAGES .	10	67 769	5 902	6 581	1 586	570	9	(D)	1	(D)
5096	PAPER AND ITS PRODUCTS	25	20 373	1 730	2 734	749	304	20	15 189	5	5 184
5097	FURNITURE AND HOME FURNISHINGS	9	4 294	430	652	133	63	8	(D)	1	(D)
5098	LUMBER AND CONSTRUCTION MATERIALS.	37	58 176	2 611	3 993	939	401	28	28 182	9	29 994
5099	MISCELLANEOUS WHOLESALERS.	42	34 920	2 447	2 962	684	428	40	(D)	2	(D)
	BRISTOL SMSA										
	WHOLESALE TRADE, TOTAL	39	(D)	(D)	(D)	(D)	(D)	33	(D)	6	(D)
501	MOTOR VEHICLES AND AUTOMOTIVE EQUIPMENT. . . .	6	3 451	546	731	133	102	6	3 451	-	-
502	DRUGS, CHEMICALS, AND ALLIED PRODUCTS.	-	-	-	-	-	-	-	-	-	-
503	PIECE GOODS, NOTIONS, AND APPAREL.	-	-	-	-	-	-	-	-	-	-
504	GROCERIES AND RELATED PRODUCTS	3	(D)	(D)	(D)	(D)	(D)	3	(D)	-	-
505	FARM PRODUCTS--RAW MATERIALS	1	(D)	(D)	(D)	(D)	(D)	1	(D)	-	-
506	ELECTRICAL GOODS	4	(D)	(D)	(D)	(D)	(D)	4	(D)	-	-
507	HARDWARE, PLUMBING, HEATING EQUIPMENT,SUPPLIES	2	(D)	(D)	(D)	(D)	(D)	2	(D)	-	-
508	MACHINERY, EQUIPMENT, AND SUPPLIES	5	(D)	(D)	(D)	(D)	(D)	3	(D)	2	(D)
5091	METALS AND MINERALS.			566	882	174	81	2			
5092	PETROLEUM AND PETROLEUM PRODUCTS				(D)	(D)	(D)				
5093	SCRAP AND WASTE MATERIALS					(D)					

FIG. 4 From 1972 *Census of Wholesale Trade, Area Statistics, Connecticut,* U.S. Department of Commerce, Bureau of the Census. A sample of the details available for local trading areas.

TABLE 2. **Standard Metropolitan Statistical Areas: 1972**—Continued

1972 SIC code	Standard metropolitan statistical area and kind of business	All establishments: Number	All establishments: Sales ($1,000)	Operated by unincorporated businesses[1]: Sole proprietorships (number)	Operated by unincorporated businesses[1]: Partnerships (number)	Establishments with payroll: Number	Establishments with payroll: Sales ($1,000)	Payroll, entire year ($1,000)	Payroll, first quarter 1972 ($1,000)	Paid employees for week including March 12 (number)
	HARTFORD SMSA									
	RETAIL TRADE, TOTAL	6 126	1 755 053	2 501	354	4 457	1 704 820	242 030	57 980	47 525
	BUILDING MATERIALS, HARDWARE, GARDEN SUPPLY, AND MOBILE HOME DEALERS									
52	TOTAL	246	66 393	73	13	188	63 967	8 484	1 864	1 166
521,3	BUILDING MATERIALS AND SUPPLY STORES	126	51 423	28	6	104	50 100	5 867	1 331	784
521	LUMBER AND OTHER BUILDING MATERIALS DEALERS	**	**	**	**	57	42 723	4 635	1 046	601
523	PAINT, GLASS, AND WALLPAPER STORES	**	**	**	**	47	7 377	1 232	285	183
525	HARDWARE STORES	82	10 368	34	5	59	9 603	1 622	346	276
526	RETAIL NURSERIES, LAWN AND GARDEN SUPPLY STORES	29	3 916	10	1	19	3 796	873	158	86
527	MOBILE HOME DEALERS	9	686	1	1	6	468	122	29	20
	GENERAL MERCHANDISE GROUP STORES									
53	TOTAL	135	280 327	30	8	106	279 374	47 761	11 472	9 310
531	DEPARTMENT STORES[2]	41	236 899	-	-	41	236 899	41 015	9 801	7 630
533	VARIETY STORES	46	27 518	16	2	32	27 204	4 936	1 238	1 252
539	MISCELLANEOUS GENERAL MERCHANDISE STORES	48	15 910	14	6	33	15 271	1 810	433	428
	FOOD STORES									
54	TOTAL	698	361 560	238	45	550	354 544	33 047	8 265	7 444
541	GROCERY STORES	419	329 464	131	29	347	325 145	27 671	6 964	6 008
542	MEAT, FISH (SEAFOOD) MARKETS, INCL. FREEZER PROV.	36	8 906	18	4	23	8 149	926	202	138
5422	FREEZER AND LOCKER MEAT PROVISIONERS	**	**	**	**	1	(D)	(D)	(D)	(D)
5423 PT.	MEAT MARKETS	**	**	**	**	13	5 049	550	124	87
5423 PT.	FISH (SEAFOOD) MARKETS	**	**	**	**	9	(D)	(D)	(D)	(D)
543	FRUIT STORES AND VEGETABLE MARKETS	23	1 462	21	1	9	1 194	87	20	21
544	... AND CONFECTIONERY STORES	33	2 110	13	2	22	1 927	323	81	106
		101	10 983	29	4	85	10 260	3 224		
	...LING	**	**	**	**	73	8 640	2 71...		
		**				12	1 620			

FIG. 5 Sample of information available in 1972 *Census of Retail Trade, Area Statistics, Connecticut*, U.S. Department of Commerce, Bureau of the Census, issued July 1974.

TABLE 2. **Standard Metropolitan Statistical Areas: 1972**

1972 SIC code	Standard metropolitan statistical area and kind of business	All establishments				Establishments with payroll				
		Number	Receipts	Operated by unincorporated businesses[1]		Number	Receipts	Payroll, entire year	Payroll, first quarter 1972	Paid employees for week including March 12
				Sole proprietorships	Partnerships					
			($1,000)	(number)	(number)		($1,000)	($1,000)	($1,000)	(number)
	BRIDGEPORT SMSA[2]									
	SELECTED SERVICES, TOTAL.	2 715	169 952	1 754	203	1 279	151 272	49 444	11 792	8 651
	HOTELS, MOTELS, TRAILERING PARKS, CAMPS									
701,3	TOTAL	34	7 792	9	4	23	7 473	2 042	473	522
7011	HOTELS, MOTOR HOTELS, AND MOTELS.	30	7 672	9	3	21	(D)	(D)	(D)	(D)
7011 PT.	HOTELS.	7	(D)	3	1	5	(D)	(D)	(D)	(D)
7011 PT.	HOTELS, 25 OR MORE GUEST ROOMS.	**	**	**	**	3	(D)	(D)	(D)	(D)
7011 PT.	HOTELS, LESS THAN 25 GUEST ROOMS.	**	**	**	**	2	(D)	(D)	(D)	(D)
7011 PT.	MOTELS, MOTOR HOTELS, AND TOURIST COURTS. . . .	23	(D)	6	2	16	6 904	1 869	438	484
7011 PT.	MOTELS, TOURIST COURTS.	**	**	**	**	15	(D)	(D)	(D)	(D)
7011 PT.	MOTOR HOTELS.	**	**	**	**	1	(D)	(D)	(D)	(D)
7032	SPORTING AND RECREATIONAL CAMPS	3	(D)	-	-	2	(D)	(D)	(D)	(D)
7033	TRAILERING PARKS AND CAMPSITES FOR TRANSIENTS . .	1	(D)	-	1	-	-	-	-	-
	PERSONAL SERVICES									
72	TOTAL	826	30 960	545	56	396	27 198	9 826	2 466	2 193
721	LAUNDRY, CLEANING, OTHER GARMENT SERVICES	184	12 750	100	18	107	11 787	4 640	1 073	887
7215	COIN-OPERATED LAUNDRIES AND DRY CLEANING. . . .	41	866	22	8	18	535	101	26	36
721 EX.7215	OTHER LAUNDRY, CLEANING, AND GARMENT SERVICES .	143	11 884	78	10	89	11 252	4 539	1 047	851
7211	POWER LAUNDRIES, FAMILY AND COMMERCIAL* . . .	**	**	**	**	10	1 374	737	183	154
7216	DRY-CLEANING PLANTS, EXCEPT RUG CLEANING* . .	**	**	**	**	56	4 096	1 703	421	385
7212	GARMENT PRESSING AND AGENTS FOR LAUNDRIES AND DRY CLEANERS	**	**	**	**	10	256	63	18	16
7218	INDUSTRIAL LAUNDERERS*.	**	**	**	**	3	2 713	951	263	130
7213	LINEN SUPPLY*	**	**	**	**	3	(D)	(D)	(D)	(D)
7217	CARPET AND UPHOLSTERY CLEANING.	**	**	**	**	3	(D)	(D)	(D)	(D)
7214,9	OTHER LAUNDRY, GARMENT ...	**	**	**	**	4	286	1...		
722	PHOTOGRAPHI...		1 794	61	1	6	(D...			
				...09	23	21...				

FIG. 6 Example of the type of information in 1972 *Census of Selected Service Industries, Area Statistics, Connecticut,* U.S. Department of Commerce, Bureau of the Census, issued July 1974.

OHIO

TABLE 2. Counties: 1972—Continued

(Excludes government employees, railroad employees, self-employed persons, etc.—see "General Explanation." Size class 1 to 3 includes reporting units having payroll during 1st quarter but no employees during mid-March pay period. "D" denotes figures withheld to avoid disclosure of operations of individual reporting units)

SIC code	Industry	Number of employees, mid-March pay period	Taxable payrolls, Jan.-Mar. ($1,000)	Total reporting units	Number of reporting units, by employment-size class							
					1 to 3	4 to 7	8 to 19	20 to 49	50 to 99	100 to 249	250 to 499	500 or more
	CUYAHOGA--CON.											
327	CONCRETE, GYPSUM, & PLASTER PRODUCTS.	705	1 852	38	6	3	16	11	2	-	-	-
3271	CONCRETE BLOCK AND BRICK.	111	295	5	1	-	2	2	-	-	-	-
3272	CONCRETE PRODUCTS N.E.C..	180	456	11	4	-	5	1	1	-	-	-
3273	READY-MIXED CONCRETE.	352	945	18	1	2	7	7	1	-	-	-
329	MISC. NONMETALLIC MINERAL PRODUCTS. .	1 432	3 120	35	4	8	5	10	3	4	1	-
3291	ABRASIVE PRODUCTS	430	1 021	14	3	2	2	4	2	1	-	-
3293	GASKETS AND INSULATIONS	311	506	8	1	2	1	2	1	1	-	-
3295	MINERALS, GROUND OR TREATED	(D)	(D)	4	-	1	1	1	-	1	-	-
3297	NONCLAY REFRACTORIES.	(D)	(D)	3	-	1	-	-	-	1	1	-
33	PRIMARY METAL INDUSTRIES.	33 430	87 752	180	12	14	43	39	21	28	12	11
331	BLAST FURNACE & BASIC STEEL PRODUCTS.	14 617	40 718	21	-	1	2	5	3	3	3	4
3312	BLAST FURNACES AND STEEL MILLS. . .	13 644	38 497	9	-	-	-	2	1	-	2	4
3315	STEEL WIRE AND RELATED PRODUCTS . .	444	962	6	-	-	-	2	2	2	-	-
3317	STEEL PIPE AND TUBES.	(D)	(D)	3	-	-	1	-	-	1	1	-
332	IRON AND STEEL FOUNDRIES.	6 071	18 512	15	-	-	1	1	3	7	1	2
3321	GRAY IRON FOUNDRIES	5 236	16 791	8	-	-	-	-	2	3	1	2
3323	STEEL FOUNDRIES	835	1 721	7	-	-	1	1	1	4	-	-
333	PRIMARY NONFERROUS METALS	(D)	(D)	2	-	-	-	1	1	-	-	-
334	SECONDARY NONFERROUS METALS	(D)	(D)	17	1	1	3	7	2	2	1	-
335	NONFERROUS ROLLING AND DRAWING. . . .	3 006	6 869	17	1	1	2	2	3	5	2	1
3351	COPPER ROLLING AND DRAWING.	839	2 111	7	-	-	1	1	1	3	1	-
3352	ALUMINUM ROLLING AND DRAWING. . . .	(D)	(D)	3	-	-	1	-	-	2	-	-
3356	NONFERROUS ROLLING AND DRAWING, NEC	(D)	(D)	2	-	1	-	-	-	-	-	1
3357	NONFERROUS WIRE DRAWING, ETC. . . .	457	1 256	5	1	-	-	1	2	-	1	-
336	NONFERROUS FOUNDRIES.	4 872	10 407	51	6	5	11	10	5	8	4	2
3361	ALUMINUM CASTINGS	3 854	8 312	33	4	3	7	5	3	6	3	2
3362	BRASS, BRONZE AND COPPER CASTINGS .	199	390	10	1	1	4	4	-	-	-	-
3369	NONFERROUS CASTINGS, N.E.C.	819	1 705	8	1	1	-	1	2	2	1	-
339	MISCELLANEOUS PRIMARY METAL	3 688	8 442	57	4	6	24	13	4			
3391	IRON AND STEEL FORG		4 466	17	-	-	3	5				
3392	NONFERROUS FORG			3	-	-	2					
	PRIMARY ME			37	4	6						

FIG. 7 From *County Business Patterns, Ohio,* U.S. Department of Commerce, Bureau of the Census, issued July 1973.

SURVEY OF CURRENT BUSINESS A monthly publication giving income figures on a national basis; total and per capita personal income on a national, regional, and state basis; income by place of work on a SMSA basis. Updates economic information.

MEASURING MARKETS: A GUIDE TO THE USE OF FEDERAL AND STATE STATISTICAL DATA A very useful guide for any marketing person, showing types of figures available for marketing and marketing research, both on a national and on a state basis. Tells where to send for the figures you need.

STATISTICAL ABSTRACT OF THE UNITED STATES The most complete single source of facts available. Annual. Includes a selection of data from many statistical publications, both government and private.[6] In my opinion, this book should be on the desk of every marketing person, particularly those who do business on a national or regional basis.

BUSINESS SERVICE CHECKLIST A weekly guide to U.S. Department of Commerce publications.[7]

OCCASIONAL STUDIES Recently there was published a study entitled *Household Furniture and Appliances.* Another was *Department Store Retailing in an Era of Change.* How extensive these special efforts will be it is hard to say. It would be wise to make an occasional check to see if the industries you may be interested in have been covered.

The preceding list is by no means a complete roster of Department of Commerce publications. As I said, a visit to a field office, in many cases, would be time well spent.

Department of Labor

EMPLOYMENT AND WAGES OF WORKERS National and state figures, by SIC code. Quarterly publication.

EMPLOYMENT AND EARNINGS STATISTICS Annual publication. Figures by states, certain SMSAs, and other labor markets.

Federal Reserve Bank Here I will cover publications available at the Boston branch of the Federal Reserve. These are probably typical of all the branches.

FEDERAL RESERVE BULLETIN National monthly publication with emphasis on financial information. May be of some assistance in directing selection of areas for research.

NEW ENGLAND ECONOMIC INDICATORS Production, employment, commercial construction, consumer and financial indicators, by region and by state. Some figures available for larger cities.

NEW ENGLAND ECONOMIC REVIEW Mostly articles, but your particular industry may have been covered. Worth investigation.

[6]U.S. Bureau of the Census, *Statistical Abstract of the United States.*

[7]Available by subscription from U.S. Department of Commerce. FCAT BR, Room 6880, Washington, D.C. 20230. Annual subscription $9.70 at this time. Checks payable to Superintendant of Documents.

Table 8.—Sales Statistics From Selected State Sources[1]

State[2]	Title of publication	SIC industry digit detail	Geographic coverage	Frequency of data	Frequency of publication	Issuing agency
California	Taxable Sales in California	1-2-3 1-2-3 1-2	State County 208 largest cities	Quarterly	Quarterly	State Board of Equalization, P.O. Box 1799, Sacramento, CA 95814
Colorado	Sales Tax Statistical Summary	1-2-3 1-2	State County	Annual	Annual	Department of Revenue, 1375 Sherman St., Denver, CO 80203
	Sales Tax Summary	1	County	Monthly with yearly summary	Monthly	
Connecticut	Sales and Use Tax Information	2	State	Quarterly	Quarterly	State Tax Department, 92 Farmington Ave., Hartford, CT 06115
Florida	Report of the Comptroller State of Florida	3	State	Annual	Annual	Comptroller, State of Florida, Tallahassee, FL 32304
Illinois	Report of Department of Revenue	2	Municipalities within counties	Annual	Annual	Department of Revenue Springfield, IL 62706
	Retailers' Occupation Tax, Service Occupation Tax, Use Tax and Service Use Tax: Report No. 1	2	Cities within counties	Quarterly	Quarterly	
Iowa	Retail Sales and Use Tax Annual Report	2-3	State and County	Quarterly	Quarterly	Research and Statistics Division, Iowa Department of Revenue, Lucas State Office Building, Des Moines, IA 50319
Kentucky	Department of Revenue Annual Report	1-2	State and County	Annual	Annual	Department of Revenue Frankfort, KY 40601
Maine	Sales and Use Tax Assessments	2-3	State	Monthly with yearly summary	Monthly	Bureau of Taxation, Sales Tax Division, State Office Building, Augusta, ME 04330
Maryland	Statistical Report of Retail Sales Tax Division	2-3 2	State County	Monthly Annual	Annual	Comptroller of the Treasury, State Office Building, Baltimore, MD 21201

FIG. 8 A sample page from *Measuring Markets, A Guide to the Use of Federal and State Statistical Data,* U.S. Department of Commerce, August 1974.

THE ECONOMICS OF THE NEW ENGLAND FISHING INDUSTRY; TRADE ADJUSTMENT ASSISTANCE; A CASE STUDY OF THE SHOE INDUSTRY IN MASSACHUSETTS Examples of special research reports that occasionally appear.

Department of Housing and Urban Development Worth investigating, if your particular study concerns these fields.

There is such a wealth of good information from the federal government that the above does not even represent a sample. Nevertheless, it is a good start, and you can go on from there. Your local librarian, as well as the Commerce field office, can help you locate pertinent publications.

State Governments

This is a hodgepodge of departments and offices of varying abilities. I would suggest that you write to the state department of commerce, or the state librarian, of any state in which you are interested, for guidance about what is available. Another source would be a state chamber of commerce. At least you will get some leads which can be followed. There often are state development commissions which can be contacted. Publication of statistics is secondary, in all these bodies, to their chief job, which is building up the economic health of present business in the state and attracting new business. I cannot hold out much hope for mines of information for your particular study, but in certain cases, it may be worth a letter or two to determine what is available.

State industrial directories These vary in size, quality, and cost. A number of state directories can be obtained from the State Industrial Directories Corporation, 2 Penn Plaza, New York, New York 10001. Another source is Manufacturers' News, 3 East Huron Street, Chicago, Illinois 60611. Most directories are classified by firm name, by cities and towns, and by product lines. Your local library, unless you are in a very small town, may have some of these directories. However, since some are quite expensive, few libraries will have all of them.

State magazines Most states have magazines which seem to have two purposes: to boost the ego of companies already in the states, and to induce outside companies to come in. In this process, they may have printed articles that would help you in any particular study. Your own library should be able to give you the names and publishers of these magazines. They are not to be confused with magazines that are designed to enhance tourism, or cater to the entertainment tastes of travelers.

CLASSIFIED SECTION — C-103 — PENS, PENCILS

ALLIED CHEMICAL CORP., Barrett Division, Round House Road, Binghamton, 13902, Broome County, 723-5368
ALLIED CHEMICAL CORP., Paving Mtls. Dept, I.C.D., P.O. Box 1118, 561 State Fair Blvd., Syracuse, 13201, (315) 468-1636
AMERICAN BITUMULS & ASPHALT CO., Cole Road, Lyons, 14489, Wayne County, 946-4848
AMFAR ASPHALT CORP., Old Northport Road, Kings Park, 11754, Suffolk County, 269-9661

CALLANAN INDUSTRIES, INC., Mingo Hollow Road, Kingston, 12400, Ulster County, 331-6868
CENTRAL ASPHALT, INC., 41 Clinton Rd., New Hartford, 13413, Oneida County, 735-8501
CHEVRON ASPHALT CO., INC., Cole Road, Lyons, 14489, Wayne County, 946-4848
CHEVRON ASPHALT CO., INC., Sub. of: Standard Oil Co. of Calif., Foot of Water Street, P.O. Box 962, Troy, 12181, Rensselaer County, 518-272-2041
COLUMBIA ASPHALT CORP., 127-50 Northern Blvd., Flushing, 11352, Queens County, 446-7000
CROWLEY TAR PRODUCTS CO., INC., 271 Madison Avenue, New York, 10016, Manhattan County, 683-1040

FLINTKOTE CO., THE, Executive Offices, 400 Westchester Ave., White Plains, 10604, Westchester County, 761-7400

GENERAL CRUSHED STONE CO., THE, P. O. Box 7836, 600 McKee Road, Rochester, 14606, Monroe County, 436-8200
GENERAL CRUSHED STONE CO., Box 1077, Syracuse, 13201, Onondaga County, 422-3103
GENESEE BITUMINOUS PRODUCTS CORP., Route 5, Stafford Road, P. O. Box 363, Batavia, 14020, Genesee County, 716-343-8362
GOSHEN ASPHALT CO., INC., Florida Road, Route ... Goshen, 10924, Orange County, 29...

WESTCHESTER COLPROVIA CORP., 92 Bedford Road, Katonah, 10536, Westchester County, 232-3151
WILLIAMS PAVING CO., 100 Katherine Street, Buffalo, 14210, Erie County, 854-0190
WORLOCK STONE COMPANY, 128 E. Center Street, Canastota, 13032, Madison County, 697-2261

PENS, PENCILS, OFFICE & ARTISTS' MATERIALS

SIC 3951-3953, 3955

A A A STAMP & SEAL MFG. CO., Sub. of: Barth Envelope, Inc., 27-02 44th Drive, Long Island City, 11101, Queens County, 361-8087
ACADEMY RUBBER STAMP CO., 307 Atlantic Avenue, Brooklyn, 11217, Kings County, 875-4582
AETNA PRODUCTS CO., INC., 11 Commercial St., P.O. Box 683, Hicksville, 11801, Nassau County, 931-3120
ALCO MANUFACTURING CORP., 1520 Stillwell Avenue, Bronx, 10461, Bronx County, 828-1310
ALLIED CARBON & RIBBON MFG. CORP., 165 Duane Street, New York, 10013, Manhattan County, 962-0762
AMERICAN IMPROVED PRODUCTS, INC., 2350 Jericho Turnpike, Garden City Park, 11040, Nassau County, 746-7300
ART SUPPLY & INSTRUMENT CO. INC., 1449 37 St., Brooklyn, 11218, Kings County, 436-2711

BALL PEN COMPANY OF AMERICA INC., Sub. of: Duro Pen co., Inc., 40 Varick Avenue, Brooklyn, 11237, Kings County, 366-9800
... 125A 12th Street, ...

Charlotte Avenue, Hicksville, 11802, Nassau County, 433-3010
FRYE COPYSYSTEMS, INC., Wheelabrator-Frye, Inc., 71 Windsor Highway, Newburgh, 12550, Orange County, 561-6040

GENERAL STENCILS, INC., 827 East 92nd Street, Brooklyn, 11236, Kings County, 649-5606
GIBSON, A. C. CO., INC., 875-881 Englewood Avenue, Buffalo, 14223, Erie County, 716-838-5960
GOTHAM PEN CO., INC., 876 Broadway, New York, 10003, Manhattan County, 475-2820

HASTINGS MARKING DEVICES, 439 Ellicott Street, Buffalo, 14203, Erie County, 852-6640

IDEAL METAL PRODUCTS CO., INC., 54 Bleecker Street, New York, 10012, Manhattan County, 226-6464
IMPERIAL CRAYON CO., 649 Lexington Avenue, Brooklyn, 11221, Kings County, 491-4000
ISLAND PEN MFG. CORPORATION, 2004 McDonald Avenue, Brooklyn, 11223, Kings County, 376-5700

J.L. HAMMETT CO., Water Street, Lyons, 14489, Wayne County, 946-4815
JAE COLOR WORKS, INC., 31-33 West 21st Street, New York, 10010, Manhattan County, 675-3456
JESSEL MARKING EQUIPMENT CO., Div. of: Consolidated Foods Corp., Box 234, 2207 Teall Ave., Syracuse, 13206, Onondaga County, 463-8641

K C PEN COMPANY, INC., 175 Pearl Street, Brooklyn, 11205, Kings County, 858-6204
KEE LOX MANUFACTURING COMPANY, Sub. of: Paterson Parchment Paper Company, 10 Kee Lox Place, P. O. Box 137, Rochester, 14608 ... County, 325-7600
KNIGHT H. W. & SON, INC ...

FIG. 9 Typical information available from state industrial directories. This is from the *New York State Industrial Directory,* 1975 edition. Published by the State Industrial Directories Corp., 2 Penn Plaza, New York, N.Y. 10001.

GEOGRAPHICAL G-25 (Brooklyn) KINGS COUNTY

BROOKLYN
Telephone Area Code—212

A A 1 QUILTING CORPORATION
161 34th Street
Brooklyn, N.Y. 11232
Phone: 768-9551
6,000 Sq. Ft.
Emp: 24
Quilted Goods
SIC 2293
Pr—Jerry Green
Sec—Harold W. Green

A A 1 STEEL EQUIPMENT CO.
199-201 Diamond Street
Brooklyn, N. Y. 11222
Phone: 383-1670
Emp: 12
Shelving
SIC 2542
Pr—A. Lieberman

A A A STEEL DRUM CO.
410 Johnson Ave.
Brooklyn, N. Y. 11237
Phone: 497-4772
Emp: 20
Barrels & Drums- Steel
SIC 3491

A B AETNA CORPORATION
147 Roebling Street
Brooklyn , N. Y. 11211
Phone: 384-2860
Emp: 42
Electrical Cords
SIC ...

Office: F,4
Plant: M,25 F,125
★Stuffed Toys
SIC 3942
Pr—A. Wessan
Ch/Ex/Off—Al Lehrer
VP—Lewis Hirsch
G/M—Rick Coronato
O/M—Reba Bloom
S/M—Al Baum
T/M—H. Lazar
R/D—Ernst Gruber

A & L TOOL & DIE & STAMPING, INC.,
43 South First Street
Brooklyn, N.Y. 11211
Phone: 384-6417
10,000 Sq. Ft.
Emp: 18
Office: M,3
Plant: M,15
Tools, Dies, Metal Fabricating
SIC 3544
Pr—Anthony D'Angelo
Sec—Leonard D'Angelo
P/F—William Rosado
P/Eng—Walter Thompson

A & S OFFSET PRINTERS, INC.
1776 Flatbush Avenue
Brooklyn, N.Y. 11210
Phone: 258-6960
2,500 Sq. Ft.
Emp: 4
Job Offset Printers
...2752

Emp: 18
Job Printers
SIC 2751
Pr—Aniello Romano
VP—Vincent Romano
O/M—Sal Stratis

ABLE CONTAINER CORP.
242 Richardson Street
Brooklyn, N. Y. 11222
Phone: 389-8304
Emp: 12
Barrels & Drums-Fibre
SIC 2655
Pr—Joel Kamen
Exec/VP—Barry Fine

ABLE-VAL CANVAS & ROPE MFG. CO., INC.
785 Fifth Avenue
Brooklyn, N.Y. 11232
Phone: 499-4064
10,000 Sq. Ft.
Emp: 18
Office: M,2 F,1
Plant: M,15
Canvas And Rope
SIC 2394
Pr—Ben Valenstein
VP—Anthony Garofalo

ABROFF, DAVID MFG. CORP.
66 Christopher Avenue
Brooklyn, N.Y. 11212
Phone: 495-0700
3,500 Sq. Ft.
Emp: 13

ACE CELLOPHANE & POLYETHYLENE CORP.,
12 Franklin Street
Brooklyn, N. Y. 11222
Phone: 383-3466
25,000 Sq. Ft.
Emp: 39
Office: M,4 F,3
Plant: M,23 F,9
Cellophane And Polyethlene Bags
SIC 2643
Pr—Murray Lederman

ACE COMBINING CO., INC.
33 Spencer Street
Brooklyn, N. Y. 11205
Phone: 858-2404
Emp: 2
Backers Of Fabrics
▲SIC 3069
Pr—M. Schwartz

ACE DIE CUTTING CO., INC.
360 Furman St.
Brooklyn, N.Y. 11201
Phone: 212-855-2300
40,000 Sq. Ft.
Emp: 75
Die Cutters
SIC 3544
Pr—Edward Feverstein
Exec/VP—Neil Feverstein
O/M—Goldie Benelsdorf
T/M—Joseph Spinelli

ACE INDUSTRIES, INC.

FIG. 10 Another page from the *New York State Industrial Directory*, published by the State Industrial Directories Corp.

City Governments and Related Offices and Commissions

These are similar to state governments in the variety of publications, and the quality of such materials. There are economic development commissions, redevelopment commissions, and so on. Some are relatively free of political influence, some not. Their chief purpose is the business, economic, and social development of their cities. Statistics may be available when they serve this purpose. How accurate and complete these figures may be is a matter for your judgment.

Sometimes these local authorities will commission a study to be done by an outside consulting agency. Such studies are likely to be done reasonably well, but may not be available to you.

It probably would be wise to contact one or more of these bodies if you are making a study where a broad knowledge of a city would be helpful. Letters may or may not produce anything worthwhile—if they are answered at all.

As a generalization I would say that little or no true research has been done by or for most cities, except the very largest.

Associations

Every industry seems to have at least one association. For some product lines there are several associations that both compete and overlap. The best source of knowledge about your own industry's associations is people in your own company, if you are a manufacturer or distributor. The best source for names of associations in other industries is probably the *Encyclopedia of Associations,* published by Gale Research Company, Book Tower, Detroit, Michigan 48226. This book is probably in your public library; it should be.

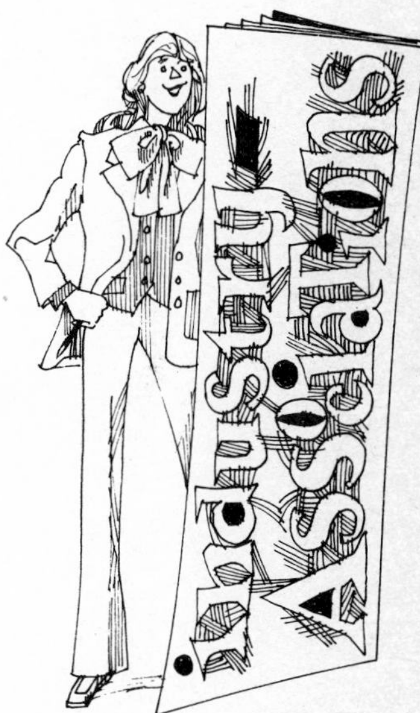

Every industry seems to have at least one association.

Associations are of highly different quality and have quite different purposes. In my own experience, I have worked with associations that were little more than public relations vehicles, influencing both the public and various government bodies. On the other hand, I have known associations that did a very good job of keeping track of the economic situation in their industry. Some associations even have their own marketing research departments. Your only real problem with associations is the probability that they will not want to release much information to nonmembers. However, a compromise position is always possible, and these groups are worth a good try.

Indexes

To be found in most libraries are a number of indexes. These include the *N.Y. Times Index, Industrial Arts Index,* and others. The two that may prove most useful to you in certain cases are:

Section 1 - TRADE, BUSINESS & COMMERCIAL ORGANIZATIONS

KNITWEAR
See Index

★1653★
LABEL MANUFACTURERS NATIONAL ASSOCIATION
2425 Wilson Blvd., Room 511 — Phone: (703) 528-8444
Arlington, VA 22201 — Francis R. Cawley, Exec.Dir.
Founded: 1916. Organized under name of Label Manufacturers National Association. In 1960, became Label Manufacturers Division of the Lithographers and Printers National Association. In 1964, resumed operation once again as a separate, independent organization, using its original name. **Convention/ Meeting**: annual.

LABOR-MANAGEMENT
See Index

★1654★
LACE IMPORTERS ASSOCIATION
420 Lexington Ave. — Phone: (212) 683-4993
New York, NY 10017 — Jean-Pierre Stern, Chm.,exec.Comm.
Founded: 1909. **Members**: 26. Importers of lace and embroideries. **Formerly:** Lace and Embroidery Association of America.

LACE
Also See Index

★1655★
AMERICAN **LADDER** INSTITUTE
C/O Smith, Bucklin And Associates, Mgrs.
111 E. Wacker Dr. — Phone: (312) 644-6610
Chicago, IL 60601 — William R. Feder, Exec.Sec.
Founded: 1922. **Members**: 75. Manufacturers of wood and metal ladders. Sponsors code developed by American National Standards Institute. **Committees**: Code; Liability; Safety; Traffic. **Publications**: Membership Newsletter, monthly; also issues pamphlet on ladder safety. **Convention/ Meeting**: semiannual.

★1661★
RLM STANDARDS INSITITUE (**Lamp**) (RLM) *
1701 Wellington Ave. — Phone: (312) 327-7200
Chicago, IL 60657 — James R. Chambers, Pres.
Founded: 1919. **Members**: 15. **Staff**: 3. Manufacturers of certifiable industrial lighting equipment. Establishes quality specifications for industrial lighting equipment. Testing and conformance procedure entrusted to the Electrical Testing Laboratories, Inc., which conducts laboratory tests of equipment and makes quarterly inspections of manufacturing plants. RLM Label Service available to certified equipment of participating manufacturers. **Committees:** Inspection and Testing; Specifications; Technical (for preparation of Standards). **Divisions:** Fluorescent Lighting; Incandescent and Mercury Lighting. **Publications:** RLM Industrial Lighting News, quarterly; also publishes specifications for industrial lighting units. **Formerly**: (1936) Reflector Lamp Manufacturers Institute. **Convention/ Meeting**: annual. Presently inactive, but in process of reorganizing.

LAND
See Index

★1662★
AMERICAN **LAND DEVELOPMENT** ASSOCIATION (ALDA)
603 Solar Bldg.
1000 16th St., N.W. — Phone: (202) 659-4582
Washington, DC 20036 — Gary A. Terry, Exec.V.Pres.
Founded: 1969. **Members**: 900. **Staff**: 12. **State Groups**: 8. Developers of recreational and planned communities; suppliers to the recreational land and second home industries. Conducts seminars and conferences; maintains library. **Committees**: Accounting Practices; Condominium; Data and Research; Land Use; Legislation and Regulation; Non-Domestic Development and Sales; Public Affairs; Special Events; Task Force on State and Federal Real Estate Registration and Disclosure Requirements. **Publications**: (1) Washington Developments, weekly; (2) ALDA Legislative Report, biweekly; (3) American Land, monthly; (4) ALDA Membership Directory, annual; (5) Land Development Law Reporter, annual; also publishes Digest of Land Sales Regulations. **Convention/ Meeting**: annual.

FIG. 11 Typical page from the *Encyclopedia of Associations,* published by the Gale Research Company, Book Tower, Detroit, Mich. Revised frequently. (*Courtesy of Gale Research Company.*)

Reader's Guide to Periodical Literature Covers many magazines and other periodicals, including some that are devoted to business.

Business Periodical Index Covers mostly business subjects. Both these guides are published by the H. W. Wilson Company, 950 University Ave., Bronx, New York 10452.

Directories

Dun & Bradstreet Million Dollar and Middle Market Directories Two of the most complete first sources when you wish to investigate a company, or the major companies within an industry. The *Million Dollar Directory* covers all businesses with a net worth of $1 million or more. The *Middle Market Directory* covers businesses with a net worth of $0.5 million to $1 million. Included in each listing are the company's full name, trade names, state of incorporation, parent company (if any), headquarters address, division names and functions, annual sales, total employment, SIC number, and correct name and title of current executives.

These directories are purchased as a service by subscription and remain the property of Dun & Bradstreet, to be returned each year when the new editions are published. Published by Dun & Bradstreet, Inc., 99 Church Street, New York, New York 10007.

Moody's manuals Cover industries, public utilities, banking and finance, and transportation. Also have biweekly updating of information. Good for getting a "feel" of an industry you are studying. Only cover the very largest corporations, however. These are not sources for facts about small, privately held companies. Available in most banks, brokerage houses, and probably in the office of your comptroller, if you work for a large company. Published by Moody's Investors Service, Inc., 99 Church Street, New York, New York 10007.

Directories of all kinds are available.

Thomas Register of American Manufacturers Used by most purchasing departments of manufacturers and distributors and many large retailers. Also available in most public libraries. Manufacturers classified by products. Also alphabetically by state and city. Codes show total assets. Gives subsidiaries, brief summary of products. Also a list of trademarks. Published by Thomas Publishing Co., 1 Penn Plaza, New York, New York 10001.

25,000 Leading U.S. Corporations Companies classified by SIC numbers, ranked by annual sales, and analyzed by twenty-five important indexes, including sales, earnings, employees, etc. Good financial information concerning the size and nature of a total market. Published by Year, Inc., 20 West 43d Street, New York, New York 10036.

Directory of Industrial Distributors Published by Morgan-Grampian, 205 E. 42 St., New York, New York 10017.

Directory of Discount Stores Published by Business Guides, Inc., an affiliate of Chain Store Age, 2 Park Avenue, New York, New York 10016.

Directory of Department Stores Published by Business Guides, Inc.

Directory of Variety and Jr. Department Store Chains Published by Business Guides, Inc.

All the above titles are self-explanatory. I just wanted you to know of their existence. The Department Store book, for example, contains information on 2,800 department store operations, local and chains, with about 12,000 stores; headquarters addresses and branch locations; resident buying office used; names of executives; etc. Obviously all the above would be most useful in planning a field study, or analyzing an industry. In addition, there is:

Directory of Supermarket, Grocery and Convenience Store Chains Also published by Business Guides, Inc.

Shopping Center Directory Information on some 17,000 shopping centers. Published by National Research Bureau, 42 N. 3d Street, Burlington, Iowa 52601.

Sales Management Annual Survey of Buying Power May be purchased separately, or as a part of a subscription to *Sales Management* magazine. Useful local data including population, individual incomes, sales of certain types of stores, and an index of market potential.

Some companies sell research reports.

Miscellaneous Sources

It is impossible to tell you all the places where a printed study on a particular topic may be found. There are private concerns that publish and sell reports on a number of topics. One of these is Predicasts, Inc., in Cleveland, Ohio. Stanford Research Institute, of Menlo Park, California, has a number of studies in various fields in its long-range planning service, but to utilize these it is necessary to sign a contract covering a period of time. There are a number of worthwhile benefits in addition to the special reports.

Other companies sell research reports. Many utilize basic government data and other published figures and attempt to analyze the present and future situation. The price is likely to be high, but the reports are worth considering if they can take the place of a few weeks of travel expense for field research.

Advertising Agencies

Up to very recently, advertising agencies had the notion of becoming the active "good right arm" of the marketing and sales departments of their clients. It appears that they have backed away from this a little. But in the process of learning marketing, they discovered sources of information that you may not know about. Some agencies installed complete marketing research departments. In such cases the agency library is almost certain to have worthwhile material. The agency marketing research director will be hungry for work, and can be a source of help at no great cost. If your company employs an agency, by all means use it to the utmost.

Banks

I have already talked about the Federal Reserve publications. In addition to the material published by the Federal Reserve branches (which, incidentally, are at Atlanta, Boston, Chicago, Cleveland, Dallas, Kansas City, Minneapolis, New York, Philadelphia, Richmond, St. Louis, and San Francisco), large city banks often have brochures of their own, issued on a regular basis. Examples of these local banks are Trust Company of Georgia; First National Bank of Boston; Security Pacific National Bank and United California Bank, both of Los Angeles; Morgan Guaranty Trust, Chase Manhattan Bank, and First National City Bank, all in New York; Mellon National Bank and Trust (Pittsburgh); and Wells Fargo Bank (San Francisco). This is by no means a complete list.

Generally speaking, only a few banks in a few large cities produce original statistics of their own. The most valuable thing that a banker can give you is a "feel" for his town. On rare occasions banks have commissioned research studies to be done by outside firms. Banks, in other words, are of value as a source where more than a casual study is being made of one or several cities. But you are very unlikely to find a marketing research department in any but the largest banks—and even then the department will operate more for the bank's own business than for outsiders.

Keep your ears open.

Keeping Your Ears Open

In addition to all the above, one of the very best receptors of information is your own hearing. Without being at all unethical, you can learn a great amount about competitors and their products by keeping your ears open around competitors' own towns. The waitress in the motel mentions a layoff at plant X, and says it is too bad because there is no promise of when the "poor fellows" are going to be called back. Or the gas station attendant says that he has heard rumors of dissatisfaction and a probable strike. Someone else says that the new production wing that was constructed to make a certain product is only working half-time because sales have not grown as fast as expected.

Granted that these sources can be completely wrong in their information, it is still possible to put two and two together, plus another two and two that you get from some other place, and conclude that the X plant is having trouble with its new product line. Perhaps this is a signal that the great new product has "filled the pipelines" and repeat sales are proving very disappointing. This is a useful rumor to check out, especially if you are planning to enter this market yourself. You cannot take the word of the waitress and the gas station attendant. But you *can* follow up such leads to see what truth may be in them.

Summary

As I have said several times, it is impossible for any book to give *all* sources of information for every product line and every sales situation. You must do some of your own searching.

What I have tried to do is to get you off to a good start. The business of finding good sources is an attitude of mind. After a little experience, it is possible to make tentative forecasts of what is *probably* available and where to get it. As an example, if you work for a big company that is tied by computer terminal with one of the large econometric models, you may be quite surprised to discover how much factual information that busy little machine can spit out at you while you are blinking your eye. It is not inexpensive, of course, but, once again, it may be a whole lot cheaper than time on the road.

So now we are ready to move into discussion of some of the most elementary ways of getting information from the field. At the very best, secondary sources usually do not quite hit the specific mark. For your own product line—your own problem—there will still be more to do before you can feel secure about giving *the* answer to your company.

FIVE

How to Conduct a Mail Questionnaire Study

Mail questionnaires have fallen into some disrepute in recent years. At least, they are not so popular as formerly. Unfortunately, they were overused, frequently by people who did not know how to use them well. So it became harder and harder to get a satisfactory return percentage.

A typical mail questionnaire package consists of the questionnaire itself, a covering letter explaining what the study is about, and a stamped, self-addressed reply envelope. It is always hoped that the combination will appear so interesting and attractive that the recipient will be moved to answer the questions and mail the questionnaire back promptly. Practically never will the researcher achieve 100 percent returns. The trick is to get the return percentage as high as possible.

Let us face a few hard truths here at the beginning. Except with one or more careful follow-up checks, it is impossible to be sure that those who do *not* answer your questionnaire are the same kind of people as those who *do*. Perhaps the people who like your product or your company answer the questionnaire. The ones who have had trouble with your product or company throw the questionnaire away. Or, busy, important executives do not answer, while less busy, less important people do. Once again, you will not *know* whether this is so unless and until you do a careful follow-up of those who did not respond, together with some effort to find why they refused. Usually, for small studies, where time is crucial, and only a small amount of money can be spent, this expensive checking cannot be done. The first mailing, plus a reminder a few days later, is about all there is.

Since you do not *know* that you have a real sample of the group you are studying, you cannot mathematically project your findings to the whole group being studied in most of the work you will be doing. Unless your return percentage is relatively high, you can only assume that you have a true picture of your whole "population," or the total of the group being studied. Getting a good return percentage is of considerable importance, therefore.

Mail questionnaires, in spite of the cautions mentioned above, have their place in your work. The larger the return percentage, as I said, the more sure you can be that you have the "right" answer to your problem. This chapter will tell how to construct a mail study that brings the highest number of returns. You are not writing a scholarly article for marketing research professionals. If your return percentage is reasonably high, if the answers are born out from your own experience and knowledge, if the differences between answers remain about the same from day to day as new batches of questionnaires come back, and finally, if the mail questionnaire bears out findings from some other work that you may have done by other methods, such as

Conducting a mail questionnaire study . . .

group interviews, you can honestly say to your company that you have a workable answer. Remember, I am talking about small studies made by nonprofessionals. If your problem is a new cereal, for example, that will sell by the thousands of cases per day, then you had better get a pro to do the research.

Types of Studies That Lend Themselves to Mail Questionnaires

You can use mail questionnaires best under these circumstances:

1. Where the "universe," or all the people that you would want to contact, is relatively small, well defined, and homogeneous. Packaging engineers of manufacturing companies, maintenance supervisors for chain grocery stores, and shipping supervisors for carpet manufacturers in the South are examples.
2. Where the same problem faces all these people, and can be expressed simply and understandably.
3. Where the particular people being addressed, although perhaps competitors, have a feeling of kinship with their counterparts in other companies.
4. In other instances, where a retailer may want to question his own customers about his faults and merits.
5. Preferably, where a mailing list of names and titles can somehow be obtained.

Return percentages of warranty cards are often low.

The above does not imply that these are the only places where mail questionnaires can be used. It simply says that, where these conditions exist, a higher return percentage is likely. And with a higher percentage return, you can feel more secure about the correctness of your findings.

One close relative of the mail questionnaire is the warranty card that is so often packed with bigger ticket items sold through the retail trade. Using the implied threat that the guarantee will be worthless unless the card is returned, immediate information flows back to the manufacturer from the ultimate customer. Even here, where the number and types of buyers are large and nonhomogeneous, return percentages are low. One very large company reports that its warranty card return never runs over 10 percent. While it considers the resulting information useful, it cannot feel that this is a true sample of customers. This company has made no effort to validate the returned cards, to see to what extent they vary from a true sample of *all* customers. However, the company believes that the type of person who fills out a warranty card, stamps and mails it, must be different than the nonreturner. Whether this difference implies a corresponding difference in buying habits for this company's products is not known.

Summarizing up to this point, I have said that mail questionnaires are most likely to be successful if the group being sampled is relatively small and homogeneous, if it has a certain identity (even though its individual members may be competitors), if the questions can be made to appear relevant and important to this group, and if these questions can be simply stated for easy understanding and answering.

Rarely can a questionnaire be written properly in its first version.

Writing the Several Drafts

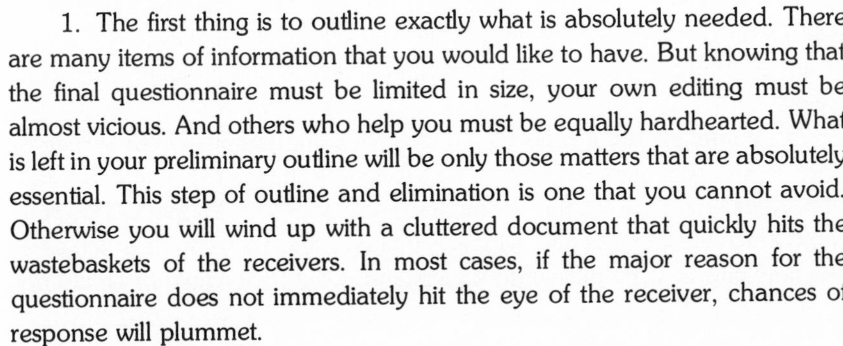

Only very rarely can a questionnaire be written properly in its first version. You must resign yourself to one revision after another until there is general agreement that the document will do the required job. It is extremely difficult for one person alone to write a good questionnaire. The help and advice of others is of the utmost importance, as was pointed out in previous chapters.

Here are the steps that lead up to a good questionnaire that produces satisfactory results:

1. The first thing is to outline exactly what is absolutely needed. There are many items of information that you would like to have. But knowing that the final questionnaire must be limited in size, your own editing must be almost vicious. And others who help you must be equally hardhearted. What is left in your preliminary outline will be only those matters that are absolutely essential. This step of outline and elimination is one that you cannot avoid. Otherwise you will wind up with a cluttered document that quickly hits the wastebaskets of the receivers. In most cases, if the major reason for the questionnaire does not immediately hit the eye of the receiver, chances of response will plummet.

2. The questionnaire must look interesting and fun to do. Your various drafts, as you develop the final questionnaire, must always keep this in mind. There is a very crucial second, when the respondent is holding the questionnaire in his hand, mentally debating what to do. If the questionnaire looks dull, then the wastebasket gets it.

If the questionnaire looks dull, the wastebasket gets it.

3. Mail questionnaires should not ask for the respondent to do much, if any, work. I have seen questionnaires that asked how many light bulbs were used last year in the factory. I am sure that the information could have been obtained, but with considerable work and time. In our company, at least, no one was willing to take this trouble. Another contribution to the wastebasket! Had the questionnaire simply asked what *brand* of bulbs was being used, it is possible that someone would have taken the trouble to find out. But the *number* of bulbs—no.

4. There is a grey area between being businesslike and being dull. And between being interesting and too cute. Again, this is why it is good to get the opinions of a number of people in your organization.

Never try to be too cute.

The questionnaires included in this book will show you various types of question-asking techniques. All these have worked where they were suitable. These methods can be adapted to your own needs. However, I hope that you will also introduce a little of your own creativity, so that none of your efforts ever looks run-of-the-mill. There is a difference between cuteness and originality.

5. To the extent possible, the receiver of the questionnaire should be able to see some relationship to his own interests. This cannot be strained to the point of ridiculousness. After all, the receiver is an intelligent person and knows very well why you are asking these questions: to help yourself. But if there is some legitimate co-interest, then you can use it honestly to win a better response rate.

6. Clarity and lack of ambiguity are of greatest importance. It is incumbent upon you to test your proposed questionnaire with enough people to make sure that there is no possible misunderstanding. It is an excellent precaution to test the questionnaire against people of different backgrounds, different education, and different intelligence (as closely as you can judge). Women and men think differently. There are ethnic differences that can lead to an unfortunate lack of understanding of what you thought you were saying.

7. If time allows, it is also good to try *several versions* of the questionnaire on groups of people. This can be a welcome change of routine for fellow employees, and you will find a real desire to cooperate. People will want to know which version was the "winner." In the testing, they can be asked what was ambiguous, what difficult to understand, what they would or would not have answered, and so on.

Women and men think differently.

8. Again, if time allows, it is desirable to send a test batch of questionnaires to a sample of your proposed sample. Sometimes these few people can be called on the phone after a few days and asked what they thought of the questionnaire. Are they going to answer it? If not, why not? You may avoid some horrendous error by using this little device, and will be able to change the questionnaire before disaster strikes.

9. Close attention to the appearance of a questionnaire pays off in return percentages. The use of cheap copying machines and cheap paper should always be avoided. Plenty of room should be left for writing, so that your respondent will not be held back by lack of space from giving you complete answers. This ties in with my next point, which concerns maximum length of questionnaire. It is true—and I hope you take my word for it—that plenty of room for answers, good margins, good reproduction, and good paper are of much greater importance than shortness. Business people are fond of the expression that "anything worth saying can be put on one page." They know better, but do like brevity. However, the Bible took over 1,300

pages of small type to get its message across to believers. A single page has no particular virtue.

10. But verboseness is a positive evil. A questionnaire should be long enough to cover its subject—and no longer. I have seen questionnaires of six or eight pages that won tremendous response. If your questionnaire looks interesting, looks fun to do, touches the special field of the respondents, is well prepared, and does not look cheap, then it can go for several pages without cutting down the response rate appreciably.

Pictures just for the sake of dressing up your questionnaire are a mistake. But pictures, drawings, and cartoons that help the respondent understand your needs are a great help. They awaken interest by appealing to the imagination. When you consider the cost of your time and the time of stenographers, paper and mailing costs, plus all the expense of tabulation, analysis, and the final report, it seems foolish to worry about the cost of reproducing a picture or two. But these are the kinds of economies that many companies like to make. Big money flows right along, while executives worry about the cost of sharpening pencils. All I am saying is, if pictures seem important to get the right answers to a questionnaire, then fight for them. Try not to let someone become a hero by cutting out this small extra cost.

Verboseness is a positive evil.

How Big Should the Sample Be?

Later in this book there will be a short chapter on sampling. All I want to say here is that you will probably never become an expert on statistics, unless you want to become a real professional researcher. Then you will *have* to know. For most of us, all that is necessary is to make the best judgment possible about whether we have *enough.*

Sometimes, with a small group like the maintenance supervisors of chain grocery stores, you will not sample at all. A questionnaire will go to every person you can find in the business. If you are in retailing, you may make an arbitrary decision to send a questionnaire to one-half of your customers with charge accounts. But recognizing that this does not represent your cash customers, you may pack questionnaires in bundles at various times during the week and the month. The charge account people will answer more readily. A smaller proportion of the cash customers will answer, depending on how skillfully you design the questionnaire.

Once, some years ago, I helped distribute questionnaires to women at subway station entrances in New York City. We hardly dared hope that anyone at all would answer. So we used every trick we could think of to arouse curiosity. The envelope was colored baby blue, and had a little flower sticker pasted on it. Inside we placed a golf pencil that could be felt through the envelope. And we even perfumed the envelope a bit. It was designed to appeal to the young working girl in New York, and asked questions about her shopping habits. I do not remember the exact return percentage, but it was over a third. These were distributed under the very worst conditions—at the going-home hour, during the rush at subway entrances. So much depends upon the quality of the questionnaire and cover letter that the number to be sent out is only a factor of the complete job.

However, you can make several judgments:

1. How many returns do you think will be adequate for this particular job? So that you feel safe in reaching a conclusion?

2. From your early tests of the questionnaire with your own people, and perhaps a pilot mailing, what return percentage do your think you are likely to get?

3. Applying item 1 to 2, you can make some sort of a guess at the total quantity that should be sent.

Importance of a Good Cover Letter and Envelope

As I have said, a market researcher must be constantly conscious of the importance of a good first impression. Unlike a salesperson, if the researcher "blows" the first few seconds of an interview or of a respondent's examination of his questionnaire, he may never get another chance. There are certain principles of a good cover letter that can be discussed separately:

1. The appearance should be the best possible. This is no place to save a few pennies. Cheap duplication methods, with the respondents' names typed in a clearly different shade of black, will argue against answering. The reaction is, "This questionnaire does not tell me that the sender believes it is very important, so I guess I will throw it away." In the few times where we were forced to use these methods, the return percentage clearly suffered.

2. The serious purpose of the questionnaire should be covered in the first paragraph of the cover letter. As with a news article, some readers will never get beyond this point, and should get the gist of the story quickly. Cuteness of any kind has no place here, or anyplace else in the cover letter or questionnaire.

3. However, a cover letter should not be dull. Some originality of expression is necessary. It is easier to say these things than for you to do them. That is why several versions of a cover letter should be written—perhaps by different people—and then tested out with another group for their reactions.

4. Where possible, the company's own letterhead should be used, instead of some dummy name like XYZ Research Associates. A made-up

name is legal and acceptable to the post office if it is not being used to defraud. But it is not a good idea, if high return percentages are needed. A known name, either national or a local retailer's, will always pull better.

5. Unless the size of the mailing absolutely prohibits it, every cover letter should be signed by hand. This seems an enormous task, but really is not for most of the mailings that you will do. I cannot prove it, but my own experience has been that respondents subconsciously know a reproduced signature. Again and again, experimentally, we tried both reproduced and hand-done signatures, and always had a higher return from the hand-signed cover letters. They do not have to be done by you personally. Your secretary can imitate your signature satisfactorily after a little practice.

6. In summary, a good cover letter for a questionnaire should be short, unambiguous, friendly, but not cute. It should get right to the point and give an honest and believable reason for the questionnaire. It should, of course, express appreciation in advance for the help which you hope the respondent will give to you. It should be addressed to a person by name and title if at all possible, and then signed by hand. A large task—but worth the effort if a mail study is to be used at all.

Writing a workable mail questionnaire.

How to Write a Questionnaire

There are only a few tricks of the trade that you need to know to write a workable mail questionnaire. It would make things very easy for us if we could ask a question like this:

> *Do you use our product Z (or patronize our store on Main Street), and do you find the service satisfactory?*

Then we could leave half a page of space for the respondent to write a small essay on the subject. It does not take a course in marketing research to tell you that such a questionnaire will not work. Few would answer at all; and fewer still would give cogent, helpful answers. Furthermore, it would be very difficult to tabulate and analyze.

A better way of asking for the same information would be:

1. Has your company bought and used product Z in the last three years?
   Yes ________ No ________
   If No, please place questionnaire in the enclosed envelope and send it to us.
2. For what purposes was it used? (Answer by using 1, 2, 3, and 4, in order of greatest use)
   Factory floor protection ________
   Office floor protection ________
   Lobby entrances ________
   Other (please explain) ____________
   ____

3. What brands have you used during the past three years? (Please check one or all.)

	For lobby	*For factory*	*For office*
Brand A	_______	_______	_______
Brand B	_______	_______	_______
Brand C	_______	_______	_______

4. We need your most honest appraisal of our own product, so that we can continue to improve it. Please rate each brand below, on the scale from *Fully satisfactory* to *Completely unsatisfactory* for us. Place a check mark at the proper place on the line for each product with which you have had experience in the last three years.

Product A	/___________/	___________/	___________/	___________/
	Fully satisfactory for our needs	Satisfactory but we felt it could be better for our needs	So-so; not very good for our needs	Completely unsatisfactory for us
etc.				

5. For each of the above, would you tell us in a few words *why* you gave it this rating?

Product A ______________________________________

____

Product B ______________________________________

____

etc.

Now, you may feel that you are introducing some bias in this questionnaire unless you send it under a dummy name. You are fearful that the respondent will consciously or unconsciously alter his answers, either to please you or because he is angry at your company. Of course, there is that chance, but if your cover letter makes an honest appeal for honest help, the chance of bias is sharply reduced. It never seemed to hurt our questionnaires too much, and we tried sending them out both ways: under our own name and under a dummy name.

Rules to Follow

1. Use screening questions early in each section of the questionnaire, to eliminate those respondents who have had no experience with the product, and whose answers would be worthless.

2. By checking with other people, as was suggested above, make absolutely sure that there can only be one way to answer each question. The question, "Where were you born?" for example, could be answered "in the U.S.A." or "in Missouri" or (I suppose) "in the hospital." One thing is as certain as tomorrow's daylight: If there is a way to foul up the answers, a large proportion of respondents will do so.

3. Avoid asking personal questions unless they are absolutely vital to the needs of the problem. And avoid asking for information that common sense

tells you will be kept confidential by the respondent's own company. With the advent of new regulations about disclosure, many companies are more open than they were. But even if the respondent knows that information is available to anyone who takes the trouble to seek it, he may still hesitate to send it to a stranger. There is no reason to kill a good questionnaire by going over the line of good sense and good taste.

4. Keep like questions together, preferably so that one question leads to the next in a logical progression.

5. Think deeply about whether any word or words are likely to cause an unwanted emotional reaction. Words that appear innocent and quite clear to you may, in fact, have a different meaning to someone else.

6. Whether your questionnaire is one or several pages, it should not appear cluttered and difficult to understand. There should be plenty of margin and plenty of room to write answers. The little boxes provided for check marks should be in line, if possible, and their use should be obvious. If you are providing space for an answer in the respondent's own words, do not force him to search for room to write what he wants to say—and what you want to hear.

Ways of Increasing the Return Percentage

Aside from all the rules above, there are other ways that can be used to increase the number of returns. The "shiny new dime" pasted at the top of the cover letter is an old, but effective, device. There is a sentence, preferably early in the cover letter, that says something to the effect that "we know that your time in answering this questionnaire is far more valuable than the shiny, new dime above. But accept it as a token of our sincere appreciation for your trouble in answering and returning the enclosed form. Give the dime to the first smiling young child whom you see on your way home tonight." Perhaps the amount should be a shiny new half-dollar in these days of inflation. At any rate, many people have used, and swear by, this technique for increasing returns. Money seems to be quite acceptable to most people. Having unglued the coin, one feels a moral obligation to comply with the researcher's wishes. Not always; there are a fair number of people who will take the money and throw the questionnaire away. But, oddly enough, even top executives, who hardly need another coin in their pockets, will be motivated to answer.

The "shiny new dime" pasted at the top of a cover letter is an old, but effective, device.

Another device is to promise some sort of present for those who return the questionnaire. Recently a large oil company did this with a sampling of its charge account customers. The present was attractive and desirable; I do not know what percentage return the company achieved, but my guess is that it was high.

If you are in a company where you can use one of your own products as a come-on, this is fortunate. Often the company is willing to charge you only a nominal cost. The respondent is doing much better than he would in the usual retail channels.

If there is a small advertising brochure describing the virtues of this giveaway, then this can be included. Again, even top executives are not immune from the happiness of getting something for nothing. One company put the address sheet for the free gift entirely separate from the cover letter and questionnaire. It found that executives were getting their people to do the work, but collecting the free gift themselves.

Every questionnaire should include a stamped, self-addressed envelope for the convenience of the respondent. Both the outgoing and the incoming envelopes should use regular postage stamps, rather than go through a postage meter. The stamp says to the respondent that *his* opinion is needed. The evidence is that he is more likely to complete the questionnaire. As with the cover letter, every effort must be made to achieve a dignified, business-like, and important atmosphere both in the questionnaire and in the way it is mailed.

Follow-up postcards increase the number of returns. If these cards offer to send another questionnaire because the first "may have been mislaid," the percentage is still further increased. Second follow-ups, and even third and fourth, are possible. Each gets fewer and fewer responses, with increasing cost and further passing of time. At some point common sense says to stop.

It is possible, especially if the mailing list is small, to telephone its receivers, to give them a little push. This can even be done with a sample of the sample. If your company has WATS lines, it becomes more economically feasible to do this.

Gathering the Mailing List

Sources of mailing lists are so varied, they cannot all be listed here. All that can be done is to give you some hints and suggestions about where to start.

1. Charge account customers of a retailer.
2. Account cards of a manufacturer—usually with names of executives and their titles.
3. Similar account records of a wholesaler or distributor.
4. People who have attended pertinent conventions. Registration lists for conventions are often available in one way or another.
5. Membership rosters of various associations. You might not be able to get such rosters directly from the associations, but you can find someone who belongs to lend you his.
6. Poor's Register of Executives and Directors.

7. Various Moody publications.

8. Form 10K of the Securities and Exchange Commission.

9. For retailers, in some cities, the telephone directories which are available by geographic area.

10. Purchased mailing lists available from several companies.

This is just the beginning. Each company will have its own sources of names to draw from. The only thing to be a little cautious about is the use of purchased mailing lists. They have proved disappointing, in several instances, by being out of date and not as complete and accurate as one should expect. But you may find a different situation in your own type of business.

Tabulation of returned questionnaires

Tabulation of Returned Questionnaires

Tabulation mechanics should have been considered in the makeup of the questionnaire. It is a terrible blow to find that tabulation is ten times as difficult as it might have been if advance thought had been given to the subject.

It is possible to "precode," that is, to put a little code mark beside each possible answer on the questionnaire. The mark tells the punch card operator what holes to punch on the tabulating card. Presumably, precoding leads to greater accuracy and greater speed. Once the cards have been punched, they can be run through the computer. Normal tabulations, cross tabulations, and all sorts of comparisons become possible.

For the smaller studies that you will probably do, however, it is questionable whether precoding is necessarily helpful. Contrary to the apparent progress of science, sometimes a questionnaire can be tabulated by hand on columnar paper, and the job will be done before the big machines can be set up.

Retailers, unless they are very big, are not likely to have access to a computer for other than normal work. The local bank's computer may keep their regular accounts, but to have a "program" written for a special and small study may cause consternation and delay.

The same thing can be said for distributors. Manufacturers are more likely to have computer availability. But to get a small study on the big machines takes time, pull, and sometimes gall. While all the fighting is going on, the questionnaire could be completely tabulated by a smart stenographer.

If you want a number of separate tabulations from your questionnaire, you may still need to use the computer. But the more complex your wants, the more returns you will need. If you want all the answers broken down by age group, by sex, and by geographical area, it is very probable that most of your studies will not have enough returns in each bracket to allow meaningful analysis. These types of breakdowns, if they are important, must be considered early in the game, so that the basic mailing is large enough.

It is usually a mistake to allow people to expect too much. It might be very nice to know, for example, what girls under twenty years of age in the Far West think of your product. But perhaps this is not important enough to quadruple your outgoing questionnaires.

At any rate, by using ingenious ways of setting up a hand-tab spread sheet, it is often quite easy to do cross tabulations without machines. There may be a bit of stenographic grumbling at the job, but it *can* be done.

Summary

A book like this cannot in itself produce mail questionnaire experts. All it can do is stimulate thought, warn against pitfalls, and point out possibilities for successful use of the technique. Mail questionnaires really need creative imagination in their construction, and that *you* must supply yourself. Just copying methods used by others leads to dullness and low return percentages. Somehow the mailing piece must sparkle with fresh thought if it is to arouse curiosity, interest, and a willingness of the respondent to cooperate.

On the following pages are examples of mail questionnaires which have worked. Almost all the types of questions that you will ever use can be found here. Knowing your own needs, you can pick certain techniques that seem to fit your purpose.

In most cases these questionnaires have been retyped and changed in size to fit book pages. In doing so, it has been necessary to eliminate much of the space which this chapter so strongly favored.

With all this in mind, I think you will find these questionnaires most useful. Perhaps they will serve best by stimulating your imagination to do something better.

RETAILER PANELING

QUESTIONNAIRE

Store Name: ____________________

Location: City __________ State ______

Person Completing Interview: __________

____

Title: ____________________

Date: ____________________

1. Approximate square feet size of your showroom:

____

2. Do you have a special wall paneling section in your store? Yes___ No___. Estimated size of wall paneling section (lineal ft.) __________

3. What paneling producer's products do you regularly carry? (Please check)

Company A___ Company B___ Company C___ etc.

Other (please indicate who) __________

4. What percent of your wall paneling (units) would you estimate is sold to:

a) Do-It-Yourselfers _____%

b) Residential remodelers? _____%

c) Residential builders? _____%

4. (cont'd)

d) Commercial builders? _____%

e) Commercial remodelers? _____%

f) Mobile home dealers/owners? _____%

5. (A) What percent of your total wall paneling sales (units) now are in the following different price ranges?

Up to $3.99____ $4.00-4.99____ $5.00-5.99____

$6.00-6.99____ $7.00-7.99____ $8.00-8.99____

$10.00+____

(B) How many patterns do you presently carry in each price range?

Up to $3.99____ $4.00-4.99____ $5.00-5.99____

$6.00-6.99 ____ $7.00-7.99____ $8.00-8.99____

$10.00+____

(C) How many patterns should you have in each price range?

Up to $3.99____ $4.00-4.99____ $5.00-5.99____

$6.00-6.99 ____ $7.00-7.99____ $8.00-8.99____

$10.00+____

(D) If you could add only one more pattern to your paneling line, which one would do the most to improve your sales?____________________________

At what retail price?__________________________

(E) Would a broad line of panels in the $3.99-8.99 retail range from one supplier in mixed carloads

5. (cont'd)

help you? Yes___ No___. Comments________________

____

6. (A) If you were to guess, how much of your paneling sales are: Hardware substrate_____%
Particleboard substrate_____% Lauan substrate_____%
Hardboard substrate_____% Plywood substrate_____%

(B) Would you have difficulty selling a good looking 3/16"-1/4" vinyl veneer particleboard panel in the $6-10 retail price category? Why?__________

____

(C) What product qualities do your customers look for in the best selling panels in the $6-10 retail price range?______________________

____

7. (A) What were your approximate total wall paneling sales units last year? Number of panels?_______

(B) How are panel sales (units) going this year?
Up_____%; Approx. the same_____; or Down_____%

8. What percent of total panels sold are decorative____% vs. wood grain patterns____%.

9. Are decorative panels increasing in popularity?
Yes____ No____. What are the best selling patterns?
Colors?____

____

10. (A) What percent of wood grain sales are now lighter? _____% Medium?_____% Darker?_____% Tones?_____%

(B) Are lighter_____medium_____darker_____ wood-grains becoming more popular? Comments?

____

11. What best selling panel patterns represent 20-25% of your unit sales? (Please indicate brand names also, if possible)

Manufacturer/Brand/Color	Approx. Retail Price
______________________________	_____________________
______________________________	_____________________
______________________________	_____________________
______________________________	_____________________

12. What percent of your wood grain panels are: Standard V-Grooved_____%; Random Board V-Grooved_____%; Ungrooved_____%

13. What percent of your total wall paneling sales have: Vinyl face____; Paper/Print face____; Plywood face____; Other____

14. What manufacturer's paneling do you like to sell best? Why?____

____

15. What manufacturers do the best job of providing you with sales aids?__________________________________

16. What promotional aids or improved/different product offerings would help you to improve your paneling sales?____

____

THANK YOU FOR YOUR HELP!!

(*Courtesy of Ducker Research Company, Birmingham, Michigan.* Names of companies have been omitted.)

THE STANLEY WORKS

Since 1843

NEW BRITAIN, CONNECTICUT 06050

MARKETING RESEARCH DEPARTMENT

Area Code 203 225-5111

Dear Sir:

This is a sincere request for information. It is not a sales device. In the development of long range plans for our Industrial Hardware Division, we need guidance to help us determine which way we should head. The experience and opinions of manufacturers such as your company will help our planning. It will help us become good, sound, substantial producers of metal parts and we are much more likely to be of assistance to you some day.

On the pages that follow, we illustrate some of the types of parts produced by this division. We would appreciate your reviewing the four sections and answering the questions related to each. If this is not in the area of your responsibility we would appreciate your passing this along to the appropriate individual in your organization.

We realize this will require some of your time. To show our appreciation for your cooperation in our market study we would like to send you a gift of one of our Stanley Hand Tool products. Please enter your name and mailing address in the place indicated on the gift sheet.

Very truly yours,

George E. Breen
Director, Marketing Research

GEB: sc
Encs.

TO SHOW OUR APPRECIATION FOR YOUR ASSISTANCE, WE WOULD LIKE TO SEND YOU THIS STANLEY TAPE RULE.

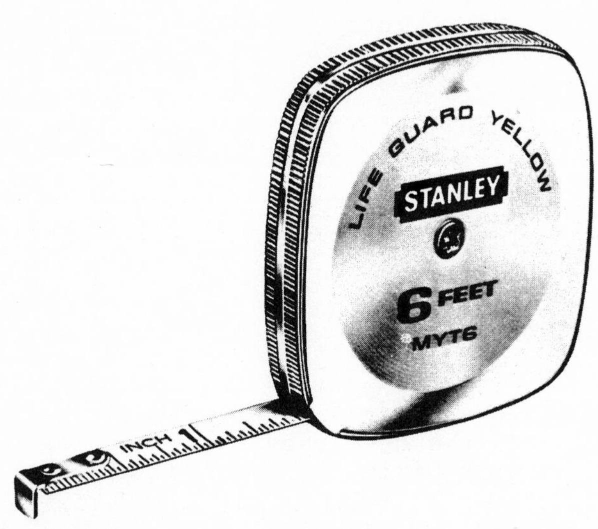

– PLEASE PRINT –

NAME ____

COMPANY ____

ADDRESS ____

CITY & STATE ____

ZIP CODE ____

Do you use parts that look like these?

If so, would you please answer the 4
questions on the following page?

COLD HEADING

1. Do you use metal parts of the types and sizes of those in the picture on page 4? ______Yes ______No

2. If so, which of the following processes are used to make the parts?

____________	Cold Heading	__________	Approx. Number of Different Parts
____________	Screw Machine	__________	Approx. Number of Different Parts
____________	Hot Forging	__________	Approx. Number of Different Parts

3. On what types of products do you use the parts? ____

4. What is the range of your annual quantity requirements of parts made by each process (such as 10M to 100M)?

Cold Heading:	________________	to	________________
Screw Machine:	________________	to	________________
Hot Forging:	________________	to	________________

5. Where do you obtain the parts made by each process?

COLD HEADING:	_______	Make Ourselves	_______	Buy on Outside	_______	Both
SCREW MACHINE:	_______	Make Ourselves	_______	Buy on Outside	_______	Both
HOT FORGING:	_______	Make Ourselves	_______	Buy on Outside	_______	Both

6. What are the ranges of part dimensions you require?

DIAMETER:	____________	Minimum to	____________	Maximum
LENGTH:	____________	Minimum to	____________	Maximum

7. What do you feel the trend will be of your future requirements in each process for making the parts?

	TOTAL NEED	QUANTITY MADE YOURSELF	QUANTITY PURCHASED
COLD HEADING:	______ Up	______ Up	______ Up
	______ Down	______ Down	______ Down
SCREW MACHINE:	______ Up	______ Up	______ Up
	______ Down	______ Down	______ Down
HOT FORGED:	______ Up	______ Up	______ Up
	______ Down	______ Down	______ Down

Do you use parts that look like these?

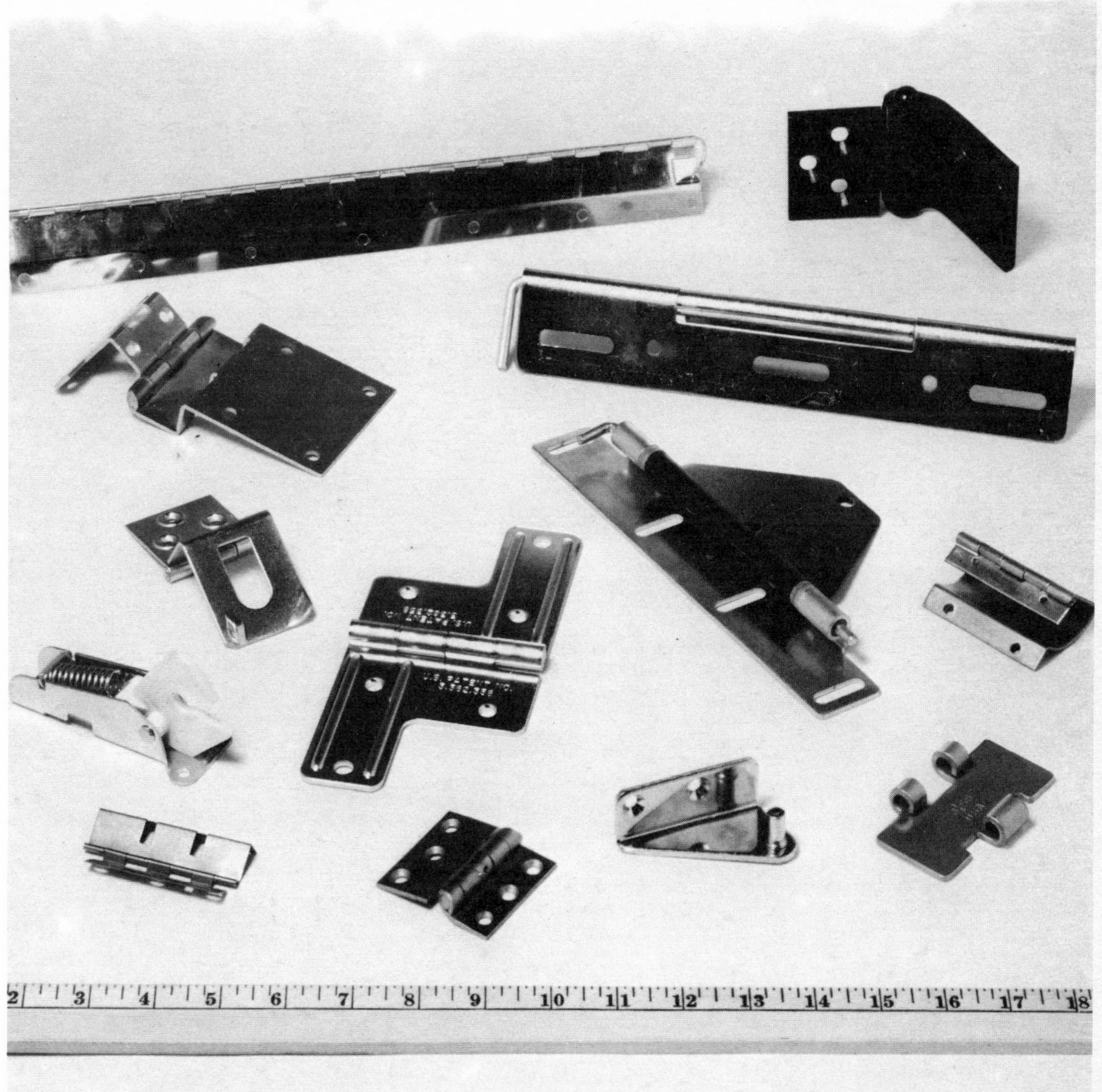

If so, would you please answer the questions on the following page? 6

SPECIAL HINGES

1. Do you use special (non-catalogued) hinges similar to those in the picture on page 6? _____ Yes _____ No

2. On what types of product do you use these hinges? ______________________________

3. If so, what are the general types of hinges used? Do you make or buy them?

		MAKE	BUY
Special Continuous	_____	_____	_____
Formed Hinges (Leaves Not Flat)	_____	_____	_____
Springloaded	_____	_____	_____
Special Hinges	_____	_____	_____
Swaged and Reverse Assembly	_____	_____	_____
Welded Hinges	_____	_____	_____
Slip Hinges	_____	_____	_____
Custom Designs	_____	_____	_____
Other ______________________	_____	_____	_____

4. What is the range of your annual requirements? (10M to 50M, etc.)

Special Continuous	_____	to	_____	Swaged/Reverse Assy.	_____	to	_____
Formed Hinges	_____	to	_____	Welded Hinges	_____	to	_____
Springloaded	_____	to	_____	Slip Hinges	_____	to	_____
Special Butts	_____	to	_____	Custom Designs	_____	to	_____

5. How do you evaluate the future trend in your requirements?

TOTAL NEED	_____ Up	_____ Down
MAKE YOURSELF	_____ Up	_____ Down
PURCHASED	_____ Up	_____ Down

Do you use parts that look like these?

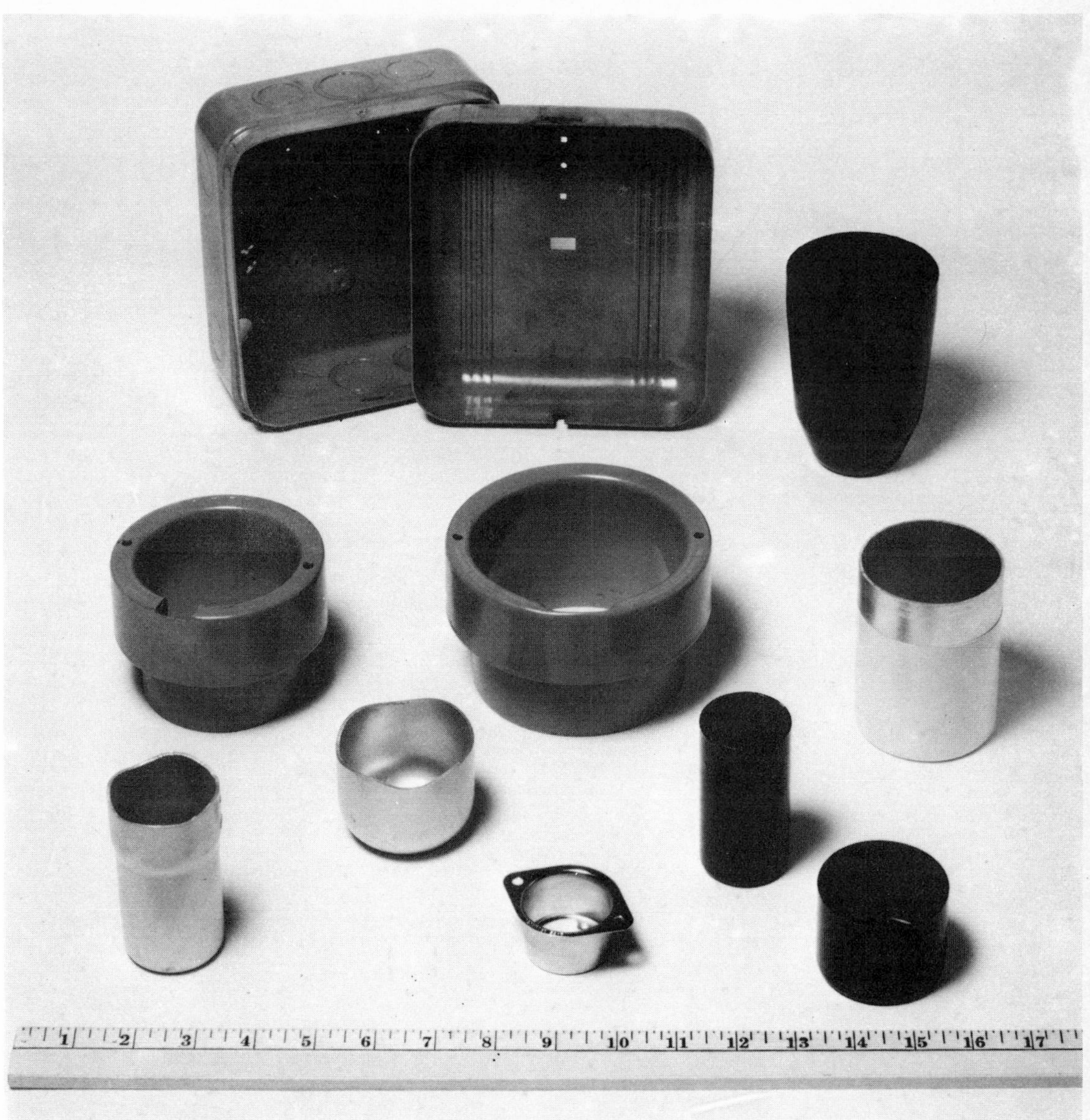

If so, would you please answer the questions on the following page? 8

DEEP DRAWING

1. Do you use metal parts of the types and sizes of those in the picture on page 8? _______ Yes _______ No

2. If so, which of the following processes are used to make the parts?

   ___________ Deep Drawing ___________ Approx. Number of Different Parts

   ___________ Fabrication ___________ Approx. Number of Different Parts

3. On what types of products do you use these parts? ______________________________

4. What is the range of your annual quantity requirements of parts made by each process (such as 10M to 100M)?

   DEEP DRAWING: ___________ to ___________

   FABRICATION: ___________ to ___________

5. Where do you obtain the parts made by each process?

   DEEP DRAWING: _____ Make Ourselves _____ Buy On Outside _____ Both

   FABRICATION: _____ Make Ourselves _____ Buy On Outside _____ Both

6. What are the ranges of part dimensions you require?

   DIAMETER: ______________ Minimum to ______________ Maximum

   LENGTH: ______________ Minimum to ______________ Maximum

7. What do you feel the trend will be of your future requirements in each process for making the parts?

	TOTAL NEED	QUANTITY MADE YOURSELF	QUANTITY PURCHASED
DEEP DRAWING:	____ Up ____ Down	____ Up ____ Down	____ Up ____ Down
FABRICATION:	____ Up ____ Down	____ Up ____ Down	____ Up ____ Down

Do you use parts that look like these?

If so, would you please answer the questions on the following page?

10

HEAVY STAMPING

1. Do you use metal parts of the type and sizes of those in the picture on page 10? _____ Yes _____ No

2. If so, which of the following processes are used to make the parts?

   ___________ Stamped ___________ Approx. Number of Different Parts
   ___________ Forged ___________ Approx. Number of Different Parts
   ___________ Cast ___________ Approx. Number of Different Parts

3. On what types of products do you use these parts? ______________________________

4. What is the range of your annual quantity requirements of parts made by each process (such as 10M to 100M)?

   Stamped: ___________ to ___________
   Forged: ___________ to ___________
   Cast: ___________ to ___________

5. Where do you obtain the parts made by each process?

   STAMPED: _______ Make Ourselves _______ Buy on Outside _______ Both
   FORGED: _______ Make Ourselves _______ Buy on Outside _______ Both
   CAST: _______ Make Ourselves _______ Buy on Outside _______ Both

6. What are the ranges of part dimensions you require?

   WIDTH: ___________ Minimum to ___________ Maximum
   LENGTH: ___________ Minimum to ___________ Maximum
   DEPTH: ___________ Minimum to ___________ Maximum

7. What do you feel the trend will be of your future requirements in each process for making the parts?

	TOTAL NEED	QUANTITY MADE YOURSELF	QUANTITY PURCHASED
STAMPED:	_____ Up	_____ Up	_____ Up
	_____ Down	_____ Down	_____ Down
FORGED:	_____ Up	_____ Up	_____ Up
	_____ Down	_____ Down	_____ Down
CAST:	_____ Up	_____ Up	_____ Up
	_____ Down	_____ Down	_____ Down

STANLEY TOOLS
NEW BRITAIN, CONNECTICUT

INDUSTRIAL QUESTIONNAIRE

Would you please encircle the number which most accurately indicates your opinion of each statement. Encircle 6 if you strongly agree with the statement or number 1 if you strongly disagree. Or, any number in between that you feel is most appropriate.

1. One source buying is important to our company.

AGREE 6 5 4 3 2 1 DISAGREE

2. The Stanley Tools line is important to our company.

AGREE 6 5 4 3 2 1 DISAGREE

3. National brands make our selling job easier.

AGREE 6 5 4 3 2 1 DISAGREE

4. Stanley products represent good value for price charged.

AGREE 6 5 4 3 2 1 DISAGREE

5. The quality of Stanley products gives us more confidence in selling.

AGREE 6 5 4 3 2 1 DISAGREE

6. I would rank Stanley's salesman in the top 20% of the manufacturers' reps calling on us.

YES ☐ NO ☐

7. This salesman gives us good support beyond taking the order.

AGREE 6 5 4 3 2 1 DISAGREE

8. Stanley's variable pricing helps us improve our gross profit margins.

AGREE 6 5 4 3 2 1 DISAGREE

NOT FAMILIAR WITH IT ☐

9. The quantity discounts on tape rules and Workmaster screwdrivers are attractive to our operation.

AGREE 6 5 4 3 2 1 DISAGREE

NOT FAMILIAR WITH IT ☐

10. We make use of Stanley's overstocking policy and it helps us maintain better stock conditions.

AGREE 6 5 4 3 2 1 DISAGREE

NOT FAMILIAR WITH IT ☐

11. The new full line #34 catalogue is an improvement over the industrial catalogue.

AGREE 6 5 4 3 2 1 DISAGREE

NOT AWARE OF IT ☐

12. We find the imprinted price sheets from Stanley helpful in our business.

AGREE 6 5 4 3 2 1 DISAGREE

NOT FAMILIAR WITH IT ☐

13. We make use of the Stanley co-op advertising allowance and think it is an important part of their industrial program.

AGREE 6 5 4 3 2 1 DISAGREE

NOT AWARE OF IT ☐

14. We believe the Stanley <u>Tool Crib News</u> can be an effective advertising and sales tool.

AGREE 6 5 4 3 2 1 DISAGREE

NOT FAMILIAR WITH IT ☐

15. The Stanley salesman conducts effective sales meetings.

AGREE 6 5 4 3 2 1 DISAGREE

16. The Stanley salesman is knowledgeable about the products he sells.

AGREE 6 5 4 3 2 1 DISAGREE

17. We have or intend to use the special Stanley "conversation starters" on our sales calls.

AGREE 6 5 4 3 2 1 DISAGREE

NOT FAMILIAR WITH THEM ☐

18. We believe the Stanley sales incentives such as the "free gas" offer is an effective way to increase sales of Stanley products.

AGREE 6 5 4 3 2 1 DISAGREE

NOT FAMILIAR WITH IT ☐

19. Would you run monthly specials if you were given special prices on products to promote?

YES ☐ NO ☐

20. Would you mail out promotion pieces (flyers) on these specials?

YES ☐ NO ☐

21. What products should Stanley add to their line to become your major supplier of small hand tools?

____

____

22. I think the following companies have a better over-all industrial program than Stanley. (Please list company names in order.)

____

____

____

CITY ____________________________

STATE ___________________________

THE STANLEY WORKS

Since 1843

NEW BRITAIN, CONNECTICUT 06050

(203) 225-5111

MARKET RESEARCH DEPARTMENT

Within the last few months you have purchased one of our Job/Master sabre saws.

Now that you have had a chance to use this tool for a while, we would like to know how well it is doing the job.

All manufacturers of quality products continually try to improve them. Electric tool manufacturers don't have "annual models" like the automobile companies. But we do change our product from time to time, and would like your experience to help guide us.

Would you be kind enough to answer the questions on the enclosed sheet, and send it back to us in the stamped envelope? Most of what we ask has to do with how our product meets your needs. We are interested in those features which you consider of greatest usefulness; we are also interested in features which you think should be changed, or which are of no real importance to you.

If you feel like writing us a letter, in addition to answering the questions, please turn the questionnaire over and do so. Everything you say will be read, considered, and acted upon, if possible, in the future.

Thank you very much for your cooperation.

Yours very truly,

George E. Breen, Director
Marketing Research Department

SABRE SAW QUESTIONNAIRE

1. Why did you choose a Stanley sabre saw?__________

____

2. Was power an important factor in making your decision? YES ☐ NO ☐

3. Also, at the time of purchase, what other things were important to you?__________

____

4. (a) Did you have a specific project in mind when you purchased the sabre saw? YES ☐ NO ☐

   (b) If Yes, what was the project?__________

   (c) What material did you cut with your sabre saw?

   ____

   Approximate thickness of material?__________

   (d) What type(s) cuts did you make?

Cut		Performance
Straight line	( )	easy to follow - Yes( ) No( )
Curved line	( )	easy to follow - Yes( ) No( )
Angle	( )	maintained angle; did not drift - Yes( ) No( )
Flush	( )	good visibility in cutting Yes( ) No( )
Pocket/plunge	( )	ease in getting blade through material with no bouncing or vibration -Yes( ) No( )

5. (a) If you had no specific job in mind, have you had the opportunity to use the saw?

YES ☐ NO ☐

(b) If Yes, what type of material have you used it on?____________________

Approximate thickness of material?__________

(c) What type(s) of cuts did you make?__________

____

(straight, curved, angle, flush, etc.)

6. How would you rate your sabre saw on the following features?

Appearance	( ) FAIR	( ) GOOD	( ) EXCELLENT
Handling ease	( ) FAIR	( ) GOOD	( ) EXCELLENT
Performance	( ) FAIR	( ) GOOD	( ) EXCELLENT

7. Did you find the following features satisfactory?

length of stroke	( ) Yes	( ) No
cutting speed	( ) Yes	( ) No
accuracy in adjustments	( ) Yes	( ) No
cord length	( ) Yes	( ) No
weight	( ) Yes	( ) No
switch position	( ) Yes	( ) No
tilting base	( ) Yes	( ) No
plastic handle	( ) Yes	( ) No

COMMENTS:____________________________________

____

8. Number the following 1, 2, 3, 4, in order of importance to you:

   cutting speed ______

   accuracy in adjustments ______

   blade life ______

   ease in installing and changing blades ______

9. If you check your instruction sheet you will note that it recommends lubrication after a certain number of performance hours. How do you feel about having to give the tool this care?

   ____

   ____

10. Approximately how many hours of <u>actual performance</u> per week or month do you think you will use your sabre saw?

    Approx. hours per week ______ or

    Approx. hours per month ______

(IF YOU HAVE ANY FURTHER COMMENTS, PLEASE USE THE REVERSE SIDE OF THIS SHEET)

THE STANLEY WORKS

Since 1843

NEW BRITAIN, CONNECTICUT 06050

(203) 225-5111

MARKET RESEARCH DEPARTMENT

Dear Stanley Tool Owner:

When you purchased your Stanley SURFORM tool some time ago, you were kind enough to furnish us some helpful information by returning an enclosed question card.

Now that you have owned your SURFORM tool for several months, we would like to ask for your help once again. By returning the enclosed questionnaire to us in the return pre-paid envelope, you will be helping us plan both new improvements to our SURFORM tools and future marketing methods for them.

We are asking only one hundred people throughout the country to participate in answering the questionnaire, and your answers are very important to us. Above all, we need your frank answers. If there is something you do not like about our SURFORM tools, we hope you will tell us about it.

As a token of our appreciation for your help, we will be pleased to forward to you free, upon receipt of your completed questionnaire, a Stanley CUSHION-GRIP PRUNER (picture enclosed). We hope you will have many pleasant hours using this fine tool.

Thank you for your help.

Sincerely yours,

George E. Breen, Director
Marketing Research Department

AT MOST, THIS QUESTIONNAIRE PROBABLY TAKES 10 MINUTES TO ANSWER

1. WHICH TYPE SURFORM TOOL DO YOU OWN?

File type ________ Plane type ________

Other type (please specify) ____________________

2. ON WHICH OF THESE KINDS OF MATERIAL HAVE YOU USED YOUR SURFORM TOOL?

Wood ________ Fiberglas ________

Plastic ________ Metal ________

Other material (please specify) ____________________

3. FOR WHAT PURPOSE HAVE YOU USED YOUR SURFORM TOOL?

Building furniture, cabinets, shelves, etc. ________

Fitting screens, doors, windows, etc. ________

Other special jobs (boatbuilding, veneering, etc.)

(Please describe) ____________________

____

4. DO YOU USE YOUR SURFORM TOOL IN PLACE OF ANOTHER TOOL?

Yes ________ No ________

IF YES, PLEASE INDICATE WHAT TOOL IT HAS REPLACED.

File or wood rasp ________

Plane ________

Other (please specify) ____________________

5. WOULD YOU PLEASE ESTIMATE THE NUMBER OF REPLACEMENT BLADES YOU HAVE BOUGHT FOR YOUR SURFORM TOOL. ____________

6. OF THESE MAGAZINES, WHICH DO YOU SUBSCRIBE TO, READ ONLY OCCASIONALLY, OR READ NOT AT ALL? (PLEASE INDICATE YOUR ANSWER BY CHECK MARK IN APPROPRIATE COLUMN).

MAGAZINE	I SUBSCRIBE TO IT	I READ IT ONLY OCCASIONALLY	I NEVER READ IT
Saturday Evening Post			
Popular Science			
Life			
Popular Mechanics			
Time			
This Week			
Work Bench			
Newsweek			
Home Craftsman			
Look			
Carpenter			
House & Home			
Other ________			

7. HAVE YOU EVER RECOMMENDED SURFORM TOOLS TO A FRIEND?

Yes ________ No ________

8. HAVE YOU EVER BOUGHT ANY SURFORM TOOLS AS GIFTS FOR OTHERS?

Yes ________ No ________

9. HOW DO YOU LIKE YOUR SURFORM TOOL?

____

____

10. DO YOU HAVE ANY SUGGESTION ON HOW WE COULD IMPROVE OUR SURFORM TOOLS?

____

____

____

THANK YOU AGAIN FOR YOUR HELP

YOUR NAME ________________________________

ADDRESS TO WHICH YOU WANT GIFT SENT ________________

____

THE STANLEY WORKS

Since 1843

NEW BRITAIN, CONNECTICUT 06050

(203) 225-5111

MARKET RESEARCH DEPARTMENT

The Stanley Tools Division recognizes the importance of mass merchandisers in the distribution of hand tools. To help us plan our marketing and sales activities, we need to know just what is important to you.

Attached is a questionnaire which we think will help us develop a better knowledge of your operation. We have tried to make it as easy as possible for you to answer and still include the subjects important to your company and to our company. We realize that this will take a few minutes of your time, but we sincerely hope that it will help us save you valuable business time in the future and contribute to more profit dollars from your tool sales.

We are sending this questionnaire to several important mass merchandisers in the industry and will give careful thought to your responses. You do not have to sign your name or indicate the name of your company.

We thank you for your contribution to this very important project.

Very truly yours,

George E. Breen, Director
Marketing Research Department

STANLEY TOOLS DIVISION
THE STANLEY WORKS
NEW BRITAIN, CONNECTICUT

1. How important is the Hardware Department in your stores? (PLEASE MARK ON SCALE)

Very Important	6	5	4	3	2	1	Not At All Important

2. What are your profit goals for hand tools? (PLEASE CIRCLE)

   a) Initial Gross Margin: 30% 32% 35% 38% 40% 42%

   b) Inventory Turns: 3 4 5 6 7 8

   c) Sales per Sq. Ft.: $75 $90 $100 $115 $125

   d) Are your normal tool selling prices discounted?

      10% 15% 20% Other____________

   e) Are retail prices for like hand tool items the same in all stores of your chain? Yes___ No___

3. Promotions:

   a) What percent of your total store sales are based on promotions? 10% 25% 33% 50% _____%

   b) How often do you promote tools?

      12 8 6 4 3 times per year

   c) What percent of your advertising costs do each of these represent?

      Newspaper ads _____% Radio _____%
      Circulars _____% Other _____%

   Do you foresee any change in the percent mix of above?________________________________

3. (cont'd)

d) Do you tie in promotions with manufacturers' national consumer advertising? Yes___ No___

e) What percent of co-op advertising costs would you expect a tool manufacturer to share?______%

f) What advertising aids do you require?

Lay outs	Yes___	No___
Line Drawings	Yes___	No___
Half Tones	Yes___	No___

Other________________________________

g) Are special promotional prices required from manufacturers to support your promotions?

Yes_____ No_____

h) What percent off of your <u>regular</u> <u>selling</u> prices are necessary for promotion?

10% 20% 25% ______%

4. Merchandising:

We would appreciate your indication of the importance of the following merchandising elements. (CIRCLE THE DEGREE OF IMPORTANCE TO YOUR CHAIN: 6 = Very Important, 1 = Not At All Important)

	Very Important					Not At All Important
a) Plan-O-Grams	6	5	4	3	2	1
b) Hook Tickets	6	5	4	3	2	1
c) Pre-ticketing	6	5	4	3	2	1

4. (cont'd)

Very Important					Not At All Important

d) Manufacturers' point of purchase displays

6 5 4 3 2 1

e) Feature end displays for tools

6 5 4 3 2 1

f) Printed hand out pieces

6 5 4 3 2 1

g) Demonstrator displays

6 5 4 3 2 1

h) Broadcast announcements for tool specials

6 5 4 3 2 1

5. In-store Service:

a) Do you allow manufacturers' personnel in your stores? Yes___ No___

b) Do you require assistance in setting up displays for a new store opening or remodeling? Yes___ No___

c) Which of the following in-store services do you expect your supplier to perform: (PLEASE CIRCLE)

Housekeeping	Yes	No
Inventorying	Yes	No
Re-ordering	Yes	No
Ticketing	Yes	No
Packing Out	Yes	No

d) Do you maintain a warehouse for hand tools?

Yes_____ No_____

e) Do you receive drop shipments of tools in your stores?

Yes_____ No_____

5. (cont'd)

f) Do you use an independent detailing service for your in-store work?

Yes_____ No_____

6. Now think of the Stanley Tools Division and rate us on the following points.

	Top Rating				Bottom Rating
a) Name Brand	6	5	4	3	2	1
b) Quality of Products	6	5	4	3	2	1
c) New Products	6	5	4	3	2	1
d) A Leader in the Industry	6	5	4	3	2	1
e) Offers Good Value to Your Customers	6	5	4	3	2	1

HOSPITAL ADMINISTRATION IN CANADA

QUESTIONNAIRE TO BE FILLED IN BY PERSON WITH THE MAJOR BUYING INFLUENCE/MOST KNOWLEDGE OF DISPOSABLES USED.

OPTIONAL

____
(Name of health care institution)

____
(Address)

____
(City or Town) (Province)

____
(Name of respondent/Job Title)

DATA ABOUT YOUR INSTITUTION - (PLEASE CIRCLE APPROPRIATE CODE IN EACH COLUMN)

TYPE	SIZE	LOCATION
Teaching hospital......1	50-99 beds.........1	Br. Columbia..1
Non-teaching general hospital............2	100-199 beds.......2	Prairies*.....2
Chronic care hospital..3	200-299 beds.......3	Ontario.......3
Convalescent..........4	300-399 beds.......4	Quebec........4
Rehabilitation........5	400-499 beds.......5	Maritimes.....5
Psychiatric...........6	500 beds and over..6	
Other __________ (specify).....7		*Includes Yukon & N.W.T.

The following are a series of types of disposable products that could be used in your hospital. For each, would you please check whether your hospital uses this item in disposable form only or re-usable form only or both. If you use the disposable form at all, please check your principal supplier and the estimated number of units purchased annually. If the number of units purchased is under or over the indicated ranges, please write, in the space provided, the actual number of units purchased.

	USE RE-USABLE ONLY	USE DISPOSABLE ONLY	USE BOTH	PRINCIPAL SUPPLIER	NUMBER OF UNITS PURCHASED
Urethral Catheter Trays	[ ]	[ ]	[ ]	Bard....................[ ]	0 - 500 (specify) ________..[ ]
				Baxter..................[ ]	501 - 1,000...............[ ]
				Cutter..................[ ]	1,001 - 1,500.............[ ]
				Kendall.................[ ]	1,501 - 2,000.............[ ]
				Pharmaseal..............[ ]	2,001 and over
				Other (specify)___________[ ]	(specify) ________...[ ]
Myelogram Trays	[ ]	[ ]	[ ]	American Hospital........[ ]	0 - 100 (specify)________...[ ]
				Baxter..................[ ]	101 - 200.................[ ]
				Monoject................[ ]	201 - 300.................[ ]
				Pharmaseal..............[ ]	301 - 400.................[ ]
				Picker..................[ ]	401 - 500.................[ ]
				Other (specify)___________[ ]	501 and over
					(specify)________......[ ]
Spinal Puncture Trays	[ ]	[ ]	[ ]	Abbott..................[ ]	0 - 150 (specify)________...[ ]
				American Hospital........[ ]	151 - 300.................[ ]
				Baxter..................[ ]	301 - 450.................[ ]
				Monoject................[ ]	451 - 600.................[ ]
				Pharmaseal..............[ ]	601 and over
				Other (specify)___________[ ]	(specify)________.......[ ]
Spinal Anaesthesia Trays	[ ]	[ ]	[ ]	Abbott..................[ ]	0 - 250 (specify)________...[ ]
				American Hospital........[ ]	251 - 500.................[ ]
				Baxter..................[ ]	501 - 750.................[ ]
				Monoject................[ ]	751 - 1,000...............[ ]
				Pharmaseal..............[ ]	1,001 and over
				Other (specify)___________[ ]	(specify)________.......[ ]
Epidural and Caudal Anaesthesia Trays	[ ]	[ ]	[ ]	Abbott..................[ ]	0 - 100 (specify)________...[ ]
				American Hospital........[ ]	101 - 200.................[ ]
				Baxter..................[ ]	201 - 300.................[ ]
				Monoject................[ ]	301 - 400.................[ ]
				Pharmaseal..............[ ]	401 and over
				Other (specify)___________[ ]	(specify)________.......[ ]

	USE RE-USABLE ONLY	USE DISPOSABLE ONLY	USE BOTH	PRINCIPAL SUPPLIER	NUMBER OF UNITS PURCHASED
Soapsud Enema	[ ]	[ ]	[ ]	American Hospital.........[ ]	0 - 1,000 (specify)________.[ ]
				Bard......................[ ]	1,001 - 2,000..............[ ]
				Baxter....................[ ]	2,001 - 3,000..............[ ]
				Cutter....................[ ]	3,001 - 4,000..............[ ]
				Davol.....................[ ]	4,001 and over
				Pharmaseal................[ ]	(specify)________.......[ ]
				Other (specify)___________[ ]	
Pre-filled Barium Enema	[ ]	[ ]	[ ]	Baxter....................[ ]	0 - 1,000 (specify)________.[ ]
				MacBick...................[ ]	1,001 - 2,000..............[ ]
				Mallinckrodt..............[ ]	2,001 - 3,000..............[ ]
				Other (specify)___________[ ]	3,001 - 4,000..............[ ]
					4,001 and over
					(specify)________.......[ ]
Vaginal Irrigation Trays	[ ]	[ ]	[ ]	American Hospital.........[ ]	0 - 200 (specify)________...[ ]
				Bard......................[ ]	201 - 400..................[ ]
				Baxter....................[ ]	401 - 600..................[ ]
				Cutter....................[ ]	601 - 800..................[ ]
				Davol.....................[ ]	801 and over
				Pharmaseal................[ ]	(specify)________.......[ ]
				Sterilon..................[ ]	
				Other (specify)___________[ ]	
Gavage Containers	[ ]	[ ]	[ ]	Bard......................[ ]	0 - 1,000 (specify)________.[ ]
				Baxter....................[ ]	1,001 - 2,000..............[ ]
				Cutter....................[ ]	2,001 - 3,000..............[ ]
				Davol.....................[ ]	3,001 - 4,000..............[ ]
				Pharmaseal................[ ]	4,001 and over
				Sterilon..................[ ]	(specify)________.......[ ]
				Other (specify)___________[ ]	
Shave Prep Trays	[ ]	[ ]	[ ]	American Hospital.........[ ]	0 - 1,500 (specify)________.[ ]
				Bard......................[ ]	1,501 - 3,000..............[ ]
				Baxter....................[ ]	3,001 - 5,000..............[ ]
				Cutter....................[ ]	5,001 - 7,000..............[ ]
				Johnson & Johnson.........[ ]	7,001 and over
				Kendall...................[ ]	(specify)________.......[ ]
				Pharmaseal................[ ]	
				Sterilon..................[ ]	
				Other (specify)___________[ ]	

	USE RE-USABLE ONLY	USE DISPOSABLE ONLY	USE BOTH	PRINCIPAL SUPPLIER	NUMBER OF UNITS PURCHASED
Skin Scrub Trays	[ ]	[ ]	[ ]	American Hospital.........[ ]	0 - 500 (specify)________....[ ]
				Baxter....................[ ]	501 - 1,000..................[ ]
				Deseret...................[ ]	1,001 - 2,000................[ ]
				Kendall...................[ ]	2,001 - 3,000................[ ]
				Pharmaseal................[ ]	3,001 and over
				Other (specify)___________[ ]	(specify)________........[ ]
Dressing Tray	[ ]	[ ]	[ ]	American Hospital.........[ ]	0 - 5,000 (specify)________..[ ]
				Bard......................[ ]	5,001 - 10,000...............[ ]
				Baxter....................[ ]	10,001 - 15,000..............[ ]
				Johnson & Johnson.........[ ]	15,001 - 20,000..............[ ]
				Kendall...................[ ]	20,001 and over
				Pharmaseal................[ ]	(specify)________.......[ ]
				Other (specify)___________[ ]	
Suture Removal Tray	[ ]	[ ]	[ ]	American Hospital.........[ ]	0 - 2,000 (specify)________..[ ]
				A.S.R.....................[ ]	2,001 - 5,000................[ ]
				Baxter....................[ ]	5,001 - 10,000...............[ ]
				Cenco.....................[ ]	10,001 - 15,000..............[ ]
				Kendall...................[ ]	15,001 and over
				Pharmaseal................[ ]	(specify)________........[ ]
				Sterilon..................[ ]	
				Other (specify)___________[ ]	
Foley Catheters	[ ]	[ ]	[ ]	Abbott....................[ ]	0 - 1,000 (specify)________..[ ]
				American Hospital.........[ ]	1,001 - 2,000................[ ]
				Bard......................[ ]	2,001 - 3,000................[ ]
				Baxter....................[ ]	3,001 - 4,000................[ ]
				Cutter....................[ ]	4,001 and over
				Escham....................[ ]	(specify)________........[ ]
				Kendall...................[ ]	
				Pharmaseal................[ ]	
				Waine.....................[ ]	
				Other (specify)___________[ ]	

	USE RE-USABLE ONLY	USE DISPOSABLE ONLY	USE BOTH	PRINCIPAL SUPPLIER	NUMBER OF UNITS PURCHASED
Foley Catheter Tray with and w/o drainage bag	[ ]	[ ]	[ ]	Abbott....................[ ]	0 - 1,000 (specify)________..[ ]
				American Hospital.........[ ]	1,001 - 2,000...............[ ]
				Bard......................[ ]	2,001 - 3,000...............[ ]
				Baxter....................[ ]	3,001 - 4,000...............[ ]
				Cutter....................[ ]	4,001 and over
				Kendall...................[ ]	(specify)________.........[ ]
				Pharmaseal................[ ]	
				Other (specify)___________[ ]	
Irrigation Tray	[ ]	[ ]	[ ]	American Hospital.........[ ]	0 - 2,000 (specify)________..[ ]
				Bard......................[ ]	2,001 - 5,000...............[ ]
				Baxter....................[ ]	5,001 - 10,000..............[ ]
				Cutter....................[ ]	10,001 - 15,000.............[ ]
				Davol.....................[ ]	15,001 and over
				Pharmaseal................[ ]	(specify)________.........[ ]
				Other (specify)___________[ ]	
Suction Catheter	[ ]	[ ]	[ ]	Aloe......................[ ]	0 - 2,000 (specify)________..[ ]
				American Hospital.........[ ]	2,001 - 4,000...............[ ]
				Bard-Parker...............[ ]	4,001 - 6,000...............[ ]
				Baxter....................[ ]	6,001 - 8,000...............[ ]
				Cutter....................[ ]	8,001 and over
				Davol.....................[ ]	(specify)________.........[ ]
				Pharmaseal................[ ]	
				Other (specify)___________[ ]	
Small Vein Infusion Sets	[ ]	[ ]	[ ]	Abbott....................[ ]	0 - 2,000 (specify)________..[ ]
				Baxter....................[ ]	2,001 - 5,000...............[ ]
				Cutter....................[ ]	5,001 - 10,000..............[ ]
				Jelco.....................[ ]	10,001 - 15,000.............[ ]
				Jintan....................[ ]	15,001 and over
				Other (specify)___________[ ]	(specify)________.........[ ]
Face Masks	[ ]	[ ]	[ ]	American Hospital.........[ ]	0 - 10,000 (specify)________..[ ]
				Bard......................[ ]	10,001 - 20,000.............[ ]
				Deseret...................[ ]	20,001 - 30,000.............[ ]
				Johnson & Johnson.........[ ]	30,001 - 40,000.............[ ]
				Kendall...................[ ]	40,001 and over
				3M........................[ ]	(specify)________.........[ ]
				Other (specify)___________[ ]	

	USE RE-USABLE ONLY	USE DISPOSABLE ONLY	USE BOTH	PRINCIPAL SUPPLIER	NUMBER OF UNITS PURCHASED
Operating Room Drapes - Disposable	[ ]	[ ]	[ ]	American Hospital.........[ ]	0 - 2,000 (specify)________..[ ]
				Bard.....................[ ]	2,001 - 5,000...............[ ]
				Johnson & Johnson.........[ ]	5,001 - 10,000..............[ ]
				Kendall...................[ ]	10,001 - 15,000.............[ ]
				Ross Disposable...........[ ]	15,001 and over
				Other (specify)___________[ ]	(specify)________.........[ ]
Endotrachial Tubes	[ ]	[ ]	[ ]	Argyle....................[ ]	0 - 2,000 (specify)_______...[ ]
				Bard.....................[ ]	2,001 - 5,000...............[ ]
				Cutter....................[ ]	5,001 - 8,000...............[ ]
				Pharmaseal................[ ]	8,001 - 11,000..............[ ]
				Portex....................[ ]	11,001 and over
				Rusch.....................[ ]	(specify)________.........[ ]
				Other (specify)___________[ ]	
Latex Surgeons Gloves - Pairs	[ ]	[ ]	[ ]	Abbott....................[ ]	0 - 5,000 (specify)_______...[ ]
				American Hospital.........[ ]	5,001 - 10,000..............[ ]
				Baxter....................[ ]	10,001 - 20,000.............[ ]
				Perry.....................[ ]	20,001 - 30,000.............[ ]
				Pharmaseal................[ ]	30,001 and over
				Pioneer...................[ ]	(specify)________.........[ ]
				Seamless..................[ ]	
				Other (specify)___________[ ]	
Latex Procedure Gloves - Pairs	[ ]	[ ]	[ ]	American Hospital.........[ ]	0 - 3,000 (specify)_______...[ ]
				Baxter....................[ ]	3,001 - 6,000...............[ ]
				Perry.....................[ ]	6,001 - 9,000...............[ ]
				Pharmaseal................[ ]	9,001 - 12,000..............[ ]
				Pioneer...................[ ]	12,001 and over
				Other (specify)___________[ ]	(specify)________.........[ ]
Latex Examination Gloves (Non-Sterile Singles)	[ ]	[ ]	[ ]	American Hospital.........[ ]	0 - 50,000 (specify)_______..[ ]
				Ardbrook..................[ ]	50,001 - 100,000............[ ]
				Perry.....................[ ]	100,001 - 200,000...........[ ]
				Pharmaseal................[ ]	200,001 - 300,000...........[ ]
				Other (specify)___________[ ]	300,001 and over
					(specify)________.........[ ]

	USE RE-USABLE ONLY	USE DISPOSABLE ONLY	USE BOTH	PRINCIPAL SUPPLIER	NUMBER OF UNITS PURCHASED
Vinyl Non-Sterile Gloves	[ ]	[ ]	[ ]	Ardbrook..................[ ]	0 - 50,000 (specify)________..[ ]
				Bard-Parker..............[ ]	50,001 - 100,000............[ ]
				Baxter....................[ ]	100,001 - 200,000...........[ ]
				Parke-Davis..............[ ]	200,001 - 300,000...........[ ]
				Seamless.................[ ]	300,001 and over
				Other (specify)___________[ ]	(specify)________.........[ ]
Vinyl Sterile Gloves	[ ]	[ ]	[ ]	American Hospital.........[ ]	0 - 10,000 (specify)________..[ ]
				Ardbrook..................[ ]	10,001 - 20,000.............[ ]
				Bard-Parker..............[ ]	20,001 - 30,000.............[ ]
				Baxter....................[ ]	30,001 - 40,000.............[ ]
				Parke-Davis..............[ ]	40,001 and over
				Pharmaseal...............[ ]	(specify)________.........[ ]
				Other (specify)___________[ ]	
Over the Needle Intravenous Catheter	[ ]	[ ]	[ ]	Abbott....................[ ]	0 - 2,500 (specify)________...[ ]
				American Hospital.........[ ]	2,501 - 5,000...............[ ]
				Baxter....................[ ]	5,001 - 8,000...............[ ]
				Deseret...................[ ]	8,001 - 11,000..............[ ]
				Sorenson..................[ ]	11,001 and over
				Other (specify)___________[ ]	(specify)________.........[ ]
Inside the Needle Intravenous Catheter	[ ]	[ ]	[ ]	Abbott....................[ ]	0 - 2,500 (specify)________...[ ]
				Argyle....................[ ]	2,501 - 5,000...............[ ]
				Becton-Dickinson..........[ ]	5,001 - 8,000...............[ ]
				Deseret...................[ ]	8,001 - 11,000..............[ ]
				Jelco.....................[ ]	11,001 and over
				Other (specify)___________[ ]	(specify)________.........[ ]
Sitz Bath	[ ]	[ ]	[ ]	American Hospital.........[ ]	0 - 100 (specify)________.....[ ]
				Baxter....................[ ]	101 - 300...................[ ]
				MacBick...................[ ]	301 - 500...................[ ]
				Volrath...................[ ]	501 - 700...................[ ]
				Other (specify)___________[ ]	701 and over
					(specify)________.........[ ]

	USE RE-USABLE ONLY	USE DISPOSABLE ONLY	USE BOTH	PRINCIPAL SUPPLIER
Diapers	[ ]	[ ]	[ ]	[WRITE IN]____________________

If you do not use disposable diapers at all, would you please write in, briefly, all of the reasons why you do not use this product? [WRITE IN BELOW]

____

____

If your hospital uses disposable diapers, I would like you to answer a few additional questions about their use in your hospital..

1) Who, of the following hospital personnel, has the major influence on the decision to use a particular brand of disposable diaper? [CHECK ONE ONLY]

Pediatrics Supervisor	[ ]	Administrator	[ ]
CSR Supervisor	[ ]	Obstetrics Supervisor	[ ]
Nursing Director	[ ]	Other __________ (please specify)	[ ]
Purchasing Agent	[ ]		

2a) Are disposable diapers being used..........

Full-time [ ] ------------ 2b) Would you please rank in order of importance, the following reasons from 1 to 4 for using disposable diapers full-time?

Emergency use only [ ]

	RANK ORDER
Better patient care	______
Cost savings	______
Time savings	______
Nursing convenience	______

(Courtesy of Southam Marketing Research Services, Don Mills, Ontario, Canada.)

HOSPITAL ADMINISTRATION IN CANADA

QUESTIONNAIRE TO BE FILLED IN BY THE PHARMACY DIRECTOR/PHARMACIST

NOTE: THIS IS A PRE-CODED QUESTIONNAIRE. PLEASE CIRCLE THE APPROPRIATE CODE NUMBERS AS INDICATED OR WRITE IN AS REQUESTED.

OPTIONAL

____
(Name of health care institution)

____
(Address)

____
(City or Town) (Province)

____
(Pharmacy Director/Pharmacist)

DATA ABOUT YOUR INSTITUTION - (PLEASE CIRCLE APPROPRIATE CODE IN EACH COLUMN)

TYPE	SIZE	LOCATION
Teaching hospital.....1	50-99 beds......1	Br. Columbia...1
Non-teaching general hospital...........2	100-199 beds....2	Prairies*......2
Chronic care hospital.3	200-299 beds....3	Ontario........3
Convalescent..........4	300-399 beds....4	Quebec.........4
Rehabilitation........5	400-499 beds....5	Maritimes......5
Psychiatric...........6	500 beds & over.6	
Other ____________ (specify)....7		

*Includes Yukon & N.W.T.

1) On what basis does this hospital employ Pharmacist(s)? (CIRCLE ONE CODE ONLY)

Full-time------------------------1
Part-time------------------------2
Consultant only------------------3
No Pharmacist--------------------4

2) Does this hospital use a formulary? (CIRCLE ONE CODE ONLY)

(IF "YES" PLEASE ANSWER Q.3)---------Yes------------------1
(IF "NO" PLEASE SKIP TO Q.5)---------No-------------------2

3) Do you dispense drugs not listed in the formulary [CIRCLE ONE CODE ONLY]

[IF "YES" PLEASE ANSWER Q.4]--------Yes---------------------------------------1
[IF "NO" PLEASE SKIP TO Q.5]--------No--2

4) Which generic areas are covered? [WRITE IN BELOW]

____

____

____

5) Do you have a central additive program? [CIRCLE ONE CODE ONLY]

Yes---------------------------------------1
No--2

6) Do you have a hyper-alimentation program? [CIRCLE ONE CODE ONLY]

[IF "YES" PLEASE ANSWER Q.7 to 9]--------Yes---------------------------------------1
[IF "NO" PLEASE SKIP TO Q.10]------------No--2

7) What is the average number of patients on this hyper-alimentation program? [WRITE IN BELOW]

Average number of patients on program ______________

8) How long is the patients' average stay on this hyper-alimentation program? [WRITE IN BELOW]

Average length of stay on program ______________

9) Which solutions do you use on this hyper-alimentation program? [CIRCLE APPROPRIATE CODES]

Amigen--------------------------------------1
Aminosol------------------------------------2
CPH---3
Freamine------------------------------------4
Intralipid----------------------------------5
Travasol------------------------------------6
Vamin---------------------------------------7
Other (please specify)______________--------8
Other (please specify)______________--------9
Other (please specify)______________--------0

10) Does this hospital have a formally organized committee (Pharmacy and Therapeutic Committee) on drugs? [CIRCLE ONE CODE ONLY]

[IF "YES" PLEASE ANSWER Q.11 & 12]--Yes---------------------------------------1
[IF "NO" PLEASE SKIP TO Q.13]-------No--2

11) Which hospital personnel serve on the Pharmacy and Therapeutic Committee? [CIRCLE APPROPRIATE CODE(S)]

Senior Physician(s)----------------------------1
Director of Nursing----------------------------2
Administrator----------------------------------3
Pharmacist-------------------------------------4
Other (please specify)__________________---------------5
Other (please specify)__________________---------------6
Other (please specify)__________________---------------7

12) Is the Pharmacy and Therapeutic Committee generally in favour of unit dose drug application? [CIRCLE ONE CODE ONLY]

Yes--1
No---2

13) In your opinion, are there any identifiable problems in establishing unit dose drug application in your hospital? If so, would you please comment on these problems. [WRITE IN BELOW]

____

____

____

14) Are you personally in favour of unit dose drug application? [CIRCLE ONE CODE ONLY]

Yes--1
No---2

15) Would you say the nursing staff in this hospital is in favour of unit drug application?

Yes--1
No---2

16) Listed below are 9 types of unit dose drugs. Would you please rate the type which, in your opinion, has the highest volume of usage in this form, by ranking it number one, second highest volume by ranking it number two, etc. [CIRCLE ONE CODE ONLY ON EACH HORIZONTAL LINE]

UNIT DOSE DRUG TYPE	RANK								
Antibiotics	1	2	3	4	5	6	7	8	9
Analgesics	1	2	3	4	5	6	7	8	9
Antacids	1	2	3	4	5	6	7	8	9
Control Drugs	1	2	3	4	5	6	7	8	9
Cardiac Preparations	1	2	3	4	5	6	7	8	9
Diabetic Preparations	1	2	3	4	5	6	7	8	9
Diuretics	1	2	3	4	5	6	7	8	9
Tranquilizers	1	2	3	4	5	6	7	8	9
Vitamins	1	2	3	4	5	6	7	8	9

NO RATING PREFERENCE [CHECK [✓] BOX] [ ]

17) Regarding usage of unit dose drug packages, does this hospital.......? [CIRCLE ONE CODE ONLY]

[PLEASE ANSWER Q.18 to 21]----------Use unit dose drugs now----------1

[THANK YOU FOR YOUR CO-OPERATION IN FILLING IN THIS QUESTIONNAIRE] ----------
- Plan to use unit dose drugs within the next 12 months----------2
- Plan to use unit dose drugs sometime in future----------3
- No plans to use unit dose drugs in future----------4

18) Does this hospital package its own unit dose drugs, other than special treatment packages? [CIRCLE ONE CODE ONLY]

Yes----------1
No----------2

19) What kind of packaging would you prefer for solid dosage? [CIRCLE APPROPRIATE CODE(S)]

Strip pack----------1
Push through----------2
Peel off----------3
Other (please specify)__________----------4
Other (please specify)__________----------5
Other (please specify)__________----------6

20) What kind of packaging would you prefer for liquid dosage? [CIRCLE APPROPRIATE CODE(S)]

Bottle----------1
Plastic pouch----------2
Plastic peel off----------3
Top container----------4
Other (please specify)__________----------5
Other (please specify)__________----------6
Other (please specify)__________----------7

21) In your experience, would it be useful to have prefilled dosage form for injectables? [CIRCLE ONE CODE ONLY]

Yes----------1
No----------2

THANK YOU FOR YOUR CO-OPERATION IN FILLING IN THIS QUESTIONNAIRE.

(Courtesy of Southam Marketing Research Services, Don Mills, Ontario, Canada.)

DEAR SIR, IN SPITE OF ITS "BILLBOARD" SIZE, THIS IS A SERIOUS REQUEST FOR YOUR OPINIONS AND EXPERIENCE CONCERNING CARPET CONTROLS WHEN YOU RETURN THIS SHEET, IT WILL GO DIRECTLY TO OUR DESIGN ENGINEERS, WHO ARE NOW WORKING ON A CARPET PROJECT. LATER WE WILL SEND YOU A "THANK YOU" GIFT FOR YOUR OWN PERSONAL USE (PLEASE CHECK YOUR CHOICE ON THE ENCLOSED SHEET.)

IN EACH BOX GIVE US YOUR THOUGHTS IN YOUR OWN WORDS

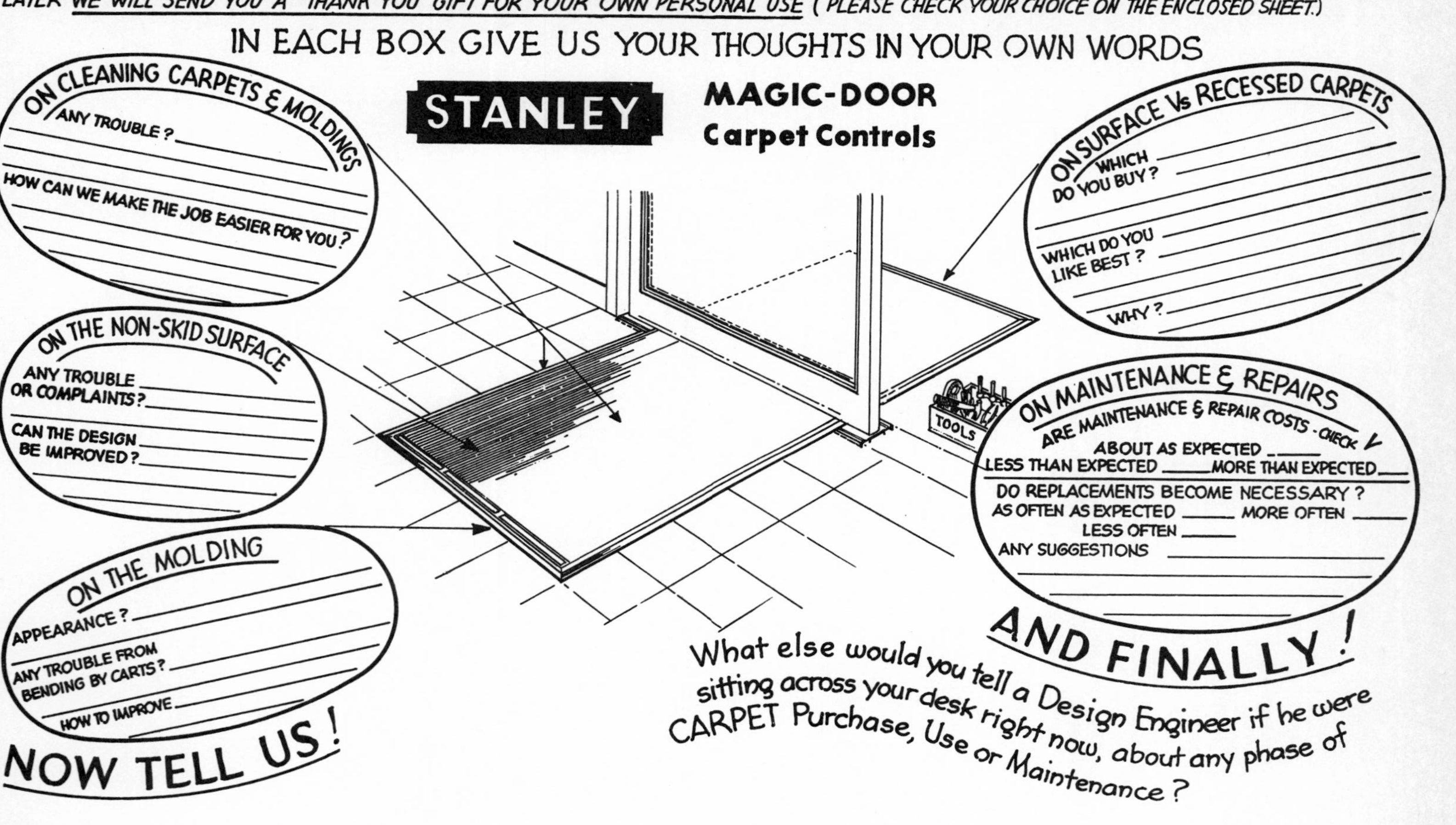

for
CUSTOMER OPERATED
TYPE DOORS UNDER YOUR SUPERVISION OR FOR WHICH YOU BUY EQUIPMENT,
APPROX. WHAT PERCENTAGE ARE AUTOMATED ? ______
APPROX. HOW MANY AUTOMATIC DOORS IS THIS ? ______

WHERE SHALL WE SEND YOUR THANK YOU GIFT ?
NAME ______ TITLE ______
COMPANY NAME ______
STREET ADDRESS ______ CITY ______ STATE ______

SIX

How to Interview

Many marketing research studies involve at least some field interviewing. This is even more true of the small studies with which this book is concerned.

This chapter describes individual interviewing; group interviews will be covered in the next chapter.

You should now start thinking how an interview study can be planned, organized, and controlled. Without such planning and organization, you would only be "out talking with the customers," just as business people have always done.

There are certain human reactions that characterize all research interviewing, whether talks are held in a shopping center or in a vice president's office. These should be considered before we discuss specific types of business interviews:

1. To induce a respondent to tell you what you want to know requires sales ability. The respondent is not necessarily antagonistic. A more usual attitude is neutrality. The respondent is willing to give you a chance, but may or may not give you the needed information. His attitude after the first minute or two is a true function of how good your planning and approach have been. A bad start is not always fatal, but it does eat into the precious, short time that this person is willing to give.

2. In spite of what I have said about sales ability, there is one large and important difference between a true selling situation and marketing research. Consciously or unconsciously, by training or basic personality, a salesperson will usually feel the need to *control* a selling interview, to "lead" the prospect toward a buying decision. In my own experience, after first "selling" myself as a person who should be helped, my best interviews have been those in which I did the least talking. It proved wiser to let the respondent do the controlling, the dominating, the impressing. An occasional question is needed; sometimes a gentle nudge back onto the track. But the logic is obvious: If you want to learn what another person knows, the best thing to do is to let him talk.

3. A good interview does not have to produce "tit for tat." If you feel the need to conjure up some artificial reason why this interview will help the interviewee, the false note will be patently obvious. If it is honestly true that he *will* be helped, say so. But do not be devious here (or in any other area of marketing research).

4. The fact of the matter is that most people are willing to help if you approach them honestly and tell them exactly what you want to know and *why* you want to know it.

When interviewing, it is best to let the other person talk.

Let me say this in a different way. It is flattering to be asked for an opinion. It makes the respondent feel good to be able to play the part of an oracle for just a few minutes. In the hard world that bears down upon him constantly, you offer him a moment of superiority; *his* opinion is being sought because of its importance. I have seen this reaction from top executives to average customers in a store.

5. Finally, it is a mistake to believe that it is unnecessary to prepare for a research interview with "good old Joe," your friend for many years. You can flub an interview with him just as easily as with a total stranger.

Some Special Strengths of Interviewing

Field interviewing obviously costs more per received answer than does mail or telephone work. There have to be clear advantages from doing the job this way before you decide on spending the necessary travel or employee-hour costs. There must be information that is available in no other way—information that is vital for your study. Or interviews can sometimes be justified to check on a mail study.

Here are some of the advantages of personal interviewing:

1. In many studies you really do not know the name of the person who has the needed information. This is true all the way up and down the line of distribution, from shopping center interviews with a sample of customers to office and factory interviews where even the purchasing agent may not have the detailed knowledge that you want. Mail or telephone research would simply not be adequate to reach the right person. There is another important aspect. In factory or office research you sometimes find that the one who is responsible for the specifying and ordering of an item may, in fact, leave the decision to subordinates. A mail questionnaire, even if addressed personally, will be sent on to a subordinate with a notation to "answer if you wish and have the time." This atmosphere does not lead to accurate or complete results.

2. Depending on the extent to which the interview has been structured, conversational leads can be quickly followed up. Lessons learned in one interview can alter and improve the next. It is possible, and actually happens frequently, that the type of person who was being sampled turns out to be quite wrong. Some other office, some other title, is the direction in which we should be going. A change in interview plans in mid-study, therefore, should be expected and allowed. The advantage of a fixed list of questions versus the use of a small "guide" outline will be covered later. Both are good in their place. Shopping center interviews may be quite structured (but not always). Executive interviews may be "in depth" (another fad expression).

3. Interviews, even in shopping centers, may begin revealing aspects of a question that had not been previously considered. Unless you have simply "hired some persons to do the work," the interview procedure should be constantly changed to take advantage of this new situation.

The advantage of an interview, in summary, is in its inherent flexibility and its probing nature. An experienced interviewer, if determinedly unbiased, can soon get a feel for the true situation. My mathematical friends may not want to agree, but after fifty store owners, chosen with honest effort at randomness and due regard for geographical differences, say that product A is a "dog" that sleeps on their shelves—and a few more interviews produce the same answer—we may safely conclude that our company should not attempt to compete in the product A market.

A combination of research methods can be effective—for example, a group interview followed by extensive mail coverage.

Types of Studies That Can Be Done Best with Interviews

Personal interviews probably should be a part of most of the studies that you plan. The best work often is a combination of several research methods. A mail questionnaire plus some field interviewing is a frequent combination. Or group interviewing followed by a more extensive mail coverage.

In many studies you will really want and need the probing nature of the interview technique. As was said before, where the particular people you need are unknown, field research can sometimes be the *only* way of doing what is required.

Indeed, it is often true that a dozen or so good interviews with the right people will give a truer answer than the mailing of a thousand questionnaires. Especially if the return percentage for the questionnaire is low and of doubtful validity.

Industrial studies that involve the purchase and use of products that become part of some other manufacturer's product, or products that are used up completely by a manufacturer or other user, such as energy-related materials or maintenance supplies, may be best tackled through direct talks.

Even with consumer products that are not used in volume, it may be quite satisfactory to have talks with wholesalers and retailers, plus some group sessions or store interviews.

There are so many types of interviews that I have had to be somewhat arbitrary in their classification. So I have chosen to describe office and factory interviewing, wholesale and retail interviewing, and consumer interviewing as categories that cover what you are most likely to be doing. Also see Chapter 10, "Special Research for Retailers."

Business Office and Industrial Interviewing

Preparation The very first thing to be done is to write out the specific objectives that you hope to accomplish in this series of interviews. In very particular terms, what knowledge do you want? These specifics are likely to

A degree of judgment is necessary in deciding about geographic coverage.

change a bit after your first few interviews, but this will give you something to do in the motel in the evening. You may have thought that you were interested in the relative sales of various sizes of a steel part, and suddenly find that plastic is being introduced. Your specifics will immediately be altered for subsequent interviews.

A decision must be made about the kind (and, if possible, the names) of people whom you want to see. This step of preparation cannot really be separated from your decision about geographic coverage. A degree of judgment is necessary. Newsprint mills will be our example. There are mills scattered around the country and Canada, but concentrations are in the Northeast, the Southeast, the Northwest, and Quebec. If your problem concerns the manufacture of newsprint, you can safely decide not to visit any areas other than the above.

Now you must eliminate a few more areas, since you probably do not have the time to go everywhere. A little use of secondary sources shows that a great part of Canadian paper is shipped to this country. Perhaps you can learn all you need to know about Canadian practices from newspapers in the United States. But is there a difference in practices in the Northeast, Southeast, and Northwest? A few exploratory telephone calls are in order if you are in the East and would prefer not to spend the money and time to fly across the country. Are there differences? Yes, in some details there are. If you are planning to manufacture a part connected with the rolling-up process, you may find that the trip is worthwhile. And, if you go to Oregon and Washington, you might as well go across the border and see some Canadian mills in British Columbia.

For some other product, you may find that a week around Chicago will be enough. You are certain, from preliminary work, that there are no significant differences between areas, and Chicago offers a good sample of nationwide practices.

Advice from trade associations, some telephone calls to users, perhaps a call or two by one of the salespersons in a questionable area may save time and travel money.

Purchased mailing lists are seldom very valuable.

For names, I have never found purchased mailing lists very valuable. They are often out of date, incomplete, and too broad to be useful. Sometimes association membership lists are available. A good source of names is attendance rosters at national and regional trade shows or business conventions. Often, one of the first people you call on—if you have gained his interest—will volunteer names of persons that you "simply *must* see." If he tells you to use his name, you are in luck.

The final bit of preparation is the decision about how much you can cover in one interview. Although it may seem efficient, it is usually unwise to attempt coverage of more than one topic at an interview. Interest rises, peaks, and then drops; it is practically impossible to rebuild the early rapport. If two topics must be covered, it would be much better to divide respondents into two groups, enlarge the list, and alternate topics as you go along.

Getting to see the right person

1. Should you call or write ahead, asking for a meeting? There are several points of view. Common sense should prevail in each instance.

Calling ahead can be most necessary when there are just a few important people to see and they are in different cities. There is no sense in flying to Chicago to see someone who has just left for New York. Moreover, calling ahead allows the respondent to prepare for the interview; it can be hoped that he will have some materials ready for you when you arrive. This makes the interview more efficient and more complete. Often, too, a prior call will allow the respondent to have another, perhaps more knowledgeable, person at the interview. Perhaps the first one you call will plead ignorance and will refer you to the right person immediately. On the other hand, it is frequently difficult to line up a series of interviews ahead of time. People's schedules do not always mesh very well, and sometimes half days, or even full days, are wasted waiting for the next appointment. An argument for not calling ahead can be made that there is always *someone* to see in a big company. If the one you want is away, frequently it is possible to interview an assistant. In a very human and understandable fashion, this second person may be willing to tell you more than the first would have done. Perhaps he wants to impress you with his knowledge. Perhaps he is bored with his position and welcomes this new diversion. Whatever his motive, a person like this is a welcome gift from the gods to the fact seeker.

Another reason for not making appointments in advance is the very real possibility that a "gold mine" of information unexpectedly will appear in an interview. It would be foolish to break off a flow of good information simply to make the next appointment on time.

There will be no agreement on this point. All I can say is that I made fewer and fewer appointments as I built up my years of experience. Seldom would I strike out completely. Almost always there would be a second person, or a "someone else," who would be available. The odds always favored me, and more often than not I would come away from an unscheduled meeting with more information than I dared hope for.

You can often come away from an interview with more information than you dared hope for.

2. There is no sure way of explaining your purpose to someone at the outer desk. The receptionist will assume that you are a salesperson, no matter what you say. The best thing is a straightforward request to see the person you want, since he has some information that you need, and you will not take more than a few minutes of his time. Anything further than that—and the name of your own company—will go in one ear and out the other.

3. If you are told by the receptionist that "he wants to talk to you on that phone over there," you are in a dilemma. Good research interviewing can

seldom be done on a lobby phone. There are only a few alternatives. You may politely urge the person to see you; or you may ask for a later appointment; or you may express your regret at not seeing the person, hoping that a future study will allow you to meet him. Or you may ask if someone else in the organization may be available. Using these approaches, the odds very much favor your getting a worthwhile interview.

Questionnaire vs. interview guide . . .

Questionnaire versus interview guide The advantages of a written questionnaire are:

1. Responses are more comparable from one interview to another.
2. Nothing important is forgotten.
3. Personal bias of the interviewer, such as reaction to the respondent, weariness built up in previous interviews, and reaction of the respondent to the interviewer are minimized.
4. Untrained interviewers, or interviewers with a minimum knowledge of the subject of the study, are less likely to cause trouble through bad interviewing procedure.
5. A questionnaire can be a welcome "crutch" to a new interviewer, making him appear more skilled than he may in fact be.

The advantages of an interview guide are equally strong. By interview guide, I mean something like a 3 by 5 card with just an outline of important points to be covered.

1. In general, the less that comes between the interviewer and the respondent the better. New interviewers tend to want a clipboard and a pad of paper. While this may seem official, it interferes with the personal rapport necessary to get good information.
2. The interview guide allows for flexibility. Leads may be followed up. The whole interview may take an entirely new, but beneficial, turn. Many interviews will have an extremely valuable surprise for the interviewer. Any fixed format can easily kill off these opportunities if the interviewer tries to keep the talk "on the track."
3. The guide allows the interview to be as short or long as need be. Sometimes the respondent really has little to say. He knows almost nothing about the subject. Kindness will dictate making the session as short as possible. On the other hand, sometimes the respondent will, in effect, suggest you ask about something else. An easy person-to-person atmosphere encourages this cooperative attitude.

In general, I would say that new interviewers in business and industrial research are more likely to use questionnaires. More experienced people will move to the guide, or simply to memory.

Tape recording versus note-taking It is possible in all large cities, and many middle-sized ones, to rent an adequate tape recorder. Or you may own a small portable model. Cost is usually low, when compared with the value of the study. Many experienced interviewers use these machines. Other equally experienced persons are opposed to them.

Here are the advantages of tape recording:

1. It is possible to bring back every word that was said, to analyze at your leisure.
2. Others can listen to the interview, and perhaps pick up points and nuances that you have missed.
3. Sometimes it is valuable to use the analytical ability of a trained psychologist at this point. He, too, may pick up significant manners of response.
4. Contrary to what you might think, the respondent soon ceases to be aware of the microphone, and talks as easily as if it were not there at all. Furthermore, a certain importance may be attached to your obvious desire to record his every word.

On the other hand, it is argued that:

1. The respondent may not *want* his every word recorded. There appears to be a loss of confidentiality, if his own voice is carried away.
2. Although it is argued that the microphone is soon forgotten, this takes a few minutes, and the first few minutes of an interview may be the most important, establishing the tone of everything that is said later.
3. There is an unavoidable bother about setting up the apparatus. Even a small, battery-operated tape recorder requires some obvious steps of preparation.
4. Tapes have to be run off—taking as much time as the interviews themselves. Often they must be transcribed, which takes the time of a secretary. It is frequently difficult to follow voices on a tape, separating out people who are talking simultaneously.
5. Less important perhaps, but always present, is the chance that the tape recorder may not work. If no recording was made, and no notes taken, important information may be completely lost.

My own belief is that a good eye-to-eye interview, with notes written immediately afterwards, is the most productive. Very little can be forgotten on the trip from an office to the parking lot. By following this procedure, nothing at all comes between interviewer and respondent. The only time that notes should be taken in front of the respondent, in my opinion, is when some figures are offered that clearly cannot be remembered. Then, after asking permission, these may be copied.

Tape recording versus note-taking.

Some people associate market research with trickery.

As I said, there are many who disagree with me. You may do what is best for you. I do suggest, however, that you try to establish the competency to remember everything that was said, and do your note-taking right after leaving the person's office.

One more point. If you write your notes immediately after the interview, you can interject your own impressions about what this new information has added, and about the competency and knowledge of the interviewee.

If you, or any of your people, are doing the interviewing, it is almost always unwise to try to hide the name of your company or the true purpose of your call. Only in interviews with consumers (whom you will never see again) can you safely hide your identity. If anonymity is necessary in calls on business people, then it would be wiser to hire an outside research firm to do the work. Often the actual interviewers working for these research companies are not told for whom they are working; your identity is absolutely safeguarded. But your own people cannot wear two hats. You are very likely to be returning to these respondents sometime in the future on another study. Complete honesty in every call is the safest rule.

Some people associate marketing research with trickery. They have had experience with the phony fellow who is doing a "heating survey of the neighborhood" and the like. The very best approach to an interview is the most honest one. You are calling on this person because he or she knows the answer to a problem that bothers you and your company. No company can afford to make major mistakes and you hope that this person will help you keep from making a bad marketing decision. This is about as direct as can be, and is almost always accepted and responded to. No trickery, no speech about how this research will help the respondent, nothing but the most transparent honesty.

Wholesale and Retail Interviewing

Interviewing a wholesaler, a manufacturers' agent, or distributors of various kinds is not essentially different from the type of business calls described above.

Calling on retailers, however, has its own special set of problems. These should be read in connection with the procedures already described.

1. Large stores, such as department stores, may be quite dissimilar in their organization. In some, the department manager, or buyer, is still king. If it is product information you want, this is the person to see.

In other stores, the department manager has little to do with the selection and purchase of goods. He or she is in charge of the sales function and the department organization. Purchases are closely supervised; major decisions are made by the merchandise manager (a person often difficult to see). In still other stores, major decisions about vendors are made by the very top management.

To complicate things further, some department store chains use a form of central buying, or committee buying, and the real person to see may be in New York.

It would be wise, if department stores are a major factor in the research, to determine in advance the buying and control practices of the chains you are about to interview. It could well be that one well-planned interview in New York will give you all you want to know about a major chain, for its stores all over the country.

Unless you know these facts about a particular store, it is always wise to begin your research at the level of the department manager.

2. Certain chain and variety stores have definite rules about research interviews in individual store units. This does not mean that you will not get to see the person you want to see, but this person may not be allowed to tell you anything. If you are guilty of visiting too many individual chain store units, you may find your own company receiving a warning from the chain store's top management. You will be asked to visit only the headquarter's buyers.

Chain stores and variety stores almost always are extremely courteous and cooperative at the head office level. When it is possible to help you, they will—just so long as you do not put too many demands on them.

3. Ignorance in calling on the retail trade is not a blessed virtue. For example, a bookstore in a shopping center may be part of a chain, which in turn is owned by a group of department stores. Any researcher should be aware of this before making a call.

Much can be learned at the local level, if the researcher knows the local unit's place in the national organization.

4. Except in the case of top management of large organizations, it is virtually impossible to make advance appointments. Buyers and department heads of local department stores are extremely difficult to pin down. Advance telephoning invites a negative answer, while a personal visit can easily lead to a talk with the right man or woman, or an assistant, or even a supervisor.

5. Locally owned stores—the myriad of groceries, hardware stores, flower shops, or whatever—simply require shoe leather and strong leg muscles.

A few hints about local retailers are in order, however. Do not ever forget that the store's own customers come first. The local store owner buys, and may also sell. His own business is more important to him than anything that you have to say. Be courteous, be understanding, and wait as long as needed. Your own patience will be appreciated, and in the end you will learn what you came after.

There are all sorts of decisions that must be made by a manufacturer or a wholesaler calling on stores for research purposes. Neither one can go to *every* city in the country, or in a sales area. Some choice must be made about what places to sample. For the most part, in spite of the advanced art of research design, these choices are made from experience, "feel," cost of travel, and how much we can spend for a particular study. To this is added information from secondary sources about the spread in types of employment, average family income, blue- versus white-collar jobs. Size of city and the number of possible calls are factors. Also, whether the city appears to be a "leading city" of its trading area. A Canadian study may use Montreal, Toronto, Edmonton, Winnipeg, and Vancouver. No one will feel the need to justify such choices; everyone knows that these metropolitan areas must be covered in a nationwide study.

For the types of studies discussed in this book it is extremely unlikely that anything approaching a statistically correct sample can be utilized. The money and the time are not available.

Once again, we must go by judgment and common sense. Having chosen the cities which seem to fit our requirements, it is now necessary to lay out a number of calls that appear to cover the territory adequately. For some research, calls on all the important local distributors, plus visits to fifteen or twenty local retailers, will appear adequate.

What we will find, in almost all cases, is a repetition that almost becomes boring. The same story is heard again and again. The product in question is

An interview at a Kansas City, Mo., shopping mall.

not selling. Or people do not like it because of certain features. Or it moved at first, but then died on the shelves. There will not be an even spread among all possible answers; instead, the picture will come fairly clear early in the game.

At some point in calling on retailers and wholesalers, all researchers are familiar with the feeling that they know in advance what is going to be said. At this point—when we are sure we have reached it—research has fulfilled its function. Assuming that the questions have been asked properly, that we have not sinned with bias, that we have successfully persuaded the trade to "tell all," we may assume that no more research is necessary. We have the answer.

One of the interesting facts discovered by most researchers is the early point at which the "truth" becomes apparent. Sometimes we find that it would have been possible to stop our work after one city. Or fifteen or twenty retailers and wholesalers. A hundred more do not change the answer, or alter the picture.

Shopping Center and Store Interviews with Consumers

This section is written especially for suppliers, manufacturers, or distributors who want to make some direct contacts with consumers at the point of purchase. Retailers should consult the special chapter for them later in the book. Group interviews, mail surveys, and telephone surveys are other techniques that are described in other chapters.

Preparation Except for a few exhibitionists who like to talk, most consumers will not allow more than a very few questions. After that they get impatient, and even if you can hold them, their answers will become less and less reliable. For this reason, it is imperative to know exactly what you want, to put your questions into as few easily understood words as possible.

A show of clipboards and recording sheets is not bad in this one kind of interviewing. Anything that makes the interviewer look official will help allay fears and induce cooperation.

One very successful shopping center study used a group of young men dressed in uniform sports jackets. They also wore a large button that said "Marketing Research, We Need Your Help." A little bit tricked-up and phony, but it got the results.

Another device can be a decorated card table, with the products in question laid out on a colored cloth. Curiosity is aroused, and it becomes much easier to stop people for a short interview.

It should go without saying that you must get the permission of the store owner, if you are doing in-store interviews. Or the management of the shopping center, if you want to do your work there. In the case of chain stores

A show of clipboards and recording sheets is not bad when interviewing shopping center or store customers.

Interviewing must not interfere with selling or customer traffic flow.

your position becomes a little more difficult. Often there is a company rule against any on-premises research, and permission would have to be obtained from headquarters. This is usually a time-consuming process, even if permission is granted.

There is a courtesy about field interviewing that your own common sense should dictate. Customers come first. Interviewing must not interfere with selling, with customer traffic flow, or with customer parking. Moreover, the researcher must be so obviously honest that he or she will not awaken fears in the most timid of people.

Some clever little "gift" can sometimes be used. It would have to be something quite inexpensive. But it should be showy enough to attract attention. Respondents will get the gifts and will "advertise" you as they walk to their cars.

If you choose a shopping center, you may find two things standing in your way:

1. The shopping center itself may be a part of a chain of such centers, with the permission-granting central office in some other city. You would have to have some correspondence with this home office in advance.
2. The shopping center management may impose a charge for permission to allow researchers on the property.

Who will do the interviewing? Several choices are possible for selecting interviewers:

1. You can do the work alone or with other people from your department or the company. If the study isn't too large and time-consuming, this will be the very best way. Talking to consumers and users can be a real and valuable learning experience for marketing people.
2. You can use interviewing companies that are present in every big city, and in most medium-size ones (see Chapter 13). These local firms can be found in the *Yellow Pages.* Often they can set up groups for you to interview, or they will do the job themselves. Such firms are used by many of the national research and consulting companies for local coverage.
3. In many cities, agencies that supply temporary help, such as Manpower, will have interviewers on their roster. Availability varies from city to city. You will have to make sure that these people are instructed and supervised well.

It is not recommended that you use your own salespeople for this job. These people are hired to sell, and that is their most important duty. You will inevitably take second place in their scale of value. Since the sale comes first, you may not be able to count on these people to be where they are supposed to be and at the right time.

Moreover, a good salesperson probably does not have the right temperament to be a researcher. We have talked about this in other chapters, and of course there are many exceptions. As a general rule, however, it is a mistake to enlist salespeople for interviewing work.

When should the interviewing take place? A moment's thought will tell you that the typical Monday customer is likely to be a different person than the Saturday shopper. The morning customer is different than the evening customer, or the afternoon customer. Your schedule of interviewing must be set up to cover all these various types of people.

Consider the reasons for these differences. Some half of the young married women are working. These women are in the accumulating time of life, and are busy stocking their homes with all the fine things that they and their husbands have decided they need for a happy home. But they will *not* be buying their wares on any morning except Saturday. And on evenings and weekends, young husbands will join to form a "shopping team," even for groceries—the exclusive province of females up to just a few years ago. The lone woman in a large car who shows up on a weekday morning is important because she will have more money to spend. But for every one of her, there are several working women whose total business is even more important to the retailer.

In case you have not thought it through: A young woman adds her own salary to her husband's, and a family income of, say, close to $30,000 results. This is not peanuts, even in the 1970s. An accumulating young couple with $30,000 a year to spend (before taxes) is not a buying unit that can be overlooked.

What to do if the merchant suddenly decides that your interviewers are causing too much trouble Leave.

How to make out a field questionnaire for this type of interviewing The best laid plans of mice and researchers "gang aft agley." An innocuous part-time researcher hired from some local source does not understand one of the questions and spends a whole day uselessly. Or a researcher unconsciously avoids interviewing large families, unshaven and rough-looking husbands, young men with long hair and beards.

Supervision and training can help ensure that something approaching a true sample of people is interviewed. But making sure the questionnaire is completely understandable is your job, and must be done well ahead of time. It is not a bad thing to try it out in a few places—the people in your office, the friendly store where your spouse shops. Ambiguities will show up quickly enough, and not much time has been lost.

There are a variety of shopping center and store interview techniques that are not discussed here because they are too complex and expensive for the average small study. Trailers are placed in the shopping center parking lot with passersby being invited to come aboard and make some judgment or other about a product. Hidden cameras have been used in stores; customer eye movements have been recorded and analyzed. Probably you will never attempt anything of this sort.

What I have tried to do in this chapter is to show each of you the way toward better interviewing practices. And better interviewing means more valuable interviewing that produces more worthwhile information.

On the following pages are examples of interview studies that have worked well. For the most part these illustrate interviewing that was done with consumers.

As in the previous chapter, many have been reduced to fit book-size pages. Much space has again had to be eliminated—space that would be necessary in a real situation. As before, my only purpose is to show *types* of questions from which you can choose for your own purposes.

GENERAL HARDWARE STORES

1. What brands of aerosol paint do you carry? Which is the best selling brand, which next, which next, etc. (Interviewer indicate by 1, 2, 3, etc.)

   (Ask for each brand) Compared with last year, is this brand gaining, losing or about the same in sales?

Brand	Sales Rank	Gaining	Losing	Same
______________	____	____	____	____
______________	____	____	____	____
______________	____	____	____	____
______________	____	____	____	____

2. What brands of brush-on paints do you carry? Which is the best selling brand, which next, which next, etc. (Interviewer indicate by 1, 2, 3, etc.)

   (Ask for each brand) Compared with last year, is this brand gaining, losing or about the same in sales?

Brand	Sales Rank	Gaining	Losing	Same
______________	____	____	____	____
______________	____	____	____	____
______________	____	____	____	____
______________	____	____	____	____

3. A) Which of the following best describes your opinion of Company A aerosol paints?

   The very best on the market ____
   One of the best on the market ____
   A little better than average ____
   About average ____
   A little below average ____
   One of the poorest on the market ____
   The very worst on the market ____

3. B) Why do you feel that way?_______________________

____

Name of Store ______________________________ Large_____
Medium_____
Address ___________________________________ Small_____

Interviewer ____________________________ Date__________

(Courtesy of Trendex, Inc.)

CONSUMER QUESTIONNAIRE

1. Have you or your husband (wife) bought paint for your own use in the past year?

   Yes_____ No_____

   (If "No", record information on interview record and end interview.)

2. Have you or your husband (wife) ever bought paint in pressurized, aerosol, push button cans?

   Yes_____ No_____

   (If "No", record information on interview record and end interview.)

Which of you bought it?		Which of you used it?	
Wife	____	Wife	____
Husband	____	Husband	____
Both	____	Both	____

   (Continue with respondent if he or she <u>used</u> it. If not ask to interview other person.)

3. How long ago did you last buy aerosol paint?__________

4. What brand was it?______________________________

5. What other brands of aerosol paint have you <u>ever</u> tried?

   ______________ ______________ ______________

   ______________ ______________ ______________

   If more than one brand, which do you prefer?

   ____

   Why do you prefer this brand?____________________

   ____

6. In addition to the aerosol paints you have already mentioned, what other brands can you name? (Any others?)

_______________ _______________ _______________

_______________ _______________ _______________

7. What, if anything, do you think are the principal advantages of aerosol paints over brush paints? (Any others?)

____

____

8. What, if anything, do you think are the principal disadvantages of aerosol paints? (Any others?)

____

____

9. Have you ever heard of Company A aerosol paints?

Yes_____ No_____

(If "No", get classification data and conclude interview.)

10. Which of the following best describes your opinion of Company A aerosol paints?

The very best on the market ____
One of the best on the market ____
A little better than average ____
About average ____
A little below average ____
One of the poorest on the market ____
The very worst on the market ____

Why do you feel that way?___________________________

____

Name______________________________ Man _____ U_____
Address____________________________ Woman_____ M_____
L_____

(Courtesy of Trendex, Inc.)

1a. Have you served any fruit flavored gelatin in the last 30 days?

Yes_____ No_____

(IF NO, SKIP TO CLASSIFICATION DATA AND END INTERVIEW.)

1b. What brand of fruit flavored gelatin do you usually serve? (IF MORE THAN ONE BRAND, CIRCLE BRAND SERVED MOST RECENTLY.) ______________________

1c. What other brands have you tried in the past year or so?

____

1d. (IF OTHER BRANDS HAVE BEEN TRIED), Is there any particular reason why you prefer_________________ (BRAND NAMED IN Q.1b)?

2. (TO BE ASKED ONLY OF THOSE WHO HAVE TRIED <u>BOTH</u> BRAND A AND BRAND B GELATIN IN THE PAST YEAR.)

Thinking back on your experience with Brand A and Brand B, I would like to ask you some questions about the difference between these brands.

a. Do you think there is any difference between Brand A and Brand B in flavor, that is, does one brand taste better than the other?

Yes_____ No_____

(IF YES) What is the difference?____________

____

b. Do you think there is any difference between Brand A and Brand B in consistency, that is, does one tend to be more thin and watery or rubbery than the other?

Yes_____ No_____

(IF YES) What is the difference?____________

____

c. Do you think there is any difference between Brand A and Brand B packages, that is, is either easier to open or pour from than the other?

Yes_____ No_____

(IF YES) What is the difference?________________
____

d. Do you think there is any difference between Brand A and Brand B in the amount of vitamins, minerals, or protein that they contain?

Yes_____ No_____

(IF YES) What is the difference?________________
____

e. Does either Brand A or Brand B tend to get lumpy in the package more than the other?

Yes_____ No_____

(IF YES) Which gets lumpy?______________________

f. Does either Brand A or Brand B dissolve more quickly than the other?

Yes_____ No_____

(IF YES) Which dissolves faster?________________

g. Does either Brand A or Brand B have a more pleasant aroma?

Yes_____ No_____

(IF YES) Which has the more pleasant aroma?
____

3. (ASK OF ALL GELATIN USERS)

Now I would like to have you help us design a gelatin best suited to your tastes and needs. As you know, in many cases you have to give up some of one quality to get more of another. In buying a car, you usually have to decide between power and economy or between the easy maneuverability of a compact and the comfort of a big car.

Now, I would like to have you play a little game. I am going to show you a page with various flavored gelatin qualities and ask you to choose between them. For example, the more sugar in a gelatin, the sweeter it would be, but the more calories it would contain. We want to know how much of one you would give up to get the other. Now, look at this table.

No Calories, Not Sweet ☐ ☐ ☐ ☐ ☐ ☐ ☐ Very Sweet but High in Calories

Now, if you are very worried about your weight, you would check the box to the far left. If you have a very sweet tooth and don't care about calories, you would check the box to the far right, or you could check any box in between. The sweeter you want it, the farther to the right you would check it, the fewer calories you want, the farther to the left you would check it. Do you understand? (IF NO, EXPLAIN AGAIN. IF YES, GO ON TO NEXT PAGE.)

No calories but not sweet	☐	☐	☐	☐	☐	☐	☐	Very sweet but high in calories
No lumps and pours easily from package but is low in vitamins	☐	☐	☐	☐	☐	☐	☐	High in vitamins, but is lumpy and difficult to pour from package
Package seals in all flavor but is hard to open	☐	☐	☐	☐	☐	☐	☐	Package is easy to open but loses some of its flavor in time
High in Vitamin C but low in proteins	☐	☐	☐	☐	☐	☐	☐	High in proteins but low in Vita- min C
No lumps & pours easily but is apt to be rubbery	☐	☐	☐	☐	☐	☐	☐	Even tender texture with no rubbery layer, but tends to be lumpy in package
True flavor but low in Vitamin C	☐	☐	☐	☐	☐	☐	☐	High in Vitamin C but less flavorful
Mixes and sets very quickly but is apt to be rubbery	☐	☐	☐	☐	☐	☐	☐	Has even, tender texture with no rubbery layer, but takes longer to mix and set
High in pro- teins but less flavorful	☐	☐	☐	☐	☐	☐	☐	True flavor but low in proteins

4. (ASK OF ALL GELATIN USERS) We all know that many improvements in products cost more money. Sometimes consumers will pay a lot for improvements; sometimes they are perfectly contented with what they have and are not in the least interested in a change. On the following table, please check the MOST you would be willing to pay for each of the following possible improvements:

	I am satisfied with present brands and would not pay anything for this "improvement"	I would pay ½¢ more per package for this "improvement"	I would pay 1¢ more per package for this "improvement"	I would pay 1½¢ more per package for this "improvement"	I would pay 2¢ more per package for this "improvement"
A heat sealed inner envelope that prevents flavor loss.	☐	☐	☐	☐	☐
A gelatin that is guaranteed to set-up firm and tender every time--no rubberiness, not thin or watery.	☐	☐	☐	☐	☐
More Vitamin C -- Twice as much as any brand now on the market.	☐	☐	☐	☐	☐
A gelatin that never lumps in the package.	☐	☐	☐	☐	☐

	Satisfied -- Would not pay	Pay ½¢	Pay 1¢	Pay 1½¢	Pay 2¢
A gelatin that mixes and sets in half the time of present brands.	☐	☐	☐	☐	☐
A package that opens easily with no tearing and no need to use a knife or scissors.	☐	☐	☐	☐	☐
More Proteins -- twice as much as any other brand.	☐	☐	☐	☐	☐
An inner envelope that pours easily with no spilling.	☐	☐	☐	☐	☐

(Courtesy of Trendex, Inc.)

CLASSIFICATION

1. Are there children in your family? Yes___ No___

   What are their ages? ____ ____ ____

   ____ ____ ____

   ____ ____ ____

   Do you serve gelatin:

   Primarily for the children _____

   Primarily for the adults _____

   For the whole family alike _____

2a. About how many packages of gelatin do you use in a typical week?

____

2b. Are these regular size or family size?

Regular _____ Family _____

3. Age of housewife 18-29 ____ Socio-Economic Class:
   30-39 ____ Upper ____
   40-54 ____ Middle____
   55 or over____ Lower ____

Respondent's Name______________________ Interviewer____________

Address________________________________ Date___________________

____

(Courtesy of Trendex, Inc.)

QUESTIONNAIRE

1. Do you now have baking powder in your home?

   ( ) Yes   ( ) No--Discontinue interview.

2. (If "Yes"): What brand?____________________

3. Have you ever heard the terms, "single-acting" and "double-acting" applied to baking powder?

   ( ) Yes   ( ) No

4. What do you think is the difference between a single-acting powder and a double-acting powder? (What exactly does each of those terms mean?)

   SINGLE:____________________

   DOUBLE:____________________

5a. What do you think might be the advantages of a single-acting powder?

 b. What do you think might be the advantages of a double-acting powder?

6. You now have (brand named in Q. 1) in your home. Is that a single-acting or a double-acting powder?

   ( )Single   ( )Double   ( )Don't know

7a. As far as you know, what ingredients are usually put into a single-acting powder?

 b. As far as you know, what ingredients are usually put into a double-acting powder?

8a. Some baking powders contain cream of tartar. What are the advantages, as you see it, of cream of tartar?

8b. What are the disadvantages?

____

____

9a. The last time you used baking powder, what were you baking?

____

b. How long ago was that?____________________

10a. Did you bake the (article named in Q. 8a) right after mixing, or did you let it stand awhile before baking?

( )Baked right after mixing
( )Let stand before baking
( )Don't know

b. (If "Let Stand"): How much time elapsed between mixing and baking?

______________hours

Age______________

Socio-Econ.

(Courtesy of Trendex, Inc.)

MARGARINE SURVEY #1

1a. Do you have margarine in your home?

Yes_____ No_____

(If "No", discontinue interview.)

b. What brand do you now have in your home?_____________

c. Do you use margarine for cooking, as a table spread, or both?

Cooking_____
Table spread_____

Here are several pairs of words, with opposite meanings, that might describe a margarine. Notice that between each pair of words there are seven boxes. Now, for each pair of words, put a check mark in whichever one of the seven boxes best tells your opinion of:

1. Your present brand of margarine;

2. A brand of margarine made from 100% pure corn oil.

Interviewer Note:

(If respondent seems slow or hesitant about making her check marks, make the point that her first, quick impressions are actually the best. Interviews should alternate - present brand first then 100% corn oil first.)

CLASSIFICATION INFORMATION

Name_________________________ Address_____________________

City_________________________ Date________________________

Age: Under 35___ 35-44____ 45 & over_____

Upper____ Middle____ Lower____

(Courtesy of Trendex, Inc.)

MY PRESENT BRAND OF MARGARINE

Good Tasting	☐	☐	☐	☐	☐	☐	☐	Poor Tasting
Pure	☐	☐	☐	☐	☐	☐	☐	Impure
Desirable	☐	☐	☐	☐	☐	☐	☐	Undesirable
Important	☐	☐	☐	☐	☐	☐	☐	Unimportant
Good Flavor	☐	☐	☐	☐	☐	☐	☐	Poor Flavor
Pleasant Aroma	☐	☐	☐	☐	☐	☐	☐	Unpleasant Aroma
Distinctive	☐	☐	☐	☐	☐	☐	☐	Commonplace
Modern	☐	☐	☐	☐	☐	☐	☐	Old-Fashioned
Healthful	☐	☐	☐	☐	☐	☐	☐	Unhealthful
High Quality	☐	☐	☐	☐	☐	☐	☐	Low Quality
Expensive	☐	☐	☐	☐	☐	☐	☐	Inexpensive
Appetizing	☐	☐	☐	☐	☐	☐	☐	Unappetizing
Fattening	☐	☐	☐	☐	☐	☐	☐	Non-Fattening
Digestible	☐	☐	☐	☐	☐	☐	☐	Indigestible
Good	☐	☐	☐	☐	☐	☐	☐	Bad
Safe	☐	☐	☐	☐	☐	☐	☐	Dangerous
For Me	☐	☐	☐	☐	☐	☐	☐	Not For Me
Fresh	☐	☐	☐	☐	☐	☐	☐	Stale
Easy to Spread	☐	☐	☐	☐	☐	☐	☐	Hard to Spread
Good for Table	☐	☐	☐	☐	☐	☐	☐	Good Only for Cooking

A BRAND OF MARGARINE MADE FROM 100% PURE CORN OIL

Good Tasting	☐	☐	☐	☐	☐	☐	☐	Poor Tasting
Pure	☐	☐	☐	☐	☐	☐	☐	Impure
Desirable	☐	☐	☐	☐	☐	☐	☐	Undesirable
Important	☐	☐	☐	☐	☐	☐	☐	Unimportant
Good Flavor	☐	☐	☐	☐	☐	☐	☐	Poor Flavor
Pleasant Aroma	☐	☐	☐	☐	☐	☐	☐	Unpleasant Aroma
Distinctive	☐	☐	☐	☐	☐	☐	☐	Commonplace
Modern	☐	☐	☐	☐	☐	☐	☐	Old-Fashioned
Healthful	☐	☐	☐	☐	☐	☐	☐	Unhealthful
High Quality	☐	☐	☐	☐	☐	☐	☐	Low Quality
Expensive	☐	☐	☐	☐	☐	☐	☐	Inexpensive
Appetizing	☐	☐	☐	☐	☐	☐	☐	Unappetizing
Fattening	☐	☐	☐	☐	☐	☐	☐	Non-Fattening
Digestible	☐	☐	☐	☐	☐	☐	☐	Indigestible
Good	☐	☐	☐	☐	☐	☐	☐	Bad
Safe	☐	☐	☐	☐	☐	☐	☐	Dangerous
For Me	☐	☐	☐	☐	☐	☐	☐	Not For Me
Fresh	☐	☐	☐	☐	☐	☐	☐	Stale
Easy to Spread	☐	☐	☐	☐	☐	☐	☐	Hard to Spread
Good for Table	☐	☐	☐	☐	☐	☐	☐	Good Only for Cooking
Worth Trying	☐	☐	☐	☐	☐	☐	☐	Not Worth Trying

Which of the statements on this card best describes how well you like:

	ICE CREAM	CAKE	(GELATIN BRAND)
I like it extremely	( )	( )	( )
I like it very much	( )	( )	( )
I like it moderately	( )	( )	( )
I like it slightly	( )	( )	( )
I neither like nor dislike it	( )	( )	( )
I dislike it slightly	( )	( )	( )
I dislike it moderately	( )	( )	( )
I dislike it very much	( )	( )	( )
I dislike it extremely	( )	( )	( )

Which of the statements on the card best describes how well you like the pie you just tasted:

I like it extremely	( )
I like it very much	( )
I like it moderately	( )
I like it slightly	( )
I neither like nor dislike it	( )
I dislike it slightly	( )
I dislike it moderately	( )
I dislike it very much	( )
I dislike it extremely	( )

NAME: ____________________

Any comments:

AGE: 12 13 14 15 16 17

SEX: Male ☐ Female ☐

(Courtesy of Trendex, Inc.)

DEODORANT SURVEY

1. Do you use an underarm deodorant?

   Yes ☐ No ☐ (DISCONTINUE INTERVIEW)

2. What brand of deodorant did you use the very last time?

   ____

3. What type was it?

   Cream ☐ Roll-On ☐ (CHECK "YES" BOX IN Q.4 AND SKIP TO Q.5)
   Spray ☐ Other ☐ ______________________ (specify)
   Stick ☐

4. Have you ever used a roll-on deodorant?

   Yes ☐ (CONTINUE WITH Q.5)

   No ☐ (SKIP TO Q.7)

5. What (other) brand or brands of roll-on have you used? (RECORD BELOW)

6. (For each brand mentioned, ask) Why are you no longer using (Name Brand) roll-on?

Q.5 Brand	Q.6 Reasons No Longer Using
______________________	______________________
	______________________
	______________________
______________________	______________________
	______________________
	______________________
______________________	______________________
	______________________
	______________________

7. Here is a statement which describes a leading brand of roll-on underarm deodorant. Would you please read it? (SHOW STATEMENT CARD)

(GIVE RESPONDENT AMPLE TIME TO STUDY STATEMENT.)

Now, would you please tell me in your own words what do you think they are trying to tell you about this deodorant in this statement? What are they trying to get across? Anything else? (PROBE)

____

____

____

8. When buying a deodorant for yourself, how important would you consider this quality--extremely important, very important, important, not very important or not at all important? (SHOW "IMPORTANCE" CARD)

- Extremely important ☐
- Very important ☐
- Important ☐
- Not very important ☐
- Not at all important ☐

9. Why? ____

____

10. Do you consider the presence of a pink or blue dye in an underarm deodorant: (SHOW "QUALITY" CARD)

- an extremely desirable quality ☐
- a very desirable quality ☐
- a fairly desirable quality ☐
- a quality of no importance ☐
- a fairly undesirable quality ☐
- a very undesirable quality ☐
- an extremely undesirable quality ☐

11. Why do you feel that way? ______________________________

____

____

12. This statement (refer to card) suggests that some roll-on deodorants contain pink or blue dye. Which roll-on deodorants do you think might fit this description? (SHOW STATEMENT CARD)

☐ None ________________ ________________ ________________

CLASSIFICATION

AGE: 18-29 ☐ 30-39 ☐ 40-54 ☐ 55 or over ☐

ECONOMIC STATUS: Upper ☐ Middle ☐ Lower ☐

EMPLOYMENT STATUS: Employed - Full Time ☐ Part Time ☐

Not Employed ☐

NAME ____

ADDRESS ________________________ CITY AND STATE ________

INTERVIEWER ________________________ DATE ________

(Courtesy of Trendex, Inc.)

DEODORANT SURVEY

1a. Which of these brands of underarm deodorants do you now have in stock? (RECORD BELOW)

b. Which of these brands do you usually carry that are temporarily out of stock?

	(a) Brands Now IN STOCK	(b) Brands Temporarily NOT IN STOCK	Brands Never Stocked
Brand A	___	___	___
Brand B	___	___	___
Brand C	___	___	___
Brand D	___	___	___
Brand E	___	___	___ (end interview)
Brand F	___	___	___
Brand G	___	___	___
Brand H	___	___	___
Brand I	___	___	___
Brand J	___	___	___
Brand K	___	___	___
Brand L	___	___	___

2. What are your four top selling brands of deodorants? (Rank in order of sales volume)

Rank 1: ______________________

Rank 2: ______________________

Rank 3: ______________________

Rank 4: ______________________

3. About how many packages of (mention each brand) would you say your store has sold in the past week?

	# Units Sold
Brand A	__________
Brand E	__________
Brand F	__________
Brand D	__________

4a. Are there any new brands of underarm deodorants on the market that seem to be making progress in terms of sales?

Yes ☐ No ☐ Don't Know ☐

b. (IF YES) What brand(s)?____________________________

c. In your opinion, why is this brand doing so well?

____

____

5a. As a selling item, that is, the dollars it might put in your cash register, what is <u>your opinion</u> of Company E's new aerosol deodorant?

Excellent ☐ Fair ☐
Good ☐ Poor ☐

b. Why?____

____

6a. Now, as a deodorant product, what is <u>your opinion</u> of Company E's new deodorant?

Excellent Product ☐
Good Product ☐
Fair Product ☐
Poor Product ☐

b. Why?____

____

c. Would you say your Company E customers are mostly men, or mostly women, or about half men and half women?

Mostly Men ☐
Mostly Women ☐
Half and Half ☐
Don't know ☐

OBSERVATION: (Brand E only)

	Yes	No
Visible to public	☐	☐
Price prominently displayed	☐	☐
On counter	☐	☐
Open shelves	☐	☐
Special display	☐	☐

Describe display: ______________________________

____

______________________________ Write in Price: $ ______

Interviewer comments: ______________________________

____

____

CLASSIFICATION:

NAME OF RESPONDENT: ____________________ POSITION: __________

NAME OF STORE: ______________________________

ADDRESS: ____________________ CITY AND STATE: __________

INTERVIEWER: ____________________ DATE: __________

SELF-SERVICE ☐ NOT SELF-SERVICE ☐ PART SELF-SERVICE ☐

STORE TYPE: CHAIN ☐ INDEPENDENT ☐

STORE SIZE: LARGE ☐ MEDIUM ☐ SMALL ☐

(Courtesy of Trendex, Inc. Interviews with store personnel.)

DEODORANT PACKAGE TEST

1a. Have you, yourself, used an underarm deodorant in the past 30 days?

Yes ☐ No ☐ (END INTERVIEW)

b. (IF YES) What brand did you use the last time?

____
(Write in Brand Name)

c. What type is it?

Roll-on (ball type) ____
Cream ____
Stick ____
Spray ____
Other (specify)________

2. I would like to show you several package designs for Company A's underarm deodorant. (SHOW FIRST TWO DESIGNS) Which of these two do you think you would prefer to buy?

	I	II	III
Package A	☐	☐	☐
Package B	☐	☐	☐
Package C	☐	☐	☐
Package D	☐	☐	☐
Package E	☐	☐	☐
Package F	☐	☐	☐
Package G	☐	☐	☐
Package H	☐	☐	☐

(INTERVIEWER: ROTATE ACCORDING TO INSTRUCTIONS.)

3. (ASK ABOUT FINAL PACKAGE SELECTED.) What is there about this package that made you like it best?

____

NAME:______________________________________
ADDRESS:___________________________________
CITY AND STATE:_____________________________

AGE: 18-24___ 25-34___ 35-44___ 45 & over___

ECONOMIC CLASS: Upper___ Middle___ Lower___

INTERVIEWER:______________________DATE:_________

(Courtesy of Trendex, Inc.)

WATER STUDY

RESPONDENT NAME: ______________________________ PHONE: ____________________

ADDRESS: ____________________________________ CITY: ____________________

Good ____________ My name is _________________ I am a representative of Southam Marketing Research Services, a national public opinion organization. We are conducting a survey in this area to obtain consumer opinions about a particular product. Would you be willing to help us in this regard? It will only take a few minutes of your time. Thank you.

[DO NOT PROCEED WITH INTERVIEW UNLESS RESPONDENT INDICATES A WILLINGNESS TO BE INTERVIEWED]

1. First of all I would like you to read these names aloud to me.

   [HAND RESPONDENT CARDS WITH PROPOSED NAMES AND RECORD CORRECTNESS AND EASE OF PRONUNCIATION BELOW - ROTATE SEQUENCE FROM INTERVIEW TO INTERVIEW]

	Pronounced Correctly	Pronounced Incorrectly	Easily Pronounced	Difficult to Pronounce
BRAND X	[ ]	[ ]	[ ]	[ ]
BRAND Y	[ ]	[ ]	[ ]	[ ]
BRAND Z	[ ]	[ ]	[ ]	[ ]

2. Now, I would like you to tell me the first thing you think of, that is, the first thing that comes to mind, when I say ____________________?

   [PROBE FULLY. ASK FOR EACH NAME ON THE CARDS AND RECORD BELOW]

	First Mentioned	Other Mentions
BRAND X	____________________	________________________
		________________________
BRAND Y	____________________	________________________
		________________________
BRAND Z	____________________	________________________

3. What kind of a product do you think would be called ________? [RECORD BELOW]
What other products might have this name? [RECORD BELOW]

	Product First Mentioned	Other Product Mentions
BRAND X	________	________
		________
BRAND Y	________	________
		________
BRAND Z	________	________
		________

4. [FOR EACH NAME, ASK.....]

A. Have you ever heard the name ____________ before? [RECORD BELOW]

[IF YES, ASK.....]

B. In what way was it used? [PROBE FULLY]

	A		B
	YES	NO	HOW USED
BRAND X	[ ]	[ ]	________
BRAND Y	[ ]	[ ]	________
BRAND Z	[ ]	[ ]	________

[STATEMENT]

[As you know, tap water in most cities is treated with chemicals such as chlorine and fluorine to ensure that it is safe for human consumption.
If a person chooses, they can buy bottled mineral water, which is pure water with a high mineral content and a distinctive mineral taste.
Suppose that ordinary pure natural water was available. That is, ordinary water, tested to ensure that it is pure with no mineral taste and no artificial additives, sold in outlets such as grocery stores, etc.]

5. [HAND RESPONDENT CONCEPT STATEMENT - ALLOW THEM TO READ IT SEVERAL TIMES IF NECESSARY THEN ASK...]

A. Do you think that you personally would want to use this product?

YES [ ] (Ask B,C,D) NO [ ] (Skip to E)

B. What are all the ways in which you think you might use this product? [PROBE FULLY]

____

____

____

C. What do you think a product such as this would be like? [PROBE FULLY]

____

____

____

D. How likely do you think you would be to use this product for the following:

	Very Unlikely	Somewhat Unlikely	Some-what Likely	Very Likely
Babies Formulas	[ ]	[ ]	[ ]	[ ]
Serve to guests as drinking water	[ ]	[ ]	[ ]	[ ]
For everyday use as drinking water	[ ]	[ ]	[ ]	[ ]
Use in cooking	[ ]	[ ]	[ ]	[ ]
Serve to old people	[ ]	[ ]	[ ]	[ ]
For medicinal use	[ ]	[ ]	[ ]	[ ]
To maintain health	[ ]	[ ]	[ ]	[ ]
For mixing with alcoholic drinks	[ ]	[ ]	[ ]	[ ]
For making non-alcoholic drinks	[ ]	[ ]	[ ]	[ ]
For special diets	[ ]	[ ]	[ ]	[ ]
Use in steam iron	[ ]	[ ]	[ ]	[ ]
For making ice cubes	[ ]	[ ]	[ ]	[ ]

5. E. Based on the information contained in this card, I would like you to try and imagine what this water would be like. Now thinking specifically about its TASTE, would you tell me what you think it would TASTE like? [PROBE FULLY - RECORD BELOW]

____

____

____

F. How would it's purity compare to ordinary tap water? [PROBE] Why do you say this? Is this important to you?

____

____

____

G. Overall, in your own words, how would you describe it's QUALITY compared to ordinary tap water or mineral water? [PROBE] Why do you say this?

____

____

____

H. How do you think it would compare to ordinary tap water in terms of freshness? [PROBE FULLY]

____

____

____

I. Just based on your impression of the product, how do you think it would compare in cost to bottled mineral water, soft drinks, fruit juices? [RECORD BELOW]

	Much Less Expensive	Less Expensive	About the same	More Expensive	Much More Expensive
Bottled Mineral Water	[ ]	[ ]	[ ]	[ ]	[ ]
Soft Drinks	[ ]	[ ]	[ ]	[ ]	[ ]
Fruit Juices	[ ]	[ ]	[ ]	[ ]	[ ]

6. [ASK FOR EACH OF THREE NAMES]
Now I would like you to try something different. Suppose a company offered this water on the market and called it ___________ I would like you to rate it for each of the following dimensions.

Example: An Olive	VERY	QUITE	SLIGHTLY	NEITHER	SLIGHTLY	QUITE	VERY	
Good Tasting	x	x	x	x	x	x	x	Poor Tasting
Oily	x	x	x	x	x	x	x	Not Oily
High Quality	x	x	x	x	x	x	x	Low Quality
Expensive	x	x	x	x	x	x	x	Inexpensive

____

High Price	x	x	x	x	x	x	x	Low Price
Good Quality	x	x	x	x	x	x	x	Poor Quality
Artificial Product	x	x	x	x	x	x	x	Natural Product
Good for Health	x	x	x	x	x	x	x	Bad for Health
Good for all Occasions	x	x	x	x	x	x	x	Not Good for all Occasions
Not Suitable for Cooking	x	x	x	x	x	x	x	Suitable for cooking
For Special Occasions	x	x	x	x	x	x	x	Not for Special Occasions
Very Clear Colour	x	x	x	x	x	x	x	Not Clear Colour
Fresh	x	x	x	x	x	x	x	Stale
For Young People	x	x	x	x	x	x	x	Not for Young People
Made by a Company that makes other Food Products	x	x	x	x	x	x	x	Not Made by a Company that makes other Food Products
For Adults	x	x	x	x	x	x	x	Not for Adults
For People Like Me	x	x	x	x	x	x	x	Not For People Like Me
Produced by a Good Company	x	x	x	x	x	x	x	Produced by a Poor Company
Modern	x	x	x	x	x	x	x	Old-Fashioned
For Babies' Formulas	x	x	x	x	x	x	x	Not For Babies' Formulas
For Mixing Alcoholic Drinks	x	x	x	x	x	x	x	Not for Mixing Alcoholic Drinks
For Making Non-Alcoholic Drink	x	x	x	x	x	x	x	Not For Making Non-Alcoholic Drink

6. [ASK FOR EACH OF THREE NAMES]
Now I would like you to try something different. Suppose a company offered this water on the market and called it ___________ I would like you to rate it for each of the following dimensions.

Example: An Olive	VERY	QUITE	SLIGHTLY	NEITHER	SLIGHTLY	QUITE	VERY	
Good Tasting	x	x	x	x	x	x	x	Poor Tasting
Oily	x	x	x	x	x	x	x	Not Oily
High Quality	x	x	x	x	x	x	x	Low Quality
Expensive	x	x	x	x	x	x	x	Inexpensive

____

High Price	x	x	x	x	x	x	x	Low Price
Good Quality	x	x	x	x	x	x	x	Poor Quality
Artificial Product	x	x	x	x	x	x	x	Natural Product
Good for Health	x	x	x	x	x	x	x	Bad for Health
Good for all Occasions	x	x	x	x	x	x	x	Not Good for all Occasions
Not Suitable for Cooking	x	x	x	x	x	x	x	Suitable for cooking
For Special Occasions	x	x	x	x	x	x	x	Not for Special Occasions
Very Clear Colour	x	x	x	x	x	x	x	Not Clear Colour
Fresh	x	x	x	x	x	x	x	Stale
For Young People	x	x	x	x	x	x	x	Not for Young People
Made by a Company that makes other Food Products	x	x	x	x	x	x	x	Not Made by a Company that makes other Food Products
For Adults	x	x	x	x	x	x	x	Not for Adults
For People Like Me	x	x	x	x	x	x	x	Not For People Like Me
Produced by a Good Company	x	x	x	x	x	x	x	Produced by a Poor Company
Modern	x	x	x	x	x	x	x	Old-Fashioned
For Babies' Formulas	x	x	x	x	x	x	x	Not For Babies' Formulas
For Mixing Alcoholic Drinks	x	x	x	x	x	x	x	Not for Mixing Alcoholic Drinks
For Making Non-Alcoholic Drink	x	x	x	x	x	x	x	Not For Making Non-Alcoholic Drink

6. [ASK FOR EACH OF THREE NAMES]
Now I would like you to try something different. Suppose a company offered this water on the market and called it ________ I would like you to rate it for each of the following dimensions.

Example: An Olive

	VERY	QUITE	SLIGHTLY	NEITHER	SLIGHTLY	QUITE	VERY	
Good Tasting	x	x	x	x	x	x	x	Poor Tasting
Oily	x	x	x	x	x	x	x	Not Oily
High Quality	x	x	x	x	x	x	x	Low Quality
Expensive	x	x	x	x	x	x	x	Inexpensive

____

High Price	x	x	x	x	x	x	x	Low Price
Good Quality	x	x	x	x	x	x	x	Poor Quality
Artificial Product	x	x	x	x	x	x	x	Natural Product
Good for Health	x	x	x	x	x	x	x	Bad for Health
Good for all Occasions	x	x	x	x	x	x	x	Not Good for all Occasions
Not Suitable for Cooking	x	x	x	x	x	x	x	Suitable for cooking
For Special Occasions	x	x	x	x	x	x	x	Not for Special Occasions
Very Clear Colour	x	x	x	x	x	x	x	Not Clear Colour
Fresh	x	x	x	x	x	x	x	Stale
For Young People	x	x	x	x	x	x	x	Not for Young People
Made by a Company that makes other Food Products	x	x	x	x	x	x	x	Not Made by a Company that makes other Food Products
For Adults	x	x	x	x	x	x	x	Not for Adults
For People Like Me	x	x	x	x	x	x	x	Not For People Like Me
Produced by a Good Company	x	x	x	x	x	x	x	Produced by a Poor Company
Modern	x	x	x	x	x	x	x	Old-Fashioned
For Babies' Formulas	x	x	x	x	x	x	x	Not For Babies' Formulas
For Mixing Alcoholic Drinks	x	x	x	x	x	x	x	Not for Mixing Alcoholic (Drinks
For Making Non-Alcoholic Drink	x	x	x	x	x	x	x	Not For Making Non-Alcoholic (Drink

7. [ASK FOR EACH BRAND NAME - ROTATE SEQUENCE FROM INTERVIEW TO INTERVIEW]

A) Suppose that this water was called ____________________, what type of container would you think would be most suitable? [RECORD BELOW]

B) What size should the container be? [RECORD BELOW]

C) What colour would you prefer to see this container? [RECORD BELOW]

NOTE: READ LIST FOR EACH OF (A), (B), and (C) FOR EACH BRAND NAME]

	(A) - (CHECK ONE)				(B) - (CHECK ONE)					(C) - (CHECK ONE)		
	CANS	GLASS BOTTLES	RIGID PLASTIC CONTAINERS	FLEXIBLE PLASTIC BAGS	1 PINT	1 QUART	3 QTS.	1 GAL.	MORE THAN 1 GAL	CLEAR	PALE GREEN	PALE BLUE
BRAND X	[ ]	[ ]	[ ]	[ ]	[ ]	[ ]	[ ]	[ ]	[ ]	[ ]	[ ]	[ ]
BRAND Y	[ ]	[ ]	[ ]	[ ]	[ ]	[ ]	[ ]	[ ]	[ ]	[ ]	[ ]	[ ]
BRAND Z	[ ]	[ ]	[ ]	[ ]	[ ]	[ ]	[ ]	[ ]	[ ]	[ ]	[ ]	[ ]

8. Here are six cards. You will see that three of these cards have a name printed on them and three have symbols printed on them. I would like you to look at the names and the symbols, and then match a name to a symbol for me. It isn't a case of matching shape to shape just put the name you think would go with each symbol. [CIRCLE ONE BELOW]

BRAND X ○ □ △

BRAND Y ○ □ △

BRAND Z ○ □ △

9. Thinking of the three names we have been discussing, BRAND X, BRAND Y and BRAND Z - Which one do you think would be the most suitable name for the type of water we have been talking about?

[IST CHOICE - ______________________

Why did you make this choice? [PROBE FULLY]

____

____

10. Which of the following products have you used before today?

Bottled Mineral Water [ ]

Bottled Drinking Water [ ]

DEMOGRAPHIC DATA

11. Into what age group should I place you?

Under 20 [ ]
21 - 29 [ ]
30 - 39 [ ]
40 - 49 [ ]
50 and Over [ ]

12. What is the occupation of the head of the household? ______________ [Write in]

13. In what country were you born?

Canada [ ] U.S.A. [ ] Other ____________ (Specify) [ ]

In what country were your parents born?

Canada [ ] U.S.A. [ ] Other ____________ (Specify) [ ]

14. What educational level did the head of the household attain?

Completed Public School	[ ]	Partially Completed Public School	[ ]
Completed High School	[ ]	Partially Completed High School	[ ]
Completed University	[ ]	Partially Completed University	[ ]

15. Into which income group should I place your family in terms of total annual income?

Under $5,000 [ ]
$5,000 - $9,999 [ ]
$10,000 - $14,999 [ ]
$15,000 - $19,999 [ ]
$20,000 and Over [ ]

DK/NA Refused [ ]

15 B What are the ages of both Adults & Children? (WRITE IN BELOW)

Children	Adults
______	______
______	______
______	______
______	______
______	______
______	______

16. Into which income group should I place your family in terms of total annual income?

Under $5,000 [ ]
$5,000 - $9,999 [ ]
$10,000 - $14,999 [ ]
$15,000 - $19,999 [ ]
$20,000 and Over [ ]
Don't Know [ ]
No Answer [ ]

17. Do you or any member of your household use Alcoholic Beverages?

YES [ ] NO [ ] DK/NA [ ]

(Courtesy of Southam Marketing Research Services, Don Mills, Ontario, Canada.)

INTERVIEWER QUESTIONNAIRE

(Interviews with hardware store managers)

I. What did you do with the Stanley News after it was received?

1. ☐ Threw it away without opening.
2. ☐ Broke seal and threw away after seeing what it was.
3. ☐ Glanced over for new products - did not read anything.
4. ☐ Began to read one or more articles or advertisements, but did not complete.
5. ☐ Read one or more articles or advertisements completely.
6. ☐ To the best of my knowledge, did not receive it.

SECTIONAL ANALYSIS - For Readers Only

II. Did you read the News Section (Page 1)?

1. ☐ Read from beginning to end.
2. ☐ Started to read, but never completed.
3. ☐ Did not read.

III. Did you read the Tool Talks Column (Page 2)?

1. ☐ Read from beginning to end.
2. ☐ Started to read, but never completed.
3. ☐ Did not read.

IV. Did you read the Handyman Merchandiser Ad (Page 3)?

1. ☐ Read from beginning to end.
2. ☐ Started to read, but never completed.
3. ☐ Looked over - did not read.

V. Did you read the "Spring Specials" Section (Pages 4-8)?

1. ☐ Read more than one tool write-up from beginning to end.

2. ☐ Read one tool write-up from beginning to end.

3. ☐ Glanced over each write-up - did not read any.

4. ☐ Started to read one or more write-ups, but never completed.

5. ☐ Passed over the entire "Spring Specials" Section.

VI. Did you read "Bolt Advertisement (Page 9)?

1. ☐ Read from beginning to end.

2. ☐ Started to read, but never completed.

3. ☐ Did not read.

VII. Did you read The Gate Hardware Ad (Page 10)?

1. ☐ Read advertisement copy completely.

2. ☐ Started to read, but never completed.

3. ☐ Did not read.

VIII. Did you read Product Knowledge Section (Page 11)?

1. ☐ Read from beginning to end.

2. ☐ Started to read but never completed.

3. ☐ Did not read.

IX. Did this copy lead you into any purchasing or inquiry action?

1. ☐ Yes (if yes, what?)

2. ☐ No

X. What is your best guess about the number of minutes you spent on this issue when it arrived?

1. ☐ 1 minute.

2. ☐ 2-5 minutes.

3. ☐ 5-10 minutes.

4. ☐ 11 minutes or more.

XI. Did anyone else in your store read the issue at all?

1. ☐ Yes (If yes, how many?)

2. ☐ No

Comments on the Stanley News:

CHEESE QUESTIONNAIRE

INSTRUCTIONS

1. Do not interview respondents who have family members employed by:
   a) An advertising agency
   b) A marketing research firm
   c) A retail food store
   d) A radio or T.V. station
   e) A newspaper or magazine pub. co.
   f) A food products manufacturer

2. Interview only housewives who have bought packaged Cheddar Cheese at least twice in the last month.

INTRODUCTION

Hello, my name is ________________. I am a representative of Southam Marketing Research Services - a national public opinion organization. We are conducting a short survey and would like to include your opinions on a food product, will you help us?

(DO NOT PROCEED WITH THE INTERVIEW UNLESS RESPONDENT AGREES)

1. First of all do you ever serve Cheddar Cheese in your home? (CHECK ONE ONLY)

   YES ( )
   NO ( ) (TERMINATE)

2. During the past month about how many times have you purchased packaged Cheddar Cheese? (CHECK ONE ONLY)

   Times Purchased

   1 - 2 times ( ) (TERMINATE)
   3 - 4 times ( )
   5 - 8 times ( )
   9 - 10 times ( )
   Over 10 times ( )

3. Out of every 10 times that you serve cheddar in your home - about how many times would you serve it to friends or guests? About how many times would you serve it to family members? (RECORD BELOW - CHECK TOTAL EQUALS 10)

   Number of times serve to friends or guests_____
   Number of times served to family _____
   Total 10

4. What brands of packaged Cheddar Cheese do you buy most frequently? (WRITE IN BRANDS IN ORDER OF MENTION - PROBE FULLY) Any others?

1st mention ________________________
2nd mention ________________________
3rd mention ________________________
4th mention ________________________
5th mention ________________________
6th mention ________________________

5. As you know Cheddar Cheese comes in two colors. You can get the yellow colored kind or the orange colored kind. Which kind do you get? (CHECK ONE ONLY BELOW)

Get orange colored only ( )
Get yellow colored only ( )
Get both yellow & orange ( )
Don't know ( )

6. I understand that you can buy mild cheddar cheese, medium cheddar cheese or old cheddar cheese. Which kind do you usually buy? (CHECK ONE ONLY BELOW)

Buy mild cheddar cheese ( )
Buy medium cheddar cheese ( )
Buy old cheddar cheese ( )
Don't know ( )

(ASK FOR EACH OF FIRST 3 BRANDS MENTIONED IN #4)

7. You mentioned that you bought ______________ brand of Cheddar Cheese. What are all your reasons for buying this brand? (PROBE FULLY)

1st brand mentioned __________________ (Reasons) ______
____

2nd brand mentioned __________________ (Reasons) ______
____

3rd brand mentioned __________________ (Reasons) ______
____

8. Now I'd like you to look at two cheese package designs (LET RESPONDENT LOOK AT DESIGNS FOR A MOMENT - TAKE THEM BACK AND PLACE OUT OF SIGHT). What was the brand name of the cheese these designs were for? (WRITE IN ANSWER BELOW)

____

9. Now I'd like to ask you some true or false questions about Cheddar Cheese. I'll read you a statement and I'd like you to tell me in your opinion if each statement is true or false as far as you are concerned. (READ EACH STATEMENT SLOWLY - ATTEMPT TO GET EITHER A TRUE OR FALSE ANSWER - IF RESPONDENT CAN'T MAKE UP HER MIND AS A LAST RESORT WRITE DON'T KNOW TO THE RIGHT OF THE ANSWER BLOCKS)

	True	False
a) All packaged Cheddar Cheese that you buy in a supermarket is the same.	( )	( )
b) There isn't much difference between Cheddar Cheese marked mild and Cheddar Cheese marked medium.	( )	( )
c) All packaged Cheddar Cheese that you buy in a supermarket is about the same price.	( )	( )
d) I prefer the square blocks of Cheddar Cheese to the wedge shaped pieces.	( )	( )
e) All packaged Cheddar Cheese that you buy in a supermarket is aged.	( )	( )
f) I switch brands of Cheddar Cheese quite often.	( )	( )
g) The higher the price of a Cheddar Cheese the better the quality.	( )	( )
h) Just the adults in our family like Cheddar Cheese.	( )	( )
i) You have to keep Cheddar Cheese in the refrigerator to keep it fresh.	( )	( )
j) I find that men prefer Cheddar Cheese more than women do.	( )	( )
k) They always have my favorite brand of Cheddar Cheese in stock where I shop.	( )	( )
l) I always buy a pre-packaged brand of Cheddar Cheese.	( )	( )

10. Now I'd like you to think back to the two package designs I showed you a few moments ago and tell me, if you can, what all the differences were between the two designs? (PROBE FULLY) Anything else? (NOTE, DO NOT SHOW THE DESIGNS TO THE RESPONDENT AGAIN UNTIL THIS QUESTION HAS BEEN ANSWERED)

____

____

____

11. (INTERVIEWER BE EXPLICIT - MAKE SURE RESPONDENT UNDERSTANDS)

As you know peoples tastes are a little different in various provinces so manufacturers sometimes change their products slightly to satisfy the different consumer tastes. When they do this they sometimes make minor changes in the labels or the package design on their products. Now use your imagination - lets imagine that these (SHOW DESIGNS) are one pound packages of Cheddar Cheese. Now I want you to just think about the Cheese that would be inside these packages. Do you understand? (SHOW CARDS - DO NOT ACCEPT A DON'T KNOW ANSWER - FORCE THE CHOICE)

	K	J	Same
a) Which do you think would be the higher priced?	( )	( )	( )
b) Which one would have the best flavor?	( )	( )	( )
c) Which one would be the easiest to prepare for serving?	( )	( )	( )
d) Which one would be the best quality?	( )	( )	( )
e) Which one would have the strongest taste?	( )	( )	( )
f) Which one would stay fresh longer?	( )	( )	( )
g) Which would be best for serving to your family?	( )	( )	( )
h) Which one would you like best?	( )	( )	( )
i) Which one would have the mildest taste?	( )	( )	( )

	K	J	Same
j) Which one would be the better cheese?	( )	( )	( )
k) Which one would be best for friends/ guests?	( )	( )	( )
l) Which one would be a product of the farm?	( )	( )	( )
m) Which one was aged longer?	( )	( )	( )
n) Which one was a product of a factory?	( )	( )	( )

Respondent's Name ______________________________

Address ______________________________

Phone ______________________________

Age 18-25 ( )
26-30 ( )
31-35 ( )
36-40 ( )
Over 40 ( )

Number in Household __________

Annual Family Income: Under $5,000 ( )
5,000 - 7,999 ( )
8,000 - 9,999 ( )
10,000 - 14,999 ( )
Over 15,000 ( )
Refused ( )
Don't Know ( )

(Courtesy of Southam Marketing Research Services, Don Mills, Ontario, Canada.)

SEVEN

Group Interviewing

A group interview is just what its name implies. A group of people (usually somewhat alike, and having an interest in the question you wish to explore) is brought together for a discussion that may last from one to two hours. For the most part, sessions like this are tape-recorded, with no effort being made to hide this fact. The group leader is either someone from the company, an outside research expert, or sometimes the research person from an advertising agency.

The discussion is free and unhampered, except that the leader must keep it centered on the subject in which he is interested. Ordinarily it is announced at the very beginning that the group has been called together to talk about subject X. And ordinarily, also, the leader gives some acceptable reason for the talk session. A well-run group that understands the reason for its existence is usually willing to cooperate to the best of its ability.

Types of Studies That Can Best Use This Research Method

Group discussions are used where new, fresh thinking is desired. The discussions can develop hypotheses about how a problem may be solved. They can show possible marketing actions, or new product lines, that deserve further exploration. For the retailer, by clearly bringing out what customers and noncustomers think about the store, group discussions can be very educational for management. Whereas a mail or telephone questionnaire is most likely to present alternatives to the respondent, asking for his choice among them, the group session looks for ideas that may not have occurred to anyone. For example:

Group interviewing . . .

1. After a few groups have been conducted by a manufacturer, it begins to appear that women like one of his product lines far better than do their husbands. Discussion groups can develop theories of why this should be so, and what can be done about it.

Some notions about a wholly new product may begin to appear. "What ifs" you might call them; what if the manufacturer made a product that did this or that? (There may be some legal complexities here that you would want to talk over with your counsel before beginning group sessions. You do not want a suit brought against you for "stealing" ideas.)

2. A group can discover human buying motivations that may not have been realized. This is much like the above, but with the difference that the very "idea" of a present or proposed product can have unexpected connotations. Men may look on a brand, or even its name, as being feminine. In this

day of "unisex," it is still important to know about such an attitude. The young man who grows a unisex head of hair also grows a beard in a heroic effort at machismo.

Further investigating buying motivations, it often surprises a new group leader to find how often Mother and Father enter into a discussion, even with entirely mature people. Without trying to be a lay psychologist, one can easily perceive, in many sessions, the influence that Father still has. Often he is still being blamed although the poor man has been dead for many years.

We do not need to belabor this point; everyone who has thought about the matter knows that a complex of emotions enters into the simplest of purchases. A hair-down, shoes-off talk-fest can sort some of these emotions out, and make them useful in merchandising. These are the sorts of motivations that would almost never be obtained from a mail or telephone questionnaire, and rarely from a face-to-face interview. To plumb these motivational depths, it is necessary to foster interplay, discussions, and even controlled arguments, among the participants. At the point where the group forgets the leader, except when he asks discreet questions to keep the subject on the track, and forgets the microphone, the true value of the group session begins to appear.

A hair-down, shoes-off talk-fest can help reveal the motivations behind purchasing.

3. A group can bring out product faults or virtues that seem too unimportant for respondents to mention in a mail or telephone study. Yet little things are often the real reason for buying or not buying. A color can be subconsciously repellent to many people—on *this* product. This is true even though the same color is perfectly acceptable on some other product.

A do-it-yourself product may "look hard to use." The instructions appear to be difficult to understand, and people impatiently refuse to go beyond the first few sentences. For example, husbands may want to please their wives with their accomplishments in the garden or the home. If they believe they may fail with a do-it-yourself product, and thus incur ridicule, they will not buy the product at all.

A group session can find features that seemed important to the manufacturer but which have no meaning or use at all to the final customer. This is added and unnecessary cost. It may even be hurting the sale.

4. Retailers can use groups of people to discuss what they are doing right or wrong in the merchandising of fashion goods. What is the real picture of the store in the minds of these persons? Merchants may be shocked to discover what people really think of their store. The store's patronage may come mostly from customers who want to park in its convenient lot. They hope to find what they want, but often end up elsewhere because the store is not stocked properly for this type of trade.

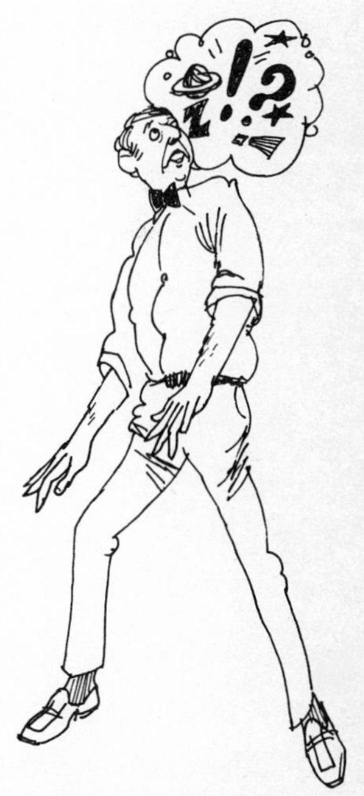

Merchants may be shocked to discover what people really think of their store.

5. A group can help find what kind of people would most likely buy a new product—or shun it. For a retailer, a group can help guide the formation of a new department, or help in the decision to begin stocking a new line of

A group can be a sort of "thinktank."

goods. It may also have some fresh, new thinking on merchandising present departments in a store. Asking about the quality of salespeople is *guaranteed* to bring about a lively discussion. A women's group under good leadership will bubble with new ideas about how to improve a store. Not all the ideas will be workable, but there will be valuable nuggets among the pebbles.

6. For a manufacturer, a group can find hidden fears about a product: fears that are groundless, but exist nevertheless. Unless a manufacturer or a retailer knows these fears, no correction is possible.

In other words, a group can be a sort of "thinktank." Its ideas, of course, are not projectable to the whole population. Further research, of a different type, may be necessary. But if a half dozen groups, without biased leadership, reach similar conclusions, one will be justified in taking these conclusions seriously, and perhaps acting upon them without further delay.

Group interviewing is relatively inexpensive. If the group is led by a professional, the cost may be as high as $700 to $800 per session. With proper forethought and preparation, this is one form of research that you can definitely do yourself, and save money. Furthermore, by leading the group yourself, you can get much more out of it than a professional who does not know your own company and your own problems as well as you do. You can be more flexible, leading the discussion into areas which may have surprised you when they arose, but which are of clear and immediate importance.

An actual group session in Kansas City, Mo.

Using a professional in group research, you might be able to benefit from some modern electronic and mechanical gadgets that would be useful, but not vital. There are interviewing rooms available in many places, fitted out with one-way windows so that the client can watch the proceedings without being seen himself. He can hear the discussion through an intercom without anyone being the wiser. There are also rooms that have been equipped with videotape recorders so that both sound and sight can be retained for later analysis. All these things are costly.

If you do the group research yourself, or have one of your own people do it, the cost will be considerably less. You can follow up leads much more quickly and thoroughly than a professional who may not even be aware of the importance of something that was just said by a participant.

How to Find or Develop a Group

Worthwhile groups are not at all difficult to find. Here are some of the methods that can be used to get a group together. (Local situations, of course, will offer other possibilities.)

1. Almost every large city, and many smaller ones, have marketing research firms which will have interviewers on their staffs. Many of these also can develop groups for you from contacts that they have in town. It is possible to get one group of men, for example, who have no interest in sports, and another of men who are very sports-minded. Or a group of young married women who are just setting up households. The possibilities are endless. The quality of these firms, however, varies among themselves and among cities. Continued use will show which can be counted upon and which cannot.
2. There are many local clubs that are anxious to find some activity that will add a little money to their treasuries. Inflation being what it is, the costs are larger than they were, but a good group from a club can probably be gathered for not much over $100. In every case, of course, you will want to find a group that can help in the specific problem now facing you.
3. If you are in a large company, wives of salesmen or other employees can sometimes get groups together. Perhaps they belong to "sororities" which need a little money. Or the money may be paid separately to each of the women who arrive. In this case, it is often possible to make a little "party" out of the affair—with the hostess furnishing some refreshments (for which you should pay).
4. Churches are sources of groups. And contrary to what might be thought, gatherings from different churches tend to think similarly about business matters. It is not really necessary to have equal representation from Protestant, Jewish, and Catholic churches. Blacks and whites do have differences, however, which may have to be taken into account in some instances.

Ordinarily the worst trouble is to keep everyone from talking at once.

5. Local service clubs, like Rotary, Kiwanis, etc., may make a group available in order to raise money for their favorite charities. This session could take the form of a lunch meeting—really one of their programs. However, programs are usually scheduled well in advance, and you might have to wait too long.

6. For groups of young people, Girl Scouts and Boy Scouts are a source. Also youth groups at the churches. Sometimes the schools will allow something of this sort—if there is no commercial aspect, nothing is being sold.

7. For stores, it is possible to gather a group of charge customers—people whose names are known. This could be in the form of a lunch program, possibly even lunch, a fashion show, and a discussion period.

Since the object of a group session is to develop new thinking, new merchandising ideas, and a better understanding of buying fears and motivations, we do not have to worry about getting statistically "pure" samples. All that is wanted is people who are interested in your subject, who are of at least average intelligence, and who can be led into being articulate.

How to Develop an Outline for the Group Session

The group session is built upon a strong foundation of informality. There have been instances in my own memory where the leader was simply unable to bring a group to life. The tape records only the leader talking—and talking. Fortunately, this is a rare happening. Ordinarily the worst trouble is to keep everyone from talking at the same time.

If you find group interviews as valuable as I have, you will probably do a number of them, and will develop your own style of leadership. However, here is a good way to start:

1. The very best way to begin is for the leader to announce who he is, tell something about his company, explain the problem at hand, and tell why it is important to get help from these people. Even though this is said with the greatest sincerity (perhaps *because* it is), the group will find itself flattered and more ready to cooperate. This, therefore, is the first thing on the outline. Obviously, it should be as short as possible, and still create the right atmosphere.

2. The next step should be for each person to introduce himself and tell a little about himself. Even though all members of the group know each other, this forces everyone to open up and talk a little right at the beginning. Some provision for name cards should be made. Blank, folded cards should be ready, together with a black crayon for each person. After each one has written his name "large and dark," the cards can be placed on the desk so

that the leader can read them. Except in the most unusual circumstances, the more quickly you can get on a first-name basis, the better the session will go.

3. Depending upon your own preference, the material that needs to be covered at the session can be written as a list of topics, or a list of questions. It is important that—so far as you can see ahead—these topics be in the best logical sequence. However, you cannot be too definite, since it is the *unexpected* and *new* that is being sought. In a well-led session, it is more than possible that the list of topics will be almost abandoned as the time goes by.

4. However, it is necessary to have topics or questions ready, to bring a wandering talk-fest back into order. To do these things takes a little experience. In the beginning, you will feel safer with a rather full list of topic sentences or questions.

5. In any case, whether you wander from your list because something new and important has been introduced, or stay fairly close to it, it is necessary to stay in the area of the main reason for the group session in the first place.

6. Finally, time should be left for the leader to make a summary and ask for confirmation from the group that this is indeed what they said.

How to Handle People at a Group Session

Standard "types" show up at a group session. Only a little experience is necessary to learn how to handle them. If the leader has explained the reason for the session, and the group has accepted this reason as being sound, then it will be found that the group unconsciously disciplines itself. However, there are a few people that can be real troublemakers, in the sense that they interfere with the purpose of the *group* session.

1. The person who talks too much is one such troublemaker, and is impulsively dominating. Intimidating the shy, if allowed, this person will fill half your tape with his or her opinions.

2. The person who hesitates too long. While he or she is drawing a breath preparing to speak, someone else has broken in.

3. The accepted "leader" of a session. Almost in a subconscious imitation of chickens, groups tend to work out a sort of "pecking order." There may be deference shown to the oldest person in the group, or to the one who appears most successful, as told by dress and mannerisms. There is always a very real tendency for certain ones to echo the opinions of the talkative person, or the accepted leader.

Groups tend to work out a sort of "pecking order."

It does not take more than a few minutes to spot these various types. And it will be up to you to throw questions at the shy ones, or to seek out people that do not agree with the head chicken. The group will be conscious of what you are doing and will aid you as much as possible.

Getting the group members to talk with each other about your problem is not as difficult a task as it sounds. Once interest has been aroused, the group members will disagree with each other, and bring out points to refute other points.

It will be of great assistance to this free discussion if your opening statement can immediately relate your problem to a problem of interest to the group. As a matter of fact, the group should have been chosen because of this likelihood. A group of middle-income women who are keeping house for their families can certainly become worked up over a problem of buying draperies and drapery hardware. Soon all their experiences come flooding out. The difficulty in getting advice, the lack of interest on the part of the salesperson, the question of how to measure the window opening for a rod and for the draperies themselves, and the changes in styles from one fad to another. And finally, the difficulty in getting friend-husband to install the fixtures, and the family fights that ensue. Out of all this may come some new ideas for merchandising this department. Or for new products. Once a group has fastened onto a topic like draperies, you may not have to say very much at all.

How to Set Up the Room; Number of People Involved

A group session can be held with as many as twenty people. Fifteen appears to work out a little better if everyone is to be given a chance to speak his piece during the hour or hour and a half that has been allotted.

A rectangular table works out well, with the leader sitting at one end, being "papa," as he might say aloud to bring a smile and help prevent any stiffness at the beginning.

Chairs should be comfortable, not the unbearable folding type.

Chairs should be comfortable, preferably not the hard, folding type that become almost unbearable for some people after a half hour. But the chairs should not be soporific either, or you may find one or two of your members "thinking" for a long time with their eyes closed.

The best sessions seem to be held in a room that is relatively bare of furniture or pictures that may distract attention. Often it is possible to rent a room in the local YMCA at a nominal charge. Or a small conference room can be had at a local motel.

One mistake that new group leaders frequently make is to have just one microphone. It seems inevitable that the most soft-spoken members arrange themselves at the end of the table (as far away as possible from the single mike). Even though it costs a bit more, it is often advisable to arrange for the rental of adequate sound equipment from some specialist in town, who will probably tell you to use two mikes and will know how to hook them up properly.

One thing you must constantly remember is the poor stenographer who must make some sense out of the sound of many voices on the tapes. Two mikes will make the level of voices more nearly the same. Not a loud one, followed by a whisper from the end of the table.

It is up to you to keep two people from speaking at once, to the extent possible without harming the free expression that is so important. If you take the time to tell them about your poor secretary back in the office, groups usually can be made to understand the need to speak in turn.

It is not necessary to hide the mikes. Or the tape recorder. In fact, these gadgets help to keep the group on the track; they can see that their every word is being recorded. Foolishness is kept to a minimum by this sight.

With a rectangular table, name signs placed so that *everyone* can see them, mikes in place, and the recorder working, everything is ready to go. But one word from experience. Make *sure* that the recorder is working!

This may be the place for one more caution. Your secretary will not be able to see who is speaking when transcribing the tapes. So, for the transcriber's benefit, use their names when you speak to people, either to ask a question or to reply to one. And it would be good to explain to the group why you do this; perhaps they will copy you, and your secretary will be very grateful.

How to Analyze the Recorded Tapes

When the value of group sessions in marketing research first began to be realized, it was often said that a trained psychologist ought to take part in the analysis of the tapes. The thought behind this attitude was that only a psychologist could perceive the feelings and motivations underlying the spoken words. For awhile, some thought that only a psychologist could effectively run a group session.

Without demeaning the noble profession of the psychologist or psychiatrist, it is utter nonsense to believe that only they can talk with a group of people for an hour or so and benefit from the results.

Because every session is so different, it is impossible to set up rules for analysis. A few thoughts are in order, however. First, it is probably necessary to transcribe the tapes. You can, and should, listen to them. But too much of the talk is fleeting and brief; you have to see the words in print fully to realize their import.

Next, perhaps, you may wish to set down on separate sheets of paper the major topics, or questions, that led you to have the session in the first place. How did these people address themselves to these points? Under each heading, it is possible to place actual quotations. As you slowly work your way

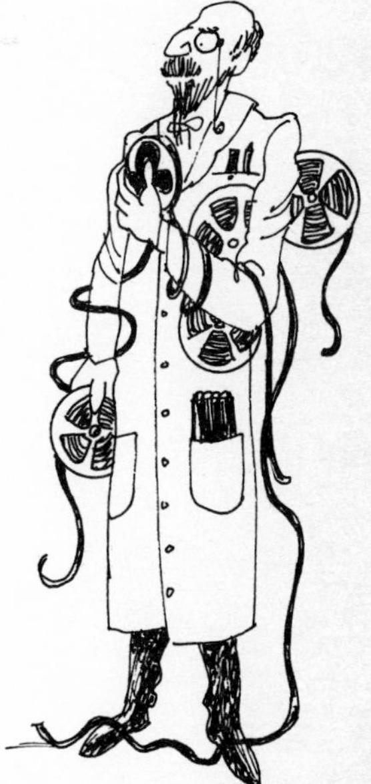

Analyzing the recorded tapes . . .

through the tapes and the evidence begins to build up on your tabulating sheets, important findings and evidence will begin to appear. You may want to use a separate section for brand new thoughts and ideas that came unexpectedly and unasked-for from the group. These new ideas can be the most valuable benefit that you will receive.

It is unlikely that only one group will be used for any problem that is important enough to do at all. The same tabulating sheets can continue to be used—separating each group, but keeping their remarks together in an organized fashion. The odds are that the groups will begin reinforcing each other; there will be some differences, of course, but these will not predominate.

If at all possible, use a second person to do the same analysis. Does he perceive something that you missed? Or does he read the meanings differently?

A bull session will end this part of the research. Can agreement be reached about what has really been learned from these sessions? What have we learned that we did not know before? Have the groups merely confirmed what we already believed?

Finally, it is necessary for all to reach agreement concerning what actions should be recommended. Have the groups pointed to the need for more thorough and extensive research, perhaps using other techniques? Or do we feel that we have the "true answer" and nothing more is needed?

What actions have the groups told us that we ought to take? Are these actions feasible? We have to be realistic; no company can do everything. Increased sales and lowered profits will not be viewed with favor by management.

The final report will be stronger if actual excerpts from things said in the sessions are used. Once it becomes clear what major recommendations should be made, it is perfectly legitimate to use actual quotations to make the report more effective.

Who Make Better Leaders: Men or Women?

It takes some courage even to raise this question in this modern day. However, to clear some misconceptions that may have been aroused by now, it is perfectly possible for a man to run a very beneficial group session of women. In some ways—for reasons which I cannot explain, and will not even try—it appears that men can sometimes get more from a women's group than can a woman leader. The exception to this, of course, is with topics that may be embarrassing to both sides. But even here, it is often quite surprising what women will say, given the right incentive.

Likewise, a woman can do a good job of group leadership with men. My inclination would be to choose a motherly type of leader rather than a sexy young thing. This only comes from a little experience, and others may not agree. In both shopping center interviews and group sessions, results have seemed to be more worthwhile when we had "mother" asking the questions.

There is no possible "right" answer. A good leader can be of either sex. The only reason for this section of the chapter is to prevent prejudice that might build up in your mind.

Choose a motherly type of group leader rather than a sexy young thing.

How Many Groups Are Enough?

Once again, there is no right answer to this question. Geographical considerations must be made. Is it possible that a group from another section of the country would give different answers? For retailers, groups must cover, as well as possible, the different ethnic and income groups that are attracted (or should be attracted) to the store. Choosing groups of varying income levels will almost automatically spread the research into different residential areas.

Realistically, the costs of research will predetermine how far we can go. So a decision will be made that four or five sessions will probably do the job. If these four or five groups produce similar or identical results, we can believe that enough has been done. If, however, radical differences are found, then it is time to stop, take a look at our procedures, determine whether we are missing the important topics, and then do a few more groups. This sounds a bit haphazard, but it is the way that most decisions of this sort are really made, and it is about the only way that you can do it.

Summary

You may have detected a certain bias in this chapter. It is true that I have a prejudice in favor of group research. It is easy to organize, can be done rather inexpensively, and can be done without too much delay. Results are very often better than anything that could have been obtained through other techniques.

But like mail questionnaires and field interviewing, this type of research should be used only where it can be cost-effective, producing the most benefit for the least cost. Where your purposes suit the group method, then fine results can be expected.

EIGHT

Telephone Research

Some telephone surveys can be done by an amateur. The decision depends upon the type of study and the kind of people to be called. Consumers are increasingly unwilling to be bothered by calls from strangers. The rapidly expanding number of unlisted telephone numbers bears witness to this. For a consumer study, therefore, the recommendation must be that you turn to experts in the field.

However, there *are* certain kinds of research that you can conduct on the phone. And even if you *do* use an outside agency to do the actual calling, the study can still be planned by you, and recommendations drawn by you. Most telephone survey companies would rather do the whole study with consumers, including writing the final report. But they can be persuaded to limit their efforts to the actual telephoning and the tabulation of results. The price for this is usually not prohibitive.

Types of Studies That Can Be Done by Telephone

Here is where the telephone technique can be used to advantage:

1. In before-and-after measuring of advertising results. More will be said about this later.

2. In quick and informal studies of a certain question, where wholesalers, retailers, or similar companies may be called for specific (and short) answers to a few questions. The only difference between this and the ordinary calls that have been made for years is your effort to maintain something approaching an unbiased sample and questioning technique.

3. Or one-shot consumer studies where it may be necessary to determine knowledge of a product and preference for a brand.

4. In studies of an industrial field, where the total number of respondents is small, and where you have reason to believe that these people will answer legitimate inquiries.

5. In certain political polls, where a very carefully selected small sample is used. It is an interesting commentary on how alike we all are in our agreements and disagreements, that just a couple of thousand "votes" in these polls can truly represent the thinking of a whole nation. We cannot go into the selection process used for these polls, and the only reason to mention it here is to emphasize that the very large samples of the early years of marketing research were never really necessary. Lately the trend has been toward smaller, well-chosen samples. Using good procedures, these small samples are as accurate as—or more accurate than—the large ones of years ago.

Consumers are increasingly unwilling to be bothered by calls from strangers.

Basic Strengths and Weaknesses of the Telephone Approach

First the strengths:

1. The greatest strength of the telephone for marketing research is our ability to get answers quickly. If you want to measure consumer awareness and attitude toward a product, or toward a store, just before and just after an advertising campaign, the telephone offers one of the few ways of doing the job before memory loss, or extraneous factors such as a competitor's promotions, make the results less accurate.

2. A complete territory—the nation, the region, the state, or even the area near a shopping center—can often be covered in just one or two days and evenings of calling. It would be very difficult to produce this speed in any other way.

3. Telephone calls may be made up to mid-evening, something that is difficult to do with personal interviewing, especially in many city neighborhoods. Additionally, few families want to be interrupted by a personal interview when they have put on nightclothes and are settled in front of the television. A phone call is perhaps less objectionable.

4. A telephone interview may produce quick, unrehearsed "gut reactions" that are very important to hear. Such reactions can be extremely revealing. They might not come out in a personal interview or a group interview.

5. Because the respondent cannot see the interviewer, and never expects to see this person (usually) in the future, it can take just a little flattery to make him "spill the beans." "You are one of a very few people that we are calling in this important quick survey. We hope that you will take a minute to tell us how you feel about ____________." Corn is not always grown in Iowa. The ego-building approach still works.

And now the weaknesses:

1. As we said, there is growing antagonism to "nuisance" telephone calls. There have been too many sales campaigns for aluminum siding, roofing, furnaces, and such things. We are talking, of course, about the consumer field. The unwillingness to bear this is understandable. Telephone selling is a significant part of our economic life, but many marketing researchers wish that it would go away before this useful instrument is denied to them for their legitimate studies.

2. For calls to consumers, it is wise to use experienced professional researchers. They have learned to bore in quickly, to stand up under abuse and rebuffs, to keep at the job until they get their quota. This is an added cost over a strictly do-it-yourself approach, but the cost is worthwhile if it means getting the results on time, or at all.

3. For calls to business people, whether industries, wholesalers, retailers, or other, you are at the mercy of circumstances. A secretary may refuse to connect you because the person you want is "in conference." If you are put through, you may still be interrupting that person in the midst of something important, and your call will receive short shrift. Complete and precious truth may even suffer a bit in the interest of getting rid of you and your problem.

4. A telephone interview does not have the flexibility of a personal interview or a group interview. Since the respondent cannot be held for long, it is better to have one or two specific things to ask. The opportunity to explore new directions and new hypotheses in depth is usually not present. If you are lucky, you will find exactly what you ask for—but with little chance of getting more. Therefore, it is wise to be well prepared with written questions, and a place to put the answers as they are given. It is possible to have your secretary on another extension taking down the respondent's answers in shorthand.

Advantages of Using an Outside Firm

As was said before, this is one kind of research which is difficult to do yourself. Especially where it is being done with consumers. Research firms have people who are especially trained for the task, and can more than balance the added cost through added productivity.

Moreover, the research firms know how to design a questionnaire that will work with consumers. They know the kinds of questions that can and cannot be used. Within the general field of what you want to know, it is wise to allow them to make out the final questionnaire. Subject to your approval, of course.

For industrial and retail calls, it is a toss-up whether you can and want to do it yourself, or hire someone else. It does take time; it does tie up WATS lines, if you have them. Or if you are doing only a regional or local survey, it still does tie up the telephones, which are presumably there for regular company business.

The outside research firm need not disclose your identity. So you can have the added advantage of anonymity, if you wish. For advertising research, or for studies of brand recognition and attitude, anonymity is wise in order to avoid bias.

Except for the small industrial studies, therefore, the recommendation must be to hire outside people to make the calls.

Anonymity is wise in order to avoid bias.

Developing a Guide for the Callers

Even though you request the research firm to draw up the final questionnaire, you should draw one up yourself in advance. It will serve as a guide to the outside firm, so that no important points are left out.

Only *you* know what the problems are. Who are the major competitors with whom you want to be compared? What comparisons do you want? Do you want measures of recognition of your brand or your store name? Attitude toward brand or store? Recognition of and attitude toward *all* competitors, or just a few? Remembrance of recent advertising? Attitude toward this advertising? Remembrance of competitors' advertising? There is a host of topics that can be covered. Probably you will want too much; the research firm will help you eliminate the unessentials.

In cooperation, you and the research firm can work out a questionnaire that gives you all you really need, and yet one that is within the limits of time that the respondent can be held on the phone.

For some hints on choosing an outside research firm, see Chapter 13.

Measuring your advertising . . .

Measuring Your Advertising

This is perhaps the most difficult of all kinds of research. At the beginning of our discussion we should agree on what we *are* discussing.

Over a period of many years there have been attempts to find surefire ways of pretesting an ad: eye-movement cameras, group discussions, split runs in local newspapers and regional issues of magazines (with follow-up checks to determine results). Better and more effective advertisements have resulted. But almost every business that sells merchandise has an advertising agency, or at least an advertising department. It is the business of these groups to do whatever pretesting is necessary. More should be done. Even now, after years of experiments with copy testing, most ads are the work of some creative person who draws on his ability and his experience. Seldom is there time, money, or inclination to research an ad before it goes to print, or on the air. Indeed, creative people still bristle at researchers. There still is a widespread belief that research is the death of creativeness. It would be good for you to know what the situation is in your own company and its advertising agency. Also, if you are in a position to do so, a little push for research might be in order. But pretesting is not something that you, yourself, should get into.

Creative people still bristle at researchers.

The other kind of research is the measurement of *results* of advertising. It was not much more than a few years ago that a top executive of one of Fortune's 500 said that the only advertising research he would believe in was the measurement of actual sales. He was theoretically right; the aim of advertising is usually to produce more sales. One should be the measure of the other. But the stumbling block has always been to establish a true and believable cause and effect relationship. How can anyone possibly say that he bought a Ford car because of a specific ad in a specific magazine? Truly the purchase is the result of many, many factors. Hundreds of advertising exposures over the years have created an *impression* of Ford cars. Friends and neighbors express opinions about Fords. Perhaps other Fords have been owned in the past, and memories are either good or bad. A wife expresses firm opinions about the appearance of the car. Some buying motivations are clear; some are less obvious. It is well-known that for many people an automobile is used to express the dream of oneself. It is Mother, Father, Wife, and all young hopes of long ago. With all this mish-mash, how can an ad be measured?

Well, ordinarily it is difficult or impossible. It is only rarely that you will get into this side of marketing research. Yet there is a trend toward such measurements being made by the company which advertises rather than by the agency. For the agency to do it is almost asking it to make out its own report card. Let me say where I think you would be in a position to do some measuring; and the reason this is placed in this chapter is because you will probably use telephone interviews to accomplish your aims.

If these conditions exist, then you are in a position to try measuring:

1. If no advertising at all will be done for a stated period of time, except for the ads that will be measured in test cities or test areas.
2. Or if only a normal amount of advertising will be done in all areas, but with the test advertising superimposed in test areas.
3. And especially if enough advertising is planned to create a noticeable "noise" in the market. If your competitor is spending $1 million, and you propose to measure the effect of $100,000, perhaps you should forget the whole measurement project.
4. If you have reason to believe that your competitors are not about to launch a large, new advertising campaign.
5. And, of course, if you have something interesting to advertise.

Almost certainly you cannot measure actual sales as a result of advertising. The person who bought the Ford could not have told you why he bought it. Sales increases in the test areas may well be due to the advertising, but there is no way to know for certain.

There are several matters that you *can* measure, however, if you have a reasonable approach to the "ideal" conditions described above:

1. You can measure any increased *awareness* of your product and your company.
2. You can measure any increase in kindly *attitudes* toward your product and company.
3. You can measure increased *belief* in your product and company.
4. You can find whether the kind of people you want to attract said they were watching or listening to the television or radio programs where you placed your advertisement. Can they describe it? Can they name the company and product? However, any measurements you do here are subject to

well-known lapses in human memory. You can get only some sort of approximation of the number watching or listening.

Many people leave for a "drink of water" during commercials.

In other words, in ideal test conditions, where there is a minimum of outside interference, you can assume that increases in awareness and favorable attitude must be a result of your ads. Or you can assume that people who were watching a certain program also had the opportunity (at least) to see your ad. This is all that the ratings of television shows do: They say that if half the country is watching Archie Bunker, half the country has the opportunity of seeing any advertising that supports Archie. But they cannot say how many people went out for "a drink of water" during the commercial break. Sudden flows of water through city mains show that many "drinks of water" are taken just at this time.

Let us assume that you have something approaching ideal conditions for a test of your advertising. Here are the steps that you might follow:

1. Work out a questionnaire that is something like the exhibits shown at the end of this chapter, or something that you dream up yourself that does the same job. Your questionnaire can ask people what companies they can name in your product field, which companies rate the best in their minds for quality, and whether they saw any ads lately for your type of product (used in control cities to establish a sort of natural error factor), plus some other questions, such as where they bought your type of product last, etc.

2. Refine the questionnaire with the help of your advertising people, or agency, to make sure that you are not missing anything important.

3. Employ a telephone research outfit, and then further work the questionnaire out with them to refine important details.

4. Schedule the test advertising to allow both a before and an after period of telephoning. Certain test cities may be chosen, and certain other and quite similar control cities where no advertising is being done. These latter are used to help eliminate the effect of unknown and uncontrollable events, such as a sudden surge of business that has nothing to do with the advertising.

5. With the advice of the research firm, you may decide on 200 or 300 completed calls in each large-size city that you have chosen, such as Atlanta or Ft. Wayne. It may well be that you do not have enough money to do test advertising in a city as large as Los Angeles. You could not make "noise" enough to have *any* effect. If you are using regional editions of magazines, the same rules hold, except that the sample would be picked differently.

6. First you will complete the telephone calls in each of the test and control areas, establishing base measurements before any advertising is done. You may find that 10 percent of the people called are aware of your company as a maker of product X, that 5 percent give you their highest rating in this

You may be shocked to find that a high percentage of people think you are in the mousetrap business.

category, and so on. These measurements are really useful only as a base to measure against in the wave of telephone calls after the advertising is completed. However, you may be shocked to find that a high percentage of people think you are in the mousetrap business. These measurements are great ego deflators for corporation executives. Just feed the figures to them gently so that they do not huff and puff and blow your house down.

7. Next you will run the advertising. While doing so you may plan to put different amounts of money into different areas. This would begin to give you a measure of what added benefits you would receive from incremental advertising expenditures. While planning the advertising, the agency can teach you some of their shop talk about gross rating points and the like.

8. Immediately after the advertising has been completed it will be necessary to telephone another sample of people in both the test and the control cities, using the same questionnaire. The sooner this is done, the better. Human memory is short, and the delay of even a few days will make a significant difference in results. The same sample does not have to be used, just so long as it is the same size and randomly chosen.

9. If the money is available, you should run another sample a few months later. This will give management some notion of the degree of "fade" that can be expected.

10. Now you can work out your findings. In the beginning, as an example, before advertising, 8 percent of the people knew your company as a maker of product X. Now this figure has risen to 11 percent. The control cities remain unchanged. It appears that the advertising has caused a 37½ percent increase in awareness. The same kind of measurements can be done for attitude. If the control cities have also changed, this can be used to adjust the figures from the test cities.

Now let us see what we have. Perhaps you find that the test advertising has increased both awareness and attitude nicely. Control cities show no difference from one wave of measurement to another. No other advertising has been done, except perhaps the regular promotion that goes right along. No one can say that you have the final answer to the value of advertising—maybe not one of these people will actually *buy*. But you do have some indication that they read or saw your advertising and that this has favorably influenced their attitude toward your products and your company. Half the battle has been won.

Variations on the above methodology can be used to measure several possible television ads. If you run some spots, and the memory of one is much better than the others, you are justified in cutting down on the weak ones and replacing them with the stronger one.

Also, variations of this technique can be used in local situations where split runs of newspapers are available. One ad can go into one-half the papers and another ad in the other half. Telephone research can establish which appears to have the better results.

Telephone companies use a version of this when they persuade a retailer to advertise in the Yellow Pages, using a telephone number that can be found only in *this* ad. The number of people using this special phone number is a measurement of the number of people who have used the Yellow Pages.

A little imagination can develop other quick and inexpensive ways of measuring advertising. Of course, these methods are by no means the final answer to sophisticated advertising research. But between no research at all, and something simple like this, it seems only sensible to get *some* idea of what your advertising dollar is bringing.

Companies, whether manufacturing or other, are sometimes strange and hard to understand about their attitudes toward advertising. At the same time as they are worrying themselves to distraction about the expenditure of $0.5 million for a new machine, they will be spending great sums for advertising without any real measure of results. This is more true the further we get from the ultimate customer. Retailers can advertise one day and see sales results the next. But manufacturers often spend promotion money in complete darkness. Does it pay off? Is it bringing business? Is *anyone* listening?

Manufacturers often spend promotion money in complete darkness.

Many companies are well aware of the results of advertising, of course. But many, many more have never taken the trouble even to begin to find out; they are relying on the assurance of their agencies that they are doing the right thing. Without any intention of questioning the motivations of advertising agencies, it must be remembered that they are not wholly neutral parties.

To emphasize this point once again: The company that spends the money for advertising should do *something,* if at all possible, to set up some sort of organized method of measuring results. I have described one kind of measurement here. Others are possible. Return coupons can sometimes be used in print ads. Smaller companies, retailers, and small divisions and sections of large corporations can exercise some ingenuity in devising methods for measurement.

Summary

Telephone research can be useful in many situations. It can help the manufacturer with small specific problems. It can be used by middlemen who have a limited customer list and some very detailed questions. For consumer research, the professional is the better bet. The professional will help set up the questionnaire, help define the problem, and—most important—have people who know how to make successful calls.

Advertising measurement has been too neglected, except by the very large companies. There are methods which can be used by small companies of all sorts to get some sort of fix on what their advertising is accomplishing. It is strongly recommended that effort along these lines be started.

On the following pages you will find several examples of telephone studies which have produced usable results. These appear in the form of instructions to those who made the calls. Again, unfortunately, it has been necessary to reduce these because of space problems. The questionnaire from Trendex is a part of a before-and-after survey of advertising.

AIR COMPRESSOR SURVEY

Respondents SIC code__________ 1: 2: 3:

Respondents SGC code__________ 4: 5: 6:

Respondents telephone No.____________________________
(area code) (number)
7: 8: 9: 10: 11: 12: 13: 14: 15: 16:

Interviewers Name____________________________________

Address___________________________City_______________

Phone No.______________________

INTERVIEWERS INSTRUCTIONS

1. Telephone the respondent company and find out from the switchboard operator the name of the person in charge of their stationary air compressors.

2. Ask to speak to him and conduct the interview.

3. NOTE: This is a pre-coded questionnaire; therefore, you must be sure to record the answers to all questions by placing a check ( ) in the correct answer block.

4. All questions must be answered.

TELEPHONE ACTIVITY

- Circle the correct number at the right to record the results of your telephone calls - Use the following codes.

1. Completed interview	1st Telephone Call
2. No answer	17) 1 2 3 4 5 6 7
3. Busy	
4. Out of town	2nd Telephone Call
5. Refused/too busy	18) 1 2 3 4 5 6 7
6. No phone listed	
7. Other	3rd Telephone Call
	19) 1 2 3 4 5 6 7

TELEPHONE INTERVIEW

Good______________ sir, I am calling on behalf of Southam Marketing Research. Could you spare a few minutes to answer some easy questions on the use of Stationary Air Compressors in your plant?

DO NOT PROCEED WITH THE INTERVIEW UNTIL THE RESPONDENT HAS SIGNIFIED A WILLINGNESS TO COOPERATE. IF THE RESPONDENT SAYS HE IS TOO BUSY NOW, REQUEST A PARTICULAR TIME WHEN HE CAN TALK FOR A FEW MINUTES.

Call-Back Date____________________ Time_________________

1a. First, do you use stationary air compressors in your plant?

Yes 20: 1 ( ) - ASK Q 2a
No 2 ( ) - THANK RESPONDENT & TERMINATE INTERVIEW
DK 3 ( ) - ASK Q 1b

b. ASK ONLY IF HE SELECTS "DON'T KNOW"

Could you refer me to someone who would be more familiar with the use of compressed air in your plant?

Name:________________________________
Position:____________________________

AFTER OBTAINING NAME & POSITION, THANK RESPONDENT AND ASK TO BE TRANSFERRED TO THE REFERRAL. BEGIN QUESTIONNAIRE ALL OVER AGAIN.

2a. How many stationary air compressors do you have in your plant? CHECK NO. BELOW - IF MORE THAN 10 RECORD NUMBER

Total No. of Stationary Air Compressors in Plant:		(1)	(2)	(3)	(4)	(5)	(6)	(7)	(8)	(9)	(10)
	21:	( )	( )	( )	( )	( )	( )	( )	( )	( )	( )

More than 10 DK
____________ ( )

b. Could you please tell me the brand names of all the Stationary Air Compressors you have in your plant? (CHECK BELOW)

2c. (FOR EACH BRAND NAME MENTIONED ASK:) How many Stationary Air Compressors do you have? (CHECK OPPOSITE BRAND BELOW)

	2b Owned		2c (1)	(2)	(3)	(4)	(5)	(6)	(7)	(8)	(9)	(10)	more than 10	DK
Atlas Copco	( )	22:	( )	( )	( )	( )	( )	( )	( )	( )	( )	( )	____	( )
Bellis & Morcom	( )	23:	( )	( )	( )	( )	( )	( )	( )	( )	( )	( )	____	( )
Broomwade	( )	24:	( )	( )	( )	( )	( )	( )	( )	( )	( )	( )	____	( )
Clark	( )	25:	( )	( )	( )	( )	( )	( )	( )	( )	( )	( )	____	( )
Devilbiss	( )	26:	( )	( )	( )	( )	( )	( )	( )	( )	( )	( )	____	( )
Gardner-Denver	( )	27:	( )	( )	( )	( )	( )	( )	( )	( )	( )	( )	____	( )
Holman	( )	28:	( )	( )	( )	( )	( )	( )	( )	( )	( )	( )	____	( )
Ingersol Rand	( )	29:	( )	( )	( )	( )	( )	( )	( )	( )	( )	( )	____	( )
Joy	( )	30:	( )	( )	( )	( )	( )	( )	( )	( )	( )	( )	____	( )
Webster	( )	31:	( )	( )	( )	( )	( )	( )	( )	( )	( )	( )	____	( )
Others	( )	32:	( )	( )	( )	( )	( )	( )	( )	( )	( )	( )	____	( )
Don't Know	( )	33:	( )	( )	( )	( )	( )	( )	( )	( )	( )	( )	____	( )

2d. How many of these compressors would be:

		(1)	(2)	(3)	(4)	(5)	(6)	(7)	(8)	(9)	(10)	more than 10	DK
Under 5 years old	34:	( )	( )	( )	( )	( )	( )	( )	( )	( )	( )	____	( )
6-10 years old	35:	( )	( )	( )	( )	( )	( )	( )	( )	( )	( )	____	( )
11-15 years old	36:	( )	( )	( )	( )	( )	( )	( )	( )	( )	( )	____	( )
16-20 years old	37:	( )	( )	( )	( )	( )	( )	( )	( )	( )	( )	____	( )
21-25 years old	38:	( )	( )	( )	( )	( )	( )	( )	( )	( )	( )	____	( )
Over 25 years old	39:	( )	( )	( )	( )	( )	( )	( )	( )	( )	( )	____	( )
Don't know	40:	( )	( )	( )	( )	( )	( )	( )	( )	( )	( )	____	( )

2e. How many of these compressors would be:

		(1)	(2)	(3)	(4)	(5)	(6)	(7)	(8)	(9)	(10)	more than 10	DK
Below 25 lbs/sq.in.	41:	( )	( )	( )	( )	( )	( )	( )	( )	( )	( )	____	( )
25-69 lbs/sq.in.	42:	( )	( )	( )	( )	( )	( )	( )	( )	( )	( )	____	( )
70-124 lbs/sq.in.	43:	( )	( )	( )	( )	( )	( )	( )	( )	( )	( )	____	( )
125-180 lbs/sq.in.	44:	( )	( )	( )	( )	( )	( )	( )	( )	( )	( )	____	( )
Over 180 lbs/sq.in.	45:	( )	( )	( )	( )	( )	( )	( )	( )	( )	( )	____	( )
Other	46:	( )	( )	( )	( )	( )	( )	( )	( )	( )	( )	____	( )
Don't know	47:	( )	( )	( )	( )	( )	( )	( )	( )	( )	( )	____	( )

2f. How many of these compressors would be:

		(1)	(2)	(3)	(4)	(5)	(6)	(7)	(8)	(9)	(10)	more than 10	DK
Type: Piston	48:	( )	( )	( )	( )	( )	( )	( )	( )	( )	( )	____	( )
Centrifugal	49:	( )	( )	( )	( )	( )	( )	( )	( )	( )	( )	____	( )
	50:	( )	( )	( )	( )	( )	( )	( )	( )	( )	( )	____	( )
	51:	( )	( )	( )	( )	( )	( )	( )	( )	( )	( )	____	( )
Other	52:	( )	( )	( )	( )	( )	( )	( )	( )	( )	( )	____	( )
Don't Know	53:	( )	( )	( )	( )	( )	( )	( )	( )	( )	( )	____	( )

2g. Could you tell me approximately the total capacity in cubic feet per minute or horsepower of all the stationary compressors installed in your plant? (RECORD BELOW THE ACTUAL CFM OR HP GIVEN)

Approximate
Total
Capacity: CFM____________ or HP________________
(write in)

Under 200	54:	1( )
200 - 999		2( )
1000 - 1999		3( )
2000 - 3999		4( )
4000 or more		5( )
Don't Know		6( )
No Answer		7( )

3. What is the average nominal discharge pressure at which the compressors in your plant operate? (CHECK ANSWER BELOW)

Less than 25 pounds/sq.in.	55:	1( )
25 - 69 pounds/sq.in.		2( )
70 - 124 pounds/sq.in.		3( )
125 - 180 pounds/sq.in.		4( )
Over 180 pounds/sq. in.		5( )
Other		6( )
Don't Know		7( )
No Answer		8( )

4. What is the compressed air used for? (RECORD ANSWER BELOW)

______________________________ For office use
56:________________

______________________________ 57:________________

____

5a. Do you have a plant requirement for oil-free air?

Yes	58:	1( )	- Go to Q 5b
No		2( )	- Go to Q 6
Don't Know		3( )	- Go to Q 6

5b. (IF YES IN QUESTION 5a) How is this achieved? (READ LIST)

Use of air filters to remove oil	58:	4( )
Use of <u>non</u>-lubricated air compressors		5( )
Other (specify)______________________		6( )
Don't Know		7( )

6a. During the last 2 years did your plant buy any stationary compressors?

```
Yes            58:  8( ) - Go to Q 6b
No                  9( ) - Go to Q 7a
Don't know         10( ) - Go to Q 7a
```

6b. (IF YES IN Q 6a) How many stationary compressors were purchased?

```
 1             59:  1( )
 2                  2( )
 3                  3( )
 4                  4( )
 5                  5( )
 6                  6( )
 7                  7( )
 8                  8( )
 9                  9( )
10 or more         10( )- Specify No.________
Don't know         11( )
```

6c. What was the total capacity of the compressors purchased? (RECORD ANSWER BELOW)

```
CFM_______________ HP_______________ or Other_______or DK
                       (write in)                     ( )
Under 200     60:  1( )
200-999            2( )
1000-1999          3( )
2000-3999          4( )
4000 or more       5( )
Don't Know         6( )
No Answer          7( )
```

(IF DON"T KNOW GO TO Q 7)

6d. What percentage of that amount would have been for replacement of old equipment, and what percentage for expansion? (RECORD BELOW ANSWER GIVEN, BE SURE TO OBTAIN A QUANTITATIVE ANSWER)(THE TOTAL SHOULD ADD UP TO 100%)

```
Replacement   61:  62: (   )%
Expansion     63:  64: (   )%
Other         65:  66: (   )% - (SPECIFY)______________
Don't Know    67:  68: (___)%
  Total                 100 %
```

7a. For the next two to three years do you anticipate any need for increase in compressed air capacity?

Yes	69: 1( )	- Go to Q 7b
No	2( )	- Go to Q 8
Don't Know	3( )	- Go to Q 8
Other	4( )	- (SPECIFY) ______________ Go to Q 8

b. Would you give me your best estimate as to the capacity of the additions that will be made? (RECORD ANSWER BELOW)

CFM______________ or HP___________ or Other_____ or DK ( )

Under 200	70: 1( )
200-999	2( )
1000-1999	3( )
2000-3999	4( )
4000 or more	5( )
Don't Know	6( )
No Answer	7( )

c. What percentage of that amount will be for replacement of old equipment, and what percentage for new expansion? (RECORD BELOW ANSWER GIVEN, BE SURE TO OBTAIN A QUANTITATIVE ANSWER) (THE TOTAL SHOULD ADD UP TO 100%)

Replacement	71:	72: ( )%	
Expansion	73:	74: ( )%	
Other	75:	76: ( )%	- (SPECIFY) ______________
Don't Know	77:	78: ( )%	
Total		100 %	

8. Could you tell me the names of some stationary air compressor manufacturers which come to your mind? (DON'T READ LIST) (CHECK ANSWERS BELOW)

Name of Manufacturer		MENTION 1st 17-18	2nd 19-20	3rd 21-22	4th 23-24	5th & more 25-26	For Office Use Only
Alley	1	( )	( )	( )	( )	( )	
Allis Chalmers	2	( )	( )	( )	( )	( )	
Atlas Copco	3	( )	( )	( )	( )	( )	
Bellis & Morcom	4	( )	( )	( )	( )	( )	80: 1
Binks	5	( )	( )	( )	( )	( )	
Bristol	6	( )	( )	( )	( )	( )	New Card
Broomwade	7	( )	( )	( )	( )	( )	Duplicate
Brunner	8	( )	( )	( )	( )	( )	1st 16 cards
Chicago Pneumatic	9	( )	( )	( )	( )	( )	
Clark	10	( )	( )	( )	( )	( )	
Cooper Bessemer	11	( )	( )	( )	( )	( )	
Curtiss Wright	12	( )	( )	( )	( )	( )	
Devilbiss	13	( )	( )	( )	( )	( )	
Elliott	14	( )	( )	( )	( )	( )	
Fairbanks Morse	15	( )	( )	( )	( )	( )	
Fuller	16	( )	( )	( )	( )	( )	
Gardner-Denver	17	( )	( )	( )	( )	( )	
Holman	18	( )	( )	( )	( )	( )	
Hydrovane	19	( )	( )	( )	( )	( )	
Ingersoll Rand	20	( )	( )	( )	( )	( )	
Jaeger	21	( )	( )	( )	( )	( )	
Joy	22	( )	( )	( )	( )	( )	
Kellogg	23	( )	( )	( )	( )	( )	
LeRoi	24	( )	( )	( )	( )	( )	
Quincy	25	( )	( )	( )	( )	( )	
Reavell	26	( )	( )	( )	( )	( )	
Schramm	27	( )	( )	( )	( )	( )	
Sullair	28	( )	( )	( )	( )	( )	
Webster	29	( )	( )	( )	( )	( )	
Worthington	30	( )	( )	( )	( )	( )	
Others(specify)	31	( )	( )	( )	( )	( )	______
Don't Know-None	32	( )	( )	( )	( )	( )	(specify)

9. Now, just a few more questions. Could you tell me your full name and position?

Name:______________________________ 27: _______

Position:__________________________

10. We have your address listed as: (READ ADDRESS) Is this correct?

Yes 28: 1( ) - ASK Q. 12
No 2( ) - ASK Q. 11

11. What is the correct address please? (RECORD BELOW)

____

____

____

12. Could you tell me approximately how many people work in your plant?

1-10 people	29:	1( )
11-25 people		2( )
26-50 people		3( )
51-100 people		4( )
101-250 people		5( )
251-500 people		6( )
501-1000 people		7( )
1001-1500 people		8( )
Over 1500 people		9( )
Don't Know		10( )
Refused		X( )

13. Thank you for your help. If I need any clarification of points in the questionnaire may I call you back?

Yes	30:	1( )	For Office Only
No		2( )	80: 2

THANK RESPONDENT AND TERMINATE INTERVIEW.

(Courtesy of Southam Marketing Research Services, Don Mills, Ontario, Canada.)

COFFEE MARKET STUDY

RESPONDENT'S NAME: ______________________________

ADDRESS: ______________________ CITY: ______________

PROVINCE: _____________________ PHONE: _____________

INTERVIEWER'S NAME: _____________________________

ADDRESS: ______________________ CITY: ______________

PROVINCE: _____________________ PHONE: _____________

INTERVIEWERS' INSTRUCTIONS

(i) You have been given a "Call Record Sheet" to record your telephone activity - write in the name and phone number of all potential respondents and indicate what transpired in the correct column.

(ii) Probe fully on all open-ended questions - that is, until the respondent states that she cannot add anything else - indicate each probe answer by a "P" placed in front of it.

(iii) CHECK QUOTAS CAREFULLY:
- interview only female household heads.
- interview only respondents who drank coffee yesterday.
- don't interview anyone where members of the family or the respondent work for any of the types of companies listed in (i).
- don't interview anyone who has been interviewed regarding food products within the past 4 months.
- interview only female household heads between 20 & 60 years of age.

(iv) Only interview those respondents who are willing to be interviewed - and those who after being told understand exactly what is expected of them - don't interview "dum-dums".

(v) Record all answers in ballpoint pen or ink - not pencil.

(vi) Read the questionnaire exactly as written - under no circumstances "ad lib".

(vii) Record exactly what the respondent tells you - do not edit or simplify the answers.

(viii) Do not leave blanks on the questionnaire. If respondent refuses to answer a question, write in "refused". If they don't know the answer, indicate this by writing in "D.K."

INTRODUCTION

Good__________Madam. My name is___________ of Southam Marketing Research Services, a national public opinion organization. We regularly conduct surveys across Canada with people like yourself, regarding the products and services that we use in our day-to-day lives. On this occasion we would like to include your ideas and opinions. The answers that you would give would remain confidential and would not be revealed to anyone except in the form of statistics along with the ideas of many other people like yourself. (DO NOT PROCEED UNLESS THE RESPONDENT IS WILLING TO COOPERATE) THANK YOU.

i. First, do you or does anyone in your household work for any of the following types of companies?

	NO	YES	
-Soft drink manufacturer or distributor.	( )	( )	RECORD ON TALLY SHEET & TERMINATE.
-Retail grocer.	( )	( )	
-Packaged foods manufacturer, wholesaler or distributor.	( )	( )	
-Advertising agency or dept.	( )	( )	
-Marketing research company or department.	( )	( )	
-A radio or T.V. station	( )	( )	
-A newspaper or magazine	( )	( )	

ii. Have you been interviewed regarding household or food products within the past four months?

No( ) Yes( ) - RECORD ON TALLY SHEET & TERMINATE

iii. Are you between the ages of 20 and 60?

Yes( ) No( ) - RECORD ON TALLY SHEET & TERMINATE.

1. Which of the following products did you, yourself, consume in your home yesterday? (RECORD BELOW)

	YES	NO	
Soft drinks	( )	( )	
Tea	( )	( )	
Coffee	( )	( )	RECORD ON TALLY SHEET & TERMINATE.
Milk	( )	( )	
Hot chocolate	( )	( )	

2. ASK EVERYONE:

a. In your own words, please tell me what you think caffeine is? (6/7:)

____

____

b. What effect, if any, do you think caffeine has on you, personally? (8/9:)

____

____

____

____

3. Would you please tell me all of the beverage products you can think of that contain caffeine? (DO NOT READ LIST: RECORD BELOW)

(IF MORE THAN ONE BEVERAGE MENTIONED ASK) Which one contains the most caffeine? (WRITE IN "1" BELOW) Which has the next most caffeine? (WRITE IN"2" BELOW) Which has the next most caffeine? (WRITE IN "3" BELOW ETC. UNTIL YOU HAVE A RANK ORDER FOR ALL BEVERAGE PRODUCTS RESPONDENTS MENTIONED AS CONTAINING CAFFEINE)

	(a) Contain Caffeine		(b) Rank Order
Coffee	( )	10:1	11:______
Tea	( )	2	12:______
Carbonated soft drinks (excluding tonic & soda water)	( )	3	13:______
Orange juice (canned or bottled)	( )	4	14:______
Fruit drinks (non-carbonated soft drinks including powdered fruit drinks)	( )	5	15:______
Cocoa (milk additives)	( )	6	16:______
Others (SPECIFY)	( )	7	17:______
D.K.	( )	8	
______________________			______
______________________			______

(IF COFFEE NOT MENTIONED ABOVE, ASK)

4. Do you think that coffee contains caffeine?

Yes ( ) 18:1
No ( ) 2]- SKIP TO 6a.
DK ( ) 3]

5. What taste effect, if any, do you think caffeine has on a cup of coffee? (19/20:) ______________________

____

____

6a. Have you ever heard of coffee being referred to as decaffeinated coffee?

ASK 6b.	— Yes	( )	21:1	
READ DESCRIPTION	No	( )	2	- SKIP 6b, BUT READ FOLLOWING DESCRIPTION
	DK	( )	3	

Decaffeinated coffee is a type of coffee from which most of the caffeine has been removed, that is, it does not have as much caffeine in it as other coffees.

b. Would you describe in your own words what decaffeinated coffee is or what the term "decaffeinated" means? Anything else that you can think of? (PROBE FULLY) (22/23:)

____

____

____

____

7a. In your own words, would you please describe what is meant by "ground coffee"? (24/25:)

____

____

b. How would you describe instant coffee? (26/27:)

____

____

c. Now what do you feel is meant by the term "freeze-dried" instant coffee? (28/29:)

____

____

Before we go on, I would like to read you some descriptions of different types of coffee other than decaffeinated so that we will know what each other means when we are discussing the different types:

We have already talked about decaffeinated coffee. Another way to describe coffee is as "ground", "instant" and "freeze-dried instant".

Ground coffee is the type of coffee that requires cooking.

There are two types of instant coffee which are manufactured differently. One is just called "instant" and the other is called "freeze-dried instant". Both are made instantly by adding hot water. No cooking is required.

8a. Would you please tell me all of the brand names of all the types of coffee you can think of? (RECORD ALL RESPONSES TO Q.8 ON FOLLOWING PAGES).

b. (FOR EACH BRAND MENTIONED ASK)
Now let's think about ______________ (brand). To your knowledge, what type of coffee is this?
(READ - REGULAR GROUND - WITH CAFFEINE OR WITHOUT CAFFEINE
REGULAR INSTANT - WITH CAFFEINE OR WITHOUT CAFFEINE
FREEZE-DRIED INSTANT - WITH CAFFEINE OR WITHOUT CAFFEINE
AND RECORD OPPOSITE EACH BRAND)

c. Would you tell me which brand and type of coffee you consider to be your main brand, that is, the coffee you serve most frequently?

d. Would you tell me which brand and type of coffee you served yesterday?

e. Now, I'd like you to think of the total number of cups of coffee served in your household yesterday - of this number, how many were served -
(READ - BLACK
BLACK WITH ANY KIND OF SWEETENER
CREAMER OR CREAM ONLY
CREAMER OR CREAM WITH ANY KIND OF SWEETENER
AND RECORD OPPOSITE BRAND SERVED YESTERDAY)

f. Would you please tell me all the other brands and types of coffee you have used in the past?

g. Of the brands and types of coffee you have used, would you please tell me which ones you would not use again?

h. (FOR EACH BRAND/TYPE OF COFFEE MENTIONED AS REJECTED, ASK)
Would you please tell me all of the reasons why you would not use ____________ again? (PROBE FULLY)(RECORD ALL INFORMATION ON FOLLOWING PAGES)

A. BRAND AWARENESS	B. TYPE OF COFFEE		C. MAIN BRAND	D. BRAND USED YESTERDAY	E. NO. OF CUPS YESTERDAY: BLACK	BLACK & SWEET	CREAM ONLY	REGULAR	F. OTHER BRANDS OR TYPES USED	G. BRANDS REJECTED	H. REASONS FOR REJECTION
______	REGULAR GROUND										
	w/out caffeine	9:1( )	10:1( )	11:1( )	12:____	21:____	30:____	39:____	48:1( )	49:1( )	50:______
	with caffeine	:2( )	:2( )	:2( )	13:____	22:____	31:____	40:____	:2( )	:2( )	51:______
	Don't Know	:3( )	:3( )	:3( )	14:____	23:____	32:____	41:____	:3( )	:3( )	52:______
	REGULAR INSTANT										
	w/out caffeine	:4( )	:4( )	:4( )	15:____	24:____	33:____	42:____	:4( )	:4( )	53:______
	with caffeine	:5( )	:5( )	:5( )	16:____	25:____	34:____	43:____	:5( )	:5( )	54:______
	Don't Know	:6( )	:6( )	:6( )	17:____	26:____	35:____	44:____	:6( )	:6( )	55:______
	FREEZE-DRIED										
	w/out caffeine	:7( )	:7( )	:7( )	18:____	27:____	36:____	45:____	:7( )	:7( )	56:______
	with caffeine	:8( )	:8( )	:8( )	19:____	28:____	37:____	46:____	:8( )	:8( )	57:______
	Don't Know	:9( )	:9( )	:9( )	20:____	29:____	38:____	47:____	:9( )	:9( )	58:______
______	REGULAR GROUND										
	w/out caffeine	9:1( )	10:1( )	11:1( )	12:____	21:____	30:____	39:____	48:1( )	49:1( )	50:______
	with caffeine	:2( )	:2( )	:2( )	13:____	22:____	31:____	40:____	:2( )	:2( )	51:______
	Don't Know	:3( )	:3( )	:3( )	14:____	23:____	32:____	41:____	:3( )	:3( )	52:______
	REGULAR INSTANT										
	w/out caffeine	:4( )	:4( )	:4( )	15:____	24:____	33:____	42:____	:4( )	:4( )	53:______
	with caffeine	:5( )	:5( )	:5( )	16:____	25:____	34:____	43:____	:5( )	:5( )	54:______
	Don't Know	:6( )	:6( )	:6( )	17:____	26:____	35:____	44:____	:6( )	:6( )	55:______
	FREEZE-DRIED										
	w/out caffeine	:7( )	:7( )	:7( )	18:____	27:____	36:____	45:____	:7( )	:7( )	56:______
	with caffeine	:8( )	:8( )	:8( )	19:____	28:____	37:____	46:____	:8( )	:8( )	57:______
	Don't Know	:9( )	:9( )	:9( )	20:____	29:____	38:____	47:____	:9( )	:9( )	58:______

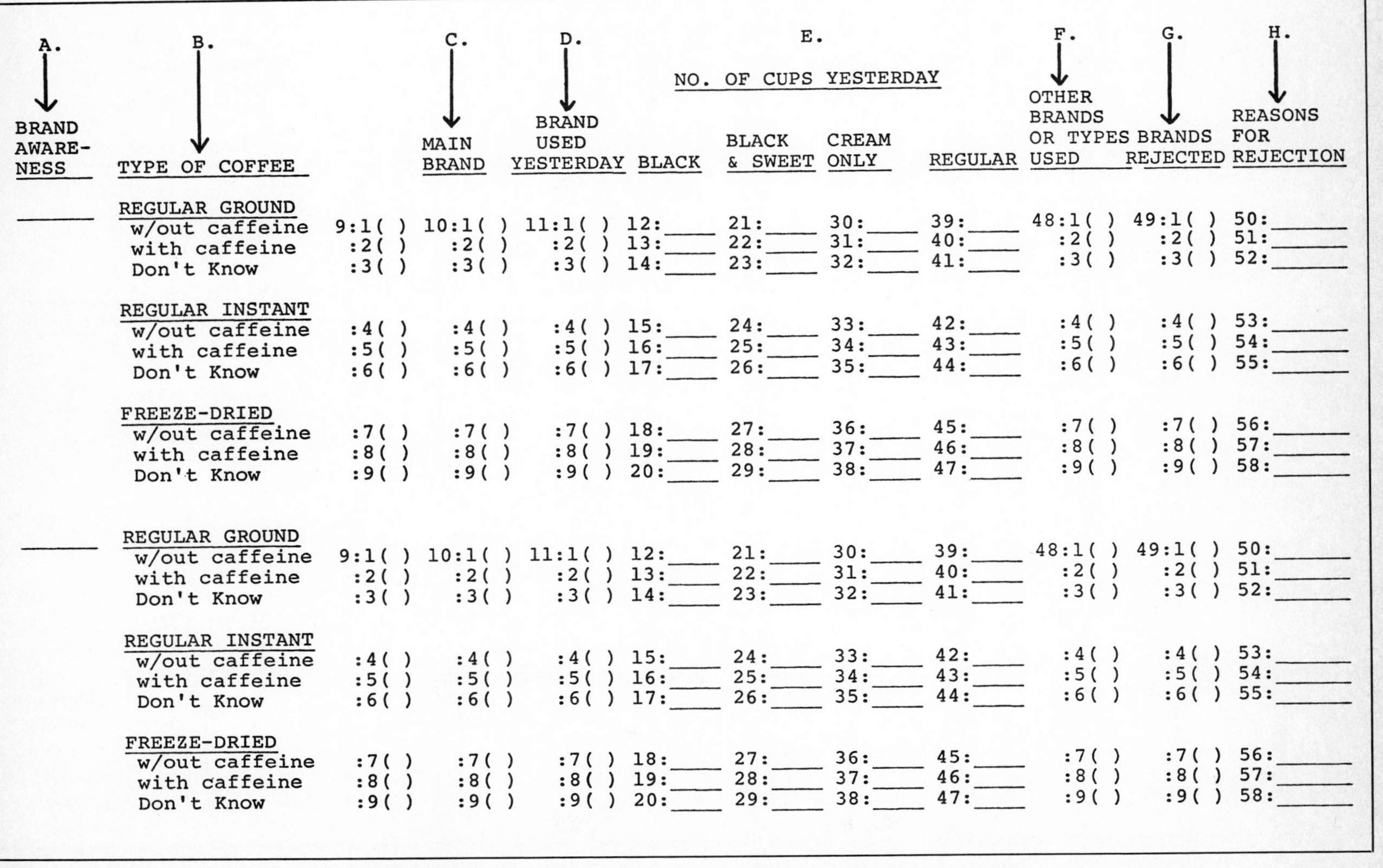

A. BRAND AWARENESS	B. TYPE OF COFFEE		C. MAIN BRAND	D. BRAND USED YESTERDAY	E. NO. OF CUPS YESTERDAY: BLACK	BLACK & SWEET	CREAM ONLY	REGULAR	F. OTHER BRANDS OR TYPES USED	G. BRANDS REJECTED	H. REASONS FOR REJECTION
______	REGULAR GROUND										
	w/out caffeine	9:1( )	10:1( )	11:1( )	12:____	21:____	30:____	39:____	48:1( )	49:1( )	50:______
	with caffeine	:2( )	:2( )	:2( )	13:____	22:____	31:____	40:____	:2( )	:2( )	51:______
	Don't Know	:3( )	:3( )	:3( )	14:____	23:____	32:____	41:____	:3( )	:3( )	52:______
	REGULAR INSTANT										
	w/out caffeine	:4( )	:4( )	:4( )	15:____	24:____	33:____	42:____	:4( )	:4( )	53:______
	with caffeine	:5( )	:5( )	:5( )	16:____	25:____	34:____	43:____	:5( )	:5( )	54:______
	Don't Know	:6( )	:6( )	:6( )	17:____	26:____	35:____	44:____	:6( )	:6( )	55:______
	FREEZE-DRIED										
	w/out caffeine	:7( )	:7( )	:7( )	18:____	27:____	36:____	45:____	:7( )	:7( )	56:______
	with caffeine	:8( )	:8( )	:8( )	19:____	28:____	37:____	46:____	:8( )	:8( )	57:______
	Don't Know	:9( )	:9( )	:9( )	20:____	29:____	38:____	47:____	:9( )	:9( )	58:______
______	REGULAR GROUND										
	w/out caffeine	9:1( )	10:1( )	11:1( )	12:____	21:____	30:____	39:____	48:1( )	49:1( )	50:______
	with caffeine	:2( )	:2( )	:2( )	13:____	22:____	31:____	40:____	:2( )	:2( )	51:______
	Don't Know	:3( )	:3( )	:3( )	14:____	23:____	32:____	41:____	:3( )	:3( )	52:______
	REGULAR INSTANT										
	w/out caffeine	:4( )	:4( )	:4( )	15:____	24:____	33:____	42:____	:4( )	:4( )	53:______
	with caffeine	:5( )	:5( )	:5( )	16:____	25:____	34:____	43:____	:5( )	:5( )	54:______
	Don't Know	:6( )	:6( )	:6( )	17:____	26:____	35:____	44:____	:6( )	:6( )	55:______
	FREEZE-DRIED										
	w/out caffeine	:7( )	:7( )	:7( )	18:____	27:____	36:____	45:____	:7( )	:7( )	56:______
	with caffeine	:8( )	:8( )	:8( )	19:____	28:____	37:____	46:____	:8( )	:8( )	57:______
	Don't Know	:9( )	:9( )	:9( )	20:____	29:____	38:____	47:____	:9( )	:9( )	58:______

A. BRAND AWARE-NESS	B. TYPE OF COFFEE		C. MAIN BRAND	D. BRAND USED YESTERDAY	E. NO. OF CUPS YESTERDAY: BLACK	BLACK & SWEET	CREAM ONLY	REGULAR	F. OTHER BRANDS OR TYPES USED	G. BRANDS REJECTED	H. REASONS FOR REJECTION
______	REGULAR GROUND										
	w/out caffeine	9:1( )	10:1( )	11:1( )	12:____	21:____	30:____	39:____	48:1( )	49:1( )	50:______
	with caffeine	:2( )	:2( )	:2( )	13:____	22:____	31:____	40:____	:2( )	:2( )	51:______
	Don't Know	:3( )	:3( )	:3( )	14:____	23:____	32:____	41:____	:3( )	:3( )	52:______
	REGULAR INSTANT										
	w/out caffeine	:4( )	:4( )	:4( )	15:____	24:____	33:____	42:____	:4( )	:4( )	53:______
	with caffeine	:5( )	:5( )	:5( )	16:____	25:____	34:____	43:____	:5( )	:5( )	54:______
	Don't Know	:6( )	:6( )	:6( )	17:____	26:____	35:____	44:____	:6( )	:6( )	55:______
	FREEZE-DRIED										
	w/out caffeine	:7( )	:7( )	:7( )	18:____	27:____	36:____	45:____	:7( )	:7( )	56:______
	with caffeine	:8( )	:8( )	:8( )	19:____	28:____	37:____	46:____	:8( )	:8( )	57:______
	Don't Know	:9( )	:9( )	:9( )	20:____	29:____	38:____	47:____	:9( )	:9( )	58:______
______	REGULAR GROUND										
	w/out caffeine	9:1( )	10:1( )	11:1( )	12:____	21:____	30:____	39:____	48:1( )	49:1( )	50:______
	with caffeine	:2( )	:2( )	:2( )	13:____	22:____	31:____	40:____	:2( )	:2( )	51:______
	Don't Know	:3( )	:3( )	:3( )	14:____	23:____	32:____	41:____	:3( )	:3( )	52:______
	REGULAR INSTANT										
	w/out caffeine	:4( )	:4( )	:4( )	15:____	24:____	33:____	42:____	:4( )	:4( )	53:______
	with caffeine	:5( )	:5( )	:5( )	16:____	25:____	34:____	43:____	:5( )	:5( )	54:______
	Don't Know	:6( )	:6( )	:6( )	17:____	26:____	35:____	44:____	:6( )	:6( )	55:______
	FREEZE-DRIED										
	w/out caffeine	:7( )	:7( )	:7( )	18:____	27:____	36:____	45:____	:7( )	:7( )	56:______
	with caffeine	:8( )	:8( )	:8( )	19:____	28:____	37:____	46:____	:8( )	:8( )	57:______
	Don't Know	:9( )	:9( )	:9( )	20:____	29:____	38:____	47:____	:9( )	:9( )	58:______

9a. What size of jar of instant coffee do you usually buy?

Small	( )	30:1
Medium	( )	2
Large	( )	3
D.K.	( )	4

b. How frequently do you purchase this size of instant coffee? (31:)

____
(write in)

(ASK ONLY OF INSTANT COFFEE BUYERS)

10a. The last time that instant coffee was bought for use in your home, what brand was purchased?

b. Was this instant or freeze-dried instant?

c. Was this coffee without caffeine or with caffeine?

(a)	(b)		(c)	
BRAND	INSTANT	FREEZE-DRIED INSTANT	WITHOUT CAFFEINE	WITH CAFFEINE
_______ 32/33:	( )2	( )3	35: ( )1	( )2

11a. What brand of instant coffee do you plan on buying for use in your home the next time coffee is purchased?

b. Will it be instant or freeze-dried instant?

c. Will the coffee be without caffeine or with caffeine?

(a)	(b)		(c)	
BRAND	INSTANT	FREEZE-DRIED INSTANT	WITHOUT CAFFEINE	WITH CAFFEINE
_______ 36/37	( )2	( )3	39: ( )1	( )2

12a. Do you or any members of your household ever use tea or iced-tea in your home?

	TEA		ICED-TEA		
Yes	( )	40:1	( )	41:1	- IF YES TO EITHER CONTINUE
No	( )	2	( )	2	- IF NO TO BOTH SKIP TO CLASSIFICATION DATA
D.K.	( )	3	( )	3	

12b. Is the tea that you or members of your household use regularly -

Loose Tea	( )	42:1
Tea Bags	( )	2
Regular Instant Tea	( )	3
Instant Iced-Tea Mix (with lemon & sugar added)	( )	4
Iced-Tea in Cans	( )	5
D.K.	( )	6

(ONLY ASK IF RESPONDENT USES TEA IN 12a.)

c. Approximately how many cups of hot tea would you and members of your household consume in an average week?

d. (ONLY ASK IF RESPONDENT USES ICED-TEA IN 12a.) During a summer week, approximately how many glasses of iced-tea would be consumed by members of your household?

(c) Cups of Hot Tea Per Average Week	(d) Glasses of Iced-Tea Per Average Week
_______43:	_______44:

CLASSIFICATION DATA

RESPONDENT'S NAME: ______________________________

ADDRESS: ______________________________

CITY: ____________________ PROVINCE: ____________

Education:

Some elementary school	( )	45:1
Completed elementary school	( )	2
Some high/secondary school	( )	3
Completed high/secondary school	( )	4
Some university	( )	5
Completed university	( )	6
Refused	( )	7

Age of Respondent:

Less than 20 years	( )	46:1
20 - 29	( )	2
30 - 39	( )	3
40 - 49	( )	4
50 years and over	( )	5
Refused	( )	6

Family Composition:

Number of children under 6	_____47:
Number of children 6-11	_____48:
Number of children 12-17	_____49:
Number of adults 18 or over INCLUDING RESPONDENT	_____50:
TOTAL	_____51/52:

Total Annual Household Income:

Under $5,000	( )	53:1
$5,000-$9,999	( )	2
$10,000-$14,999	( )	3
$15,000-$19,999	( )	4
$20,000 or over	( )	5
Refused	( )	6

Employment of Respondent:

Is not employed outside the house	( )	54:1
Works part-time outside the house	( )	2
Works full-time outside the house	( )	3

Occupation of Household Head:

Job Title:________________________________(55:)

Type of Company:__________________________

Day of the Week Interviewing was Conducted:

Monday	( )	56:1
Tuesday	( )	2
Wednesday	( )	3
Thursday	( )	4
Friday	( )	5
Saturday	( )	6

(Courtesy of Southam Marketing Research Services, Don Mills, Ontario, Canada.)

HARDWARE SURVEY - JOB NO: ______________ INTERVIEW # ________

DATE INTERVIEWER INITIALS INTERVIEWER NUMBER _ _ _ _ _
5 6 7 8 9

RESPONDENT'S TELEPHONE NUMBER ______________ CITY & STATE ______________

RESPONDENT'S NAME ______________________________

RESPONDENT'S ADDRESS ______________________________
Street & No. City or Town State ZIP

Time interview started: ___A.M.___P.M.

Female 10-2

Age: 25-34 11-4

1A. WITHIN THE "DO-IT-YOURSELF" CATEGORY, WHAT MANUFACTURERS CAN YOU NAME? BY THE "DO-IT-YOURSELF" CATEGORY I MEAN MANUFACTURERS OF PRODUCTS USED IN HOME IMPROVEMENT PROJECTS AND HOME REPAIRS SUCH AS PUTTING UP SHELVES, REFINISHING FURNITURE, PUTTING UP CURTAINS AND DRAPERIES, REPAIRING DOORS OR DRAWERS, CRAFT PRODUCTS AND SO FORTH. (Record in grid below)

1B. (For each company/brand mentioned, ask) WHAT PRODUCTS DOES (Insert company) MAKE? WHAT OTHERS? (Record in grid below)

Companies - Q.1A		Products - Q.1B	
1st: ______________	13-	______________	22-
	14-	______________	23-
	15-	______________	24-
		______________	25-
2nd: ______________	16-	______________	26-
	17-	______________	27-
	18-	______________	28-
		______________	29-

Companies - Q.1A		Products - Q.1B	
3rd: ________________	19-	________________	30-
	20-	________________	31-
	21-	________________	32-
		________________	33-

NOTE: If the respondent has named any name listed on the "Brand Card", circle, on the card, the number or numbers corresponding to the brand or brands mentioned.

2. NOW, WOULD YOU PLEASE NAME A LEADING BRAND OF WOOD WORKING HAND TOOLS, SUCH AS HAMMERS, CHISELS, LEVELS, SCREWDRIVERS, PLANES, TAPE RULES AND SO FORTH. DON'T STOP TO THINK - JUST NAME THE FIRST BRAND THAT POPS INTO YOUR MIND. (Do not read off list. Circle number for one brand only, in grid below, then ask Q.3.)(Write in brand, if not listed)

3. WHAT OTHER BRANDS OF WOOD WORKING HAND TOOLS CAN YOU RECALL? WHAT OTHERS? (Do not read off list. Circle in grid below, the number or numbers corresponding to each brand mentioned.)(Write in brand(s) if not listed)

	Q.2 First Brand		Q.3 Other Brand(s)	
Don't Know	34	-1	37	-1
No answer		-2		-2
Company A		-3		-3
Company B		-4		-4
Company C		-5		-5
Company D**		-6		-6
Company E		-7		-7
Company F		-8		-8
Company G		-9		-9
Company H		-0		-0
Company I		-x		-x
Company J		-y		-y
Company K**	35	-1	38	-1
Company L		-2		-2
Company M**		-3		-3
Company N		-4		-4
Company O		-5		-5
Company P**		-6		-6
Company Q**		-7		-7
Company R		-8		-8
Company S		-9		-9
Other (write in)	____________	36-	____________	39-

NOTE: If respondent mentioned any brands marked (**) above, circle corresponding number or numbers on "Brand Card".

4. PLEASE THINK ABOUT HOME HARDWARE AND BUILDERS HARDWARE FOR A MOMENT - ITEMS SUCH AS HINGES, LOCK HASPS, DOOR BOLTS, WINDOW LATCHES AND SO FORTH. PLEASE NAME ONE LEADING BRAND OF HOME OR BUILDERS HARDWARE. (Do not read off list)(Circle number for one brand only in grid below)(Write in brand if not listed)

5. WHAT OTHER BRANDS OF HOME HARDWARE OR BUILDERS HARDWARE CAN YOU RECALL? WHAT OTHERS? (Do not read off list) (Circle, in grid below, number(s) corresponding to each brand mentioned)(Write in brand(s) if not listed)

	Q.4 First Brand		Q.5 Other Brand(s)	
Don't Know	40	-1	42	-1
No answer		-2		-2
Company AA		-3		-3
Company BB		-4		-4
Company CC		-5		-5
Company DD**		-6		-6
Company EE		-7		-7
Company FF		-8		-8
Company GG		-9		-9
Company HH**		-0		-0
Other (Write in)	________ 41-		________ 43-	

NOTE: If respondent mentioned any brands marked (**) above, circle corresponding number or numbers on "Brand Card".

6. WOULD YOU NAME A LEADING BRAND OF DRAPERY HARDWARE, SUCH AS WOOD OR METAL CURTAIN RODS, TRAVERSE RODS AND SO FORTH? JUST THE FIRST BRAND THAT COMES TO MIND. (Do not read off list)(Circle number for one brand only, in grid below. Write in brand, if not listed)

7. AND WHAT OTHER BRANDS OF DRAPERY HARDWARE CAN YOU NAME? WHAT OTHERS? (Do not read off list. Circle in grid below, the number or numbers corresponding to each brand mentioned. Write in brand, if not listed)

	Q.6 First Brand		Q.7 Other Brand(s)	
Don't Know	44	-1	46	-1
No answer		-2		-2
Company AAA		-3		-3
Company BBB		-4		-4
Company CCC		-5		-5
Company DDD		-6		-6
Company EEE**		-7		-7
Company FFF		-8		-8
Company GGG		-9		-9
Company HHH**		-0		-0
Company III		-x		-x
Other	________	45-	________	47-

NOTE: If respondent mentioned any brands marked (**) above, circle corresponding number or numbers on "Brand Card".

IMPORTANT:
Look at the brand(s) circled on the "Brand Card". If a brand is circled, circle the number corresponding to that brand under the "Yes" column under Q.8 below. Then ask Q.8 for each brand not circled on the "Brand Card".

8. (For each brand not circled on the "Brand Card", ask) HAVE YOU EVER HEARD OF (insert brand)? (Record under Q.8 in grid below) (You must have a "Yes" or "No" answer for each of the brands listed in the grid below)

9. (For each brand answered "Yes" in Q.8 ask) WHAT PRODUCTS DOES (insert brand) MAKE? WHAT OTHERS? ANY OTHERS? (Record under Q.9 in grid below)

Brand	Q.8 Heard of Yes	No	Products - Q.9	
Company B	13-1	-2	____________________	21-
				22-
			____________________	23-
				24-
Company D	14-1	-2	____________________	25-
				26-
			____________________	27-
				28-

Brand	Q.8 Heard of Yes	Q.8 Heard of No	Products - Q.9
Company DD	15-1	-2	____ 29- 30- ____ 31- 32-
Company EEE	16-1	-2	____ 33- 34- ____ 35- 36-
Company K	17-1	-2	____ 37- 38- ____ 39- 40-
Company M	18-1	-2	____ 41- 42- ____ 43- 44-
Company P	19-1	-2	____ 45- 46- ____ 47- 48-
Company Q	20-1	-2	____ 49- 50- ____ 51- 52-

IMPORTANT:

Look at the brands listed in the next series of questions. If any of these brands have not been heard of..."No" to Q.8--draw a line through the brand or brands and ask the Q.10 series for only those brands the respondent has heard of.

NOW, I'D LIKE YOU TO RATE SOME BRANDS ON SPECIFIC POINTS. EVEN IF YOU HAVE NEVER USED THESE BRANDS, PLEASE GIVE YOUR IMPRESSION BASED ON ANYTHING YOU MAY HAVE SEEN OR HEARD. USE A SCALE OF 1 TO 5. IF YOU FEEL A BRAND RATES HIGH ON A CHARACTERISTIC, GIVE IT A HIGH NUMBER. THE MORE YOU LIKE IT THE HIGHER THE NUMBER YOU SHOULD GIVE IT. IF YOU THINK A BRAND RATES LOW ON A POINT, GIVE IT A LOW NUMBER...THE LESS YOU LIKE IT, THE LOWER THE NUMBER.

10A. THE FIRST CHARACTERISTIC IS OVERALL QUALITY OF PRODUCTS. ON OVERALL QUALITY OF PRODUCTS, HOW WOULD YOU RATE (insert brand)? (Circle number corresponding to answer below.) (Repeat for each brand respondent has heard of)

	Overall Quality of Products					
Company B	53	-1	-2	-3	-4	-5
Company D	54	-1	-2	-3	-4	-5
Company DD	55	-1	-2	-3	-4	-5
Company EEE	56	-1	-2	-3	-4	-5
Company P	57	-1	-2	-3	-4	-5

10B. AND HOW DO YOU FEEL ABOUT THESE BRANDS ON GOOD VALUE FOR THE MONEY. ON A SCALE OF 1 TO 5, HOW WOULD YOU RATE (insert brand) ON GOOD VALUE FOR THE MONEY? (Circle number corresponding to answer below. Repeat for each brand respondent has heard of)

	Good Value for the Money					
Company B	58	-1	-2	-3	-4	-5
Company D	59	-1	-2	-3	-4	-5
Company DD	60	-1	-2	-3	-4	-5
Company EEE	61	-1	-2	-3	-4	-5
Company P	62	-1	-2	-3	-4	-5

10C. AND FINALLY WOULD YOU PLEASE RATE THESE BRANDS ON MANUFACTURER'S GUARANTEE OR WARRANTY. ON A SCALE OF 1 TO 5, HOW WOULD YOU RATE (insert brand) FOR ITS GUARANTEE OR WARRANTY? (Circle number corresponding to answer below. Repeat for each brand respondent has heard of)

	Guarantee or Warranty					
Company B	63	-1	-2	-3	-4	-5
Company D	64	-1	-2	-3	-4	-5
Company DD	65	-1	-2	-3	-4	-5
Company EEE	66	-1	-2	-3	-4	-5
Company P	67	-1	-2	-3	-4	-5

NOTE: If "Company P" ever heard of (Q.8), ask Q.11. Otherwise, skip to Q.12.

11. DURING THE PAST TWO YEARS HAVE YOU BOUGHT ANY "COMPANY P" BRAND PRODUCTS?

Yes	68 -1
No	-2

NOW, I WOULD LIKE TO ASK YOU ABOUT ANY ADVERTISING YOU MAY HAVE SEEN OR HEARD ON TELEVISION, RADIO, IN NEWSPAPERS, MAGAZINES OR ON BILLBOARDS. WE ARE INTERESTED IN WHAT ADVERTISING YOU REMEMBER ABOUT BRANDS OF HAND TOOLS, DRAPERY HARDWARE OR HOME AND BUILDERS HARDWARE.

Note: (Start with the question marked with a red checkmark and continue, as directed, until you have asked each question in the Q.12-15 series. If Q.12 is checked, read Q.12, 13, 14 & 15 in order. If Q.15 is checked, read Q.15, 14, 13 & 12 in reverse order.)

Start with:

____ 12. WHAT DOES ANY ADVERTISING YOU HAVE SEEN OR HEARD SAY ABOUT COMPANY B? WHAT ELSE? 13-

____________________ 14-

15-

____________________ 16-

13. WHAT DOES ANY ADVERTISING YOU HAVE SEEN SAY ABOUT COMPANY P? WHAT ELSE? 17-

____________________ 18-

19-

____________________ 20-

14. WHAT DOES ANY ADVERTISING YOU HAVE SEEN OR HEARD SAY ABOUT COMPANY E? WHAT ELSE? 21-

____________________ 22-

23-

____________________ 24-

____ 15. WHAT DOES ANY ADVERTISING YOU HAVE SEEN OR HEARD SAY ABOUT COMPANY D? WHAT ELSE? 25-

____________________ 26-

27-

____________________ 28-

16. WOULD YOU CONSIDER YOURSELF A "DO-IT-YOURSELFER" AROUND YOUR HOME? THAT IS, DO YOU DO SOME HOME IMPROVEMENT PROJECTS YOURSELF OR AT LEAST DO MINOR REPAIRS AND MAINTENANCE AROUND YOUR HOME YOURSELF?

Yes (Do-it-yourselfer)	29 -1
No	-2

AND NOW, JUST A FEW QUESTIONS FOR CLASSIFICATION PURPOSES...

17. FIRST OF ALL, WOULD YOU PLEASE TELL ME...

(If talking to a woman) WHAT IS THE OCCUPATION OF THE HEAD OF THE HOUSEHOLD?
(If talking to a man) WHAT IS YOUR OCCUPATION?

____ 30-

18. DO YOU OWN OR RENT YOUR HOME?

Own	31-1
Rent	-2

19. DO YOU LIVE IN A HOUSE OR AN APARTMENT?

House	32-1
Apartment	-2

Other(write in) ______________________

20. PLEASE TELL ME HOW MANY PERSONS, INCLUDING YOURSELF, ARE LIVING IN YOUR HOUSEHOLD?______________ 33-

21. AND FINALLY, CAN YOU TELL ME THE APPROXIMATE NUMBER OF WOODWORKING HAND TOOLS THAT (YOU OWN)(THE HEAD OF THE HOUSEHOLD OWNS). BY THAT, I MEAN SUCH TOOLS AS SAWS, HAMMERS, CHISELS, PLANES AND SO FORTH. WOULD YOU SAY IT WAS LESS THAN 10, 10 to 24, OR 25 OR MORE?

Less than 10	34-1
10 - 24	-2
25 or more	-3
Don't Know	-4

THANK YOU SO MUCH FOR YOUR HELP...MAY I PLEASE HAVE YOUR NAME AND ADDRESS.

Time interview finished: _____A.M. _____P.M.

(Courtesy of Trendex, Inc.)

NINE

How to Do Sales Tests, Store Audits, and Certain Other Types of Marketing Research

This chapter concerns itself with types of research that are often considered too difficult for an amateur to do properly. Sales tests and store audits, especially, may not seem a viable activity for a small manufacturer, a retailer, or even a small division of a large manufacturer (one that does not have ready access to a professional department or outside firm).

This difficulty is certainly true if large amounts of money are riding on the results. A new powdered coffee that has a bit of chocolate taste will certainly receive the most thorough and accurate marketing research, including sales tests in spot locations. A second manufacturer who wants to jump on the bandwagon of an apparent market success may not have to do so much research. But it is hoped that he will at least do *some*.

Small retailers and small chains may be able to do experimental sales tests quite well without outside help. Large chains will usually have their own marketing research departments. But even in this instance, a local manager may want to do a bit of experimenting before putting in a line of goods offered by the central buying office.

For all stores, manufacturers, and departments such as the above (where the last degree of statistical accuracy is not really necessary), this chapter's research methods can be profitably used.

A sales test is used to predict sales.

How to Do A Sales Test

A test of sales of a product can occur only if the product is in existence in sufficient quantities. This clearly eliminates many products. An automobile manufacturer cannot put a few hundred 1979 models on sale in test cities in 1976. Yet, we are told, many of his major decisions about product features and appearance must be made that far in advance. For many products, the tooling up to make test units would cost so much that the manufacturer might as well go ahead and go to market completely.

However, if the product is available, or can be made available, with little trouble and cost, then a sales test becomes feasible and advisable. For example, an American company can bring over from Europe a small quantity of an item that is selling very well over there. A retailer can buy just enough to try an item out under varying conditions of display and price. The benefits of sales tests can be summarized:

1. Obviously, a sales test is used to predict sales. If done well, it is a microcosm of the whole market, and an inexpensive way of forecasting.
2. It can be used to test sales at different locations within the store.
3. For a manufacturer or for a retailer with his own label, it can be used

to test packaging concepts, including color and graphics. Are the labels clearly legible? Do they seem to attract the customer's eye? How do they compare in such matters with competitors' items?

4. The sales test can be used to test pricing policies. This becomes possible for a manufacturer who sells nationally, or locally, or for a chain with at least a few stores separated widely enough not to affect each other. A product that is not yet on the market may be tested at different prices at different locations. Care must be taken that it is *only* price that is affecting sales. Locations within the test stores can be varied, according to a predetermined plan, so that, at the end of the experiment, all factors other than price have been eliminated to the extent possible. For more, see the items that follow.

5. The variable that you may want to test is location within the store. Again, locations should be shifted in the test stores according to a predetermined plan. Prices should remain constant. So should packaging, etc. It is possible, through somewhat more elaborate test planning, to experiment with more than one variable at a time. But perhaps you ought to stick to one variable per test. If you wish to test another, a new group of test stores can be chosen.

6. Other possible variables that might be tested will occur to you. Slight differences in the product itself may lend themselves to sales testing. Yellow handles versus green; slightly different angles in some part of the product, and so on. Things that can be done without incurring too much expense.

The fact that this chapter talks mostly about sales testing in several locations does not mean that one store cannot do the job at its own location. What store does not move merchandise around to see where it will sell best? What store does not experiment with pricing, perhaps keeping certain items low in price to help bring customers into the store, and other items high? Any successful store manager knows where the customer is most likely to do price comparisons. On infrequently bought merchandise, where the customer is ignorant of what the price *should* be, and where the price is not high enough to warrant going someplace else, a higher-than-average margin can be obtained. What store does not try out several kinds of displays? There is a difference, however, between just "trying something out" and planning an experiment.

Pricing tests should keep careful account of the weather, days of the week, competitors' promotions, and other activities. Only by keeping a record of all these, and making judgments about how they have affected sales, can some conclusion be reached concerning the variable being tested. The test plan, in other words, as stated earlier, should be so closely controlled that all factors other than the variable being tested are eliminated to the greatest extent possible.

What store doesn't price some items low to bring in customers?

Choose areas and cities where tests can best be conducted.

Sales test using a number of stores Manufacturers wishing to test a new product before it is put into the market, or chain stores wishing to try out a new product before completely committing themselves, will follow a conceptual path something of this nature:

1. Choosing areas and cities where the test can be best conducted. This has to be a judgment by you, after consultation with others in the company, particularly those most closely connected with the geographic areas under consideration. Comparisons of cities, of areas within cities, even of census tracts and blocks, can be made from Department of Commerce publications described in Chapter 4. In addition, of course, your own sales statistics will be of great value. There is no reason to test a product for possible addition to stock in an area, city, or region where the *stores themselves* are doing a poor job. On the other hand, you do not want all "star" stores—those happy locations where almost anything will sell. What you need is a group of stores that can be described as representative of the type that you must depend upon if this new line is to succeed. It is much better to use several cities, since economic conditions may unduly affect the product's sales in any one city.
2. Choosing the number of stores to be included in the test is again a matter of judgment. I am not dodging the issue when I say that you will probably end up with a number of stores in each city that you can describe to yourself, and to others, as "a good sample." And so it will be if you have adhered to the principles of objectivity and good sense.

How to set up the test A group of stores under one management has a distinct advantage over a manufacturer who must somehow persuade people to cooperate with his test. The single management can "instruct" its managers in what to do. But knowing something about human nature and human fallibility, I suspect that even here things can go wrong, and there will be managers who do not do what they were told to do.

Most ongoing research of the type described here is felt to be on a sounder basis if some sort of control is established. This can be accomplished by keeping track of the sales of an older and known product during the period of the test. If a screwdriver with a new shape of handle is to be sales-tested in a group of hardware stores, then we can, at the same time, keep track of the sales of all screwdrivers during the period of the test. It would even be good to measure the sales of some other product entirely—such as hammers or rules. Knowing something about the sales rate for these older products, we can detect any significant variation in their sales during the period of the test. If a sudden drop, or a sudden spurt, in the sales of the old products should occur during the test period, we would have to alter our conclusions about the test product sales rate.

Since we cannot eliminate seasonality in the sale of many products, the control products should be those which would presumably be affected by the same outside factors. So, if the control products are expected to increase roughly by 10 percent during the test period, but actually increase by 30 percent, it would have to be assumed that the test product's sales were abnormally and beneficially affected by an extra and unexpected 20 percent increase from some nonrecurring economic factor.

On the other hand, if the older products sold as expected during the test period, we may assume that the test stores faced a normal economic situation, and the test product sales were valid (if all other variables were under control).

The greatest trouble in a sales test, as with a store audit, arises from a lack of cooperation from both the retailers and your own sales force (if you are a manufacturer). If your sales test plan has set up a schedule of moving the displays around to eliminate variables due to location within the stores, it is necessary that someone actually do this job *on the appointed day*.

It's far better that you do as much of the work as possible yourself.

Unhappy experience tells me that you cannot really count on anyone in a sales test. Your needs take second place to others' needs. It is probable, as I said before, that even orders issued by central management of a chain will not necessarily be carried out on the very day specified.

It is certain that a manufacturer who counts on a group of retailers to do what they have agreed to do is looking for trouble. They mean well, but they forget. And counting on your own salespeople to do this job is nearly as dangerous. A local salesperson is accountable for sales, but is accountable to his own boss first. If *you* are the boss, you have more leverage. But even then, with you sitting in your office in Chicago, for example, and the salesperson working in Indiana, you cannot *know* that he indeed moved the displays as requested. Or changed the prices on the day you asked. Or, if you are testing two concepts of the same product side by side, that he switched positions from right to left. Or whatever.

It is by far better that you do as much of the work as possible, or have someone in your own department do it. Whoever does it, constant supervision is vital to avoid errors that could ruin the validity of the complete test.

What can go wrong? Aside from the troubles mentioned above, a number of events can spoil a sales test. A sudden splurge of competitive activity (sometimes deliberately done, I am afraid, to spoil your test), a sudden run of bad weather, or an unexpected strike that affects a test city adversely. Your control products will help balance off such disasters but if business in a store is off 50 percent because of a plant shutdown, it is hard to be sure that your product on test would have done better in normal times.

A run of bad weather or an unexpected strike can adversely affect a test city.

Retailers can harm a test simply from their own desire to "help." A statement that "here is a product that the X company has on test," if repeated often enough, can certainly affect the sales rate.

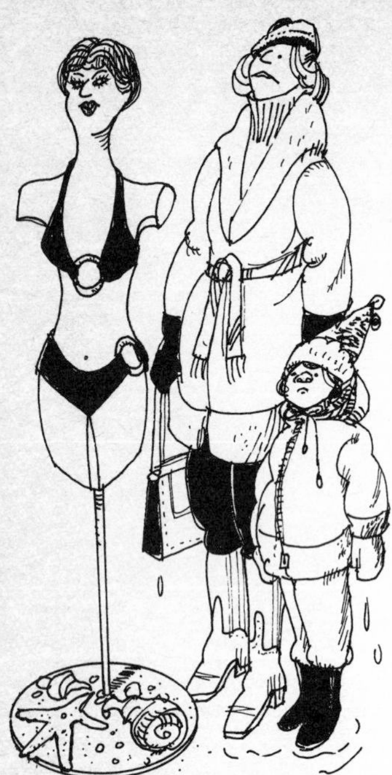
There is no way that spring and summer items can be adequately tested in Northern stores in November.

Final statement about sales tests With all its troubles and cost, a sales test is a very good thing, if conditions permit. It measures that most important happening of all—whether the customer is willing to spend money for *this* product. And in a *real* situation. A sales test at the point of purchase can be combined with some spot interviewing in the store. Between the two efforts, a good picture can usually be obtained of what the product will do when it hits the market seriously. It is unfortunate that practical circumstances prevent the testing of many new products.

How to Do a Store Audit

A sales audit at the retail level is similar to a sales test. But there are differences that call for explanation and caution.

In a sales test, we are determining the likelihood of successful sales under varying conditions of pricing, packaging, displaying, etc. For the most part, we are dealing with a new product—either one that a manufacturer is considering adding to his line, or a new product that a store, or group of stores, may put into stock. Not all products lend themselves to such tests, as was said in the last chapter. Often, retailers do not have time for such testing. They must order months ahead in seasonal goods. There is no way that spring and summer items can be given an adequate test at retail in a Northern store in November. Buying is still an art.

A store audit, particularly designed for a manufacturer or wholesaler, will attempt to show how a present product is doing:

1. As a result of certain forces applied to it, such as additional advertising. Telephone surveys can show whether brand recognition and favorable attitudes have been created by advertising. But a better ultimate measure is an increase in sales which can be tied to increased advertising. A store audit can do this job, if all other variables are held constant in the test area.
2. In comparison with competitors' products over a period of time, with normal advertising and merchandising taking place. Store audits can give a manufacturer that very important figure, share of market, and can indicate whether his share is going down, going up, or holding. Many manufacturers are still sadly ignorant of their share of market.

Store audits are based on a very simple formula. Beginning inventory, plus purchases, minus ending inventory, equals sales plus shrinkage. (Shrinkage means merchandise that disappears without being paid for. The amount can be as great as 5 percent of sales in some locations and with some kinds of goods.) If such figures could be obtained on a regular basis from a true sample of retail outlets, the manufacturer would have constant knowledge of his position vis-á-vis his competitors.

Unfortunately, the process is not so simple for most companies. For certain kinds of merchandise, particularly in the drug and grocery store fields, continuing audits can be purchased from auditing firms. But for the majority of goods sold over the counter, no such outside service exists.

How to set up a store audit If no outside service exists, and it still seems worth the time and money involved to find out how you are doing, or to measure actual sales results of advertising as best you can, or to determine whether a competitor is creeping up on you in his share of market, here is how a manufacturer can set up a store audit. After these steps have been considered, please read the next section, which will tell all the things that can go wrong, or which should be anticipated.

1. The purpose of the audit must be clearly understood by everyone concerned. It may be one or more of the matters already mentioned. But at any rate, the results of the audit must be actionable. More advertising, or less. More sales effort. Better and more appealing product. Better retailer relations. More cooperative advertising. All these things may result from the findings of a well-run audit.
2. As in other types of research, it is necessary to pick areas, cities, and particular stores within the cities which are the closest thing possible to a true sample of all your outlets.
3. It is usually necessary, thereafter, to visit these merchants, sell them on the idea, and make arrangements for cooperation. It is possible to give some information in return: You may be in a position to tell each merchant how he is doing in comparison with *all* merchants, or all merchants in his area.
4. Ordinarily, even if the merchant agrees to cooperate, it will be necessary for you, or one of your employees, to do the actual counting of stock and figuring of sales. This will probably mean visiting each store several times during the audit period.
5. In order to obtain cooperation from the merchants, it is possible that you will have to pay a fee.
6. Purchase invoices must be made available to you at preset intervals. Each time an audit is made, therefore, it will be necessary to count inventory and subtract what is now in stock from the earlier inventory plus purchased goods received during the intervening period. With good persuasion, it may be possible to do this for competitive goods as well.
7. If advertising or new merchandising techniques are under test in the sample areas, it is wise to use control stores that will be unaffected by these forces. Very similar stores in other cities or areas will help show what might have happened in the test stores if no special efforts were being made.
8. The results will be a continuing record of sales of your product in a

Chain stores may not welcome you.

sample of stores over either a finite or a continuing period of time. These sales results can be compared with whatever advertising and merchandising you are doing. Or whatever efforts your competitors are making.

This job, which can be described so easily, is unfortunately much more difficult in practice. Here are some of the difficulties:

1. Many stores will not allow such audits as a matter of policy. Chain stores may not welcome you. Department stores will be difficult to convince. A few giant retailers can make an audit program impossible, or completely inaccurate. Your company may know how much it is selling to the chain central buyers, but you will not know where your goods are going after that, or how fast they are selling. Even wholesalers in many fields and distributors of all types are guilty of keeping very poor records of the actual types of goods sold to particular stores.

So, in many lines of goods, you can be faced with large retailers which will not cooperate. And, if your goods go to such outlets through distributors, you will almost certainly find that no records are being kept of where your particular items are sold and delivered.

2. Most smaller stores mean well when they promise to keep their purchase records for you to see. But something happens. To start with, too many stores do not really *know* what they have in inventory. Six electric skillets of a brand that did not sell very well have been gathering dust on a top shelf. Quite literally, they have been forgotten. Your beginning inventory will be incorrect by that amount. Even though it was agreed by all that you would return on a certain date, and that the records would be ready for you, it is more than possible that some part-time bookkeeper is working with them at home on his kitchen table. The storekeeper expresses his sorrow, but you do not have time to run around looking for the kitchen table.

3. And to repeat what was said above, if you depend upon your own sales force to do the auditing job, it is almost inevitable that the job will not be done correctly. Even with direct orders from the sales manager, you can never by really *sure* that these salespeople have not arrived at the store on a different day than scheduled, or that they have taken a proper inventory and accounting of purchases. As noted, these people are paid to *sell;* if a large customer wants them in another city on the day you want your audit to be made, you know who is going to win.

Final statement about audits Store audits that are attempted by amateurs, people without a great amount of money and time to spend, are likely to be disappointing and inaccurate. They have their place, but the chances are they will be of decreasing importance in research in future years.

The new industry-wide marking system, and future use of optical scanners in the grocery trade, can mean almost perpetual sales and inventory records store by store. Similar schemes are under test, or consideration, in other types of stores. With such computer-based accuracy, store audits will become unnecessary. I think you should know about audits, and keep them in mind for possible use in special cases, but not as a regular device of marketing research.

Coupon and Catalog Research

It used to be said that the coupon was the best form of marketing research. A hard-hitting ad in a magazine was accompanied by a coupon to be sent in for additional information, or for purchasing some item like a course of instruction. No other advertisements were used. Different forms of advertising messages could be tested, to see which brought the most responses. A quick inspection of today's newspapers and magazines will show that this kind of selling is still very much with us. The advertiser does not call it research, but, in fact, he is constantly experimenting to find which headline, which copy, appears to pull best.

Coupons that must be sent in are still a valid way of measuring the response to a new item before it hits the regular retail shelves. The trouble is, of course, that unless the method has been used on a regular basis, it is difficult to know what to measure the response against. Is a 5 percent response rate good or bad? Does it indicate that the merchandise would sell well over the counter?

Catalogs offering a number of possible items can be sent to specific territories. Customers, or those being researched, are offered an opportunity to buy what they want. The "dogs" quickly appear: No one buys them, even when they are described in glowing terms as they would be in future advertising and copy on a display.

At the other end of the scale, the big runaway items also are very visible. The mild sellers, the in-betweeners, will probably require other kinds of research, if any interest in them remains.

This kind of research has its weaknesses. The kind of person who "sends in" may, in fact, not be the same kind of person as the regular retail purchaser over the counter. Also, the goods must be immediately available for delivery if ordered. Government agencies take a dim view of those who offer goods for sale without being able to make delivery in a reasonable time. Especially if you ask for money in advance.

Government agencies take a dim view of those offering goods for sale without being able to deliver them on time.

How to Use Salespeople for a "Quickie"

It is tempting for a distributor or a manufacturer to use salespeople for a quick and inexpensive research job. There are so many surface reasons why this is a

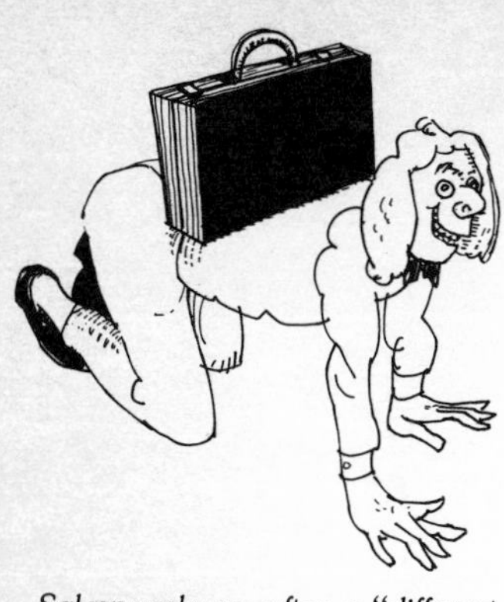

Salespeople are often a "different sort of animal."

good way of doing things that it becomes difficult to find anything wrong with the idea. Let me point out a few possible sources of error, however.

As has been discussed several times, the salesperson is paid to *sell.* His own job will always come first in his own mind—at least, if he is a good salesperson. You cannot blame these individuals for putting sales ahead of research.

Salespeople are often a "different sort of animal." They are enthusiastic, tend to want to dominate an interview, are outgoing and not analytical by nature. These are the qualities that many salespeople display. That is the way they have gotten ahead, and the person on display almost becomes the *real* person.

Whether these traits are real or a "front" does not matter. They are the antithesis of what is needed for research. It is often very difficult for a salesperson to do adequate research on a temporary basis.

Another factor sometimes overlooked in the desire to save money is that the salesperson has an entirely different relationship with the customer than does a researcher, or someone from the home office doing research. Research seeks what is *wrong* as well as what is *right.* If research proves that a proposed product will not sell if put on the market, it has done a good job for the company. Salespeople do not make a living by seeking faults in their own companies, or in the products that they may be asked to sell at some future time.

In my opinion, therefore, it is not fair to the company or to the salespeople to ask them to do "quickie" studies. Only when this is the very last resort should it be attempted. The facts sent back will always be more suspect than if the job were done by someone from the office.

In my experience, salespeople will welcome a research assignment because they believe that it is a break in their daily routine. But then they do as they have to do—put sales ahead of research.

Summary

This has been an odds-and-ends sort of a chapter. Perhaps not a one of the readers will ever actually *do* sales tests or sales audits, or catalog research. But it is well to know something about these techniques. One of the greatest blessings that come to a professional marketing research person is the opportunity to "do things a little different." For most of us, every study is a little different than any that have gone before. Using this chapter as a place from which to leap, you may discover some variation of techniques that will exactly suit your needs. So, if this chapter has sparked your imagination, it has served its purpose.

TEN

Special Research for Retailers

At the moment this chapter is being written, W. T. Grant Company has just sought protection of the court in an effort to reorganize itself and become a profitable company once again. (It has since filed for bankruptcy.)

Another large chain has also embarked upon a program of massive store closings to eliminate losses.

All over the country, downtown shopping areas are in difficulty. It becomes harder each day to bring shoppers so far from their homes.

Even in suburban shopping centers there is continuing evidence of failure; stores close and new stores take their place. Hope springs eternal among those people who want to become retailers. The card shop, the bookshop, the franchised something-or-other, announce themselves with all the publicity they can afford. Then a few years later the boards go up; another retail firm has bitten the dust.

It is very clear that retail establishments, from the largest to the smallest, simply are not doing a very good job of defining their objectives. They are not placing themselves in the right locations for the kind of stores they want to be, and then stocking and merchandising for their own chosen markets.

For proof, take almost any shopping area of which you have long personal knowledge. Think back as far as you can and count the changes that have occurred. I am almost sure that travel agencies, gift shoppes, appliance stores, etc., one after another, will have come and gone.

The only conclusion that can be reached is that these losers have not done an adequate job of studying their market, their position in the market, and their proposed location. Even when a study has been completed—as *must* have happened when a big chain chooses a site—the research *had* to be incorrect to some degree. Otherwise, why the boarded up doors and windows within just a few years?

This chapter cannot make research experts out of its retail readers. But I can repeat what was said earlier in the book: There are many times when *some* research is better than none. Even in the case of the large chains, some of the sites chosen can only make one wonder about the quality of thinking and active factfinding that went into the research. Whatever research you may do, therefore, must be done after a great deal of planning and thought, and must be done quite objectively and with as much thoroughness as possible.

Contrary to what a great many retailers think, research is both possible and advisable. I am often shocked at the excuses given for failure to execute even the most elementary factfinding. It can only be concluded that the typical retailer views himself as a man of *action* rather than one who engages in

Hope springs eternal among those who want to become retailers.

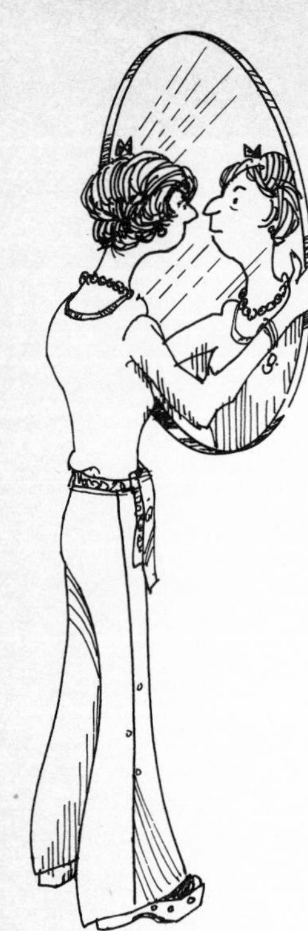
There is nothing so important as a good look at yourself and your store.

"academic studies." He knows he must buy well in advance; in many lines of goods he prides himself on having a feel for the market and what it is going to be like in the future. When changing styles and tastes are important, this "feel" cannot be discounted. But there are still many, many places in the retail operation where good research can be done on a do-it-yourself basis, with resulting benefits in sales and profits. Resulting benefits often keep the wolf from the door.

The rest of this chapter will be directed toward the independent retailer, rather than the chain. Not that chains do not need research. But most chains have their own research departments. The local manager is limited in what he can do. He can still benefit from some of the procedures to be recommended, however, so I hope that everyone stays with me.

Defining Yourself and the Personality of Your Store

There is nothing so important as a good look at yourself and your store. First let us consider you, yourself, and urge you to decide whether you are in the right business at all. You may *not* be.

These questions come from years of experience working in stores, calling on them as a salesperson, and as a marketing research person.

Do you "hate" the business? This is not an idle question at all. I cannot tell you how many retailers over the years have told me that they really wished they had gone into some other line of business, or some other activity. Brooding about this "other life that might have been" will show in the store's own atmosphere, and in the treatment of customers by the employees as well as by yourself. Retailing is a hard life, with long hours, and not necessarily high income. If, to all this, is added a personal distaste, the dice will really be loaded against you. So, before we discuss research, I suggest a little personal factfinding. If you really *know* that you should be in some other kind of life, then the time to leave retailing is while you are relatively young. Do not let yourself become an embittered person of forty to sixty, too old to change, but not yet old enough to take what life gives with complacency. Research for a store that is *hated* by its owner is useless. His heart would not be in the research, its findings, or in any recommendations that would call for extra work or extra money. Nothing would be done—so what would be the purpose of research?

Does your store say, "Come in, welcome"? Once again, before we begin talking about research with customers, or research connected with site selection, I would like to invite you to walk into your store with an open mind, just as a new customer might do. Now really, do you feel a welcoming ambience?

Does the store seem to give you a friendly greeting, through decoration, color schemes, easily traveled aisles, plenty of light, and so on? If not, then more formal kinds of research with customers can wait until you have made clear changes.

I'll never forget an incident of several years ago in an Eastern city. A man in his fifties was sitting in the sun in front of his hardware store. Inside, there were no lights on, and only the open door gave any hint of expected business. Chatting for awhile with the store owner (he did not offer to get me a chair), I found that business was being "stolen" by Sears, Roebuck, and the "little man" had no chance against such a giant. There would have been no use arguing. A few months later, I noticed that the store was closed for good. Where the man and his rocking chair went, I do not know. I am sure that Sears, Roebuck did not hire him.

Do some "heart research"—a do-it-yourself study of yourself and your store.

I only tell this story to illustrate an exaggerated instance of a situation that is common enough in all kinds of retailing. The "poor little merchant" fears his competition, gives up trying to do better, literally or figuratively sits in his rocking chair in the sun, and soon departs, leaving another empty store to be rented by another hopeful. Sears, Roebuck did not steal the hardware business; the merchant simply gave it away.

Only a minority of merchants are as bad as this man was. But too many store owners do not do their best. Without research, many could do better if they just put their hearts and minds into the business that is supporting them and their families. As difficult as it may be, any merchant should regularly try to size himself up, and size up his store in the eyes of his customers. Is he the right man for his particular kind of trade? Is he liked? Is the store designed for his trade, or for the trade that he would *like* to get?

I guess what I am advocating here at the beginning might be called "heart research." Perform some do-it-yourself study of yourself and your store. Then, if you are still satisfied that everything is as it should be, you can do outside work of the kind that this chapter will cover.

Site location will be discussed in a separate section. Most of what follows is for the merchant already in business who wants to do a better job.

Take the trouble to make yourself a written credo.

Statement of Purpose and Objective of Store; Questions to Be Asked

I suspect that very few store owners have set down on paper what *kind* of business they really want to be in. A quality store, a price store, one appealing to one or several income classes, high markup and relatively lower volume, or low markup and relatively higher volume. And so on. Every store owner *thinks* about these things, but rarely goes to the trouble of making a written credo for himself. Force yourself, if you own or manage a store, to consider your own personality, your own likes and dislikes in people, the cheerful ambience (or lack of it) of your physical surroundings, and your own taste (or lack of it). Then decide what kind of store would be the very best for you. And therefore most likely to be successful.

Who are my customers now? The typical store owner's ignorance of who his customers really are is sometimes beyond belief. What is the typical family income? Are the wives likely to be working? What age groups are represented? If the typical customer is young and married, are there a great many children in the families of all the customers? How do these people entertain? Are the men typically sports-minded? How do the women spend their leisure hours? It does not need to be spelled out how such knowledge can help in pricing, in stocking, in level of inventories, in kinds of merchandise to carry.

Do these customers make a good "fit" with me, and with my store? This is a matter of judgment, but research will help in both this and the last question. You are asking yourself whether you are in the right business at the right time and in the right location. If not, then the very big and important question is: Do you want to go sliding slowly downhill together, you and your store?

What kind of customers do I want? Should you be adding a new group of customers to your present trade? Is it possible to think of changing your image a bit, to make a better fit between your store, yourself, and your customers? Where do these new customers live? Do the kinds of customers you want and need even exist within your present trading area?

What is my trading area? From how far away can you expect to attract customers? If you are in a big regional shopping area, you can expect people from miles away. If you are on a string street, or have a small store downtown, a different situation exists.

After I have decided on the type of customers I have and need, what quality and price of merchandise should I stock? This is the other side of the coin. First you find out what kind of customers you now have; next, you decide on how you want to change this customer mix; and finally, you decide on what kinds, quality, and price of merchandise will best fit this new customer group.

Far too much advertising money is wasted.

How can I best reach my present customers and future customers with my advertising message? This has to be a part of your analysis. Far too much advertising money is wasted. And the great trouble is that we often do not even know that it has been wasted. Rarely do you know that customer X came into your store because he saw a specific advertisement placed in a certain issue of a certain newspaper. Or because of a thirty-second commercial on a local TV station. Coupons can do something to help measure print ads. Specials can be advertised on TV alone, so that you have some knowledge of how customers obtained their information. More exact planning of your advertising dollar is worthwhile, however. Most retailers cannot afford to lose very much through advertising the wrong merchandise to the wrong people—or to no one at all.

Find out what your customers really think of you.

What kind of advertising message will reach the people I want to attract? A hard-hitting price ad, or a "quality" ad? One chock-full of specials, or one that features a single product? Do you want to raise your image through quality ads, even at the expense of losing immediate trade that would be attracted by price?

No matter what I think of myself and my store, what do my customers really think of me? This is a crucial question in your planning. Are you fooling yourself about how much people love you? Maybe you are only getting trade that comes because your parking is easy. They would leave you in a minute if some other easy shopping opened up. Customers are fickle by nature; no matter how much loyalty you believe you have built, you can lose your trade overnight if conditions change. Merchants have learned this sad fact about human nature in the past, often learning the hard way by a downhill slide to bankruptcy.

These are the kinds of questions that a merchant must ask if he is to devise a viable and thorough plan for future growth and profits. Unhappily, they are not asked often enough. Or, being asked, they are quickly dismissed as something that can be answered sometime in the future. Right now he has to worry about trimming the window for Halloween, or whatever. Planning is forever put off for the future. With luck, the merchant without plans survives. But the closed stores, the empty stores, testify to the frequency with which planning is postponed until too late.

Troubles of local units of chain stores indicate that this lack of planning and analytical thought is not only a disease of small merchants. Within the limits allowed by central office policy, much more planning can and should be done by local managers.

This is especially true of those stores which are members of voluntary or cooperative chains, tied by some sort of a contract to a wholesaler. Even though the wholesaler offers merchandising helps, combined buying power and resulting lower costs, cooperative advertising, and many other benefits, it is still up to the local unit to know its own market. Lower merchandise costs, and benefits of national or regional cooperation, cannot make up for ignorance of local needs.

I have been "preachy" in these first pages of this chapter, since I have such a high regard for the difficult task of a retailer, and am so sure that many could do so much better in their business if they would do just a bit more planning, a bit more anaysis, a bit more research. The benefits would far surpass the small costs in time and money. Benefits would include a better-informed management. They could also include those things that every retailer wants and needs: higher turnover, better margins, lower inventories.

How to Find the Answers to These Questions

The kinds of research that will be described in the remainder of this chapter can be performed by a local retailer, a unit manager of a chain, an owner or a manager of a shopping center. Nothing is too difficult. These questions should be asked:

Where do my customers live? What is my territory? There are several ways of getting the answer to these questions:

1. It is possible, of course, to map the home addresses of charge account customers. This is at least a start. Frequency of purchase can be indicated by some coding device on the map, so that your map will clearly show those areas which are giving you most of your regular charge business.

2. But many stores do not have charge accounts. Or the charge business is only a fraction of total sales. To find out where your cash customers live is a bit more difficult.

You can slip a questionnaire in a sample of bundles or bags. These questionnaires should be accompanied with stamped return envelopes. By using such a questionnaire at different times of the day, and different times of the week, a fairly objective sample can be obtained. There is no harm in urging people to fill out and return the *unsigned* questionnaire. You will not get a great many returns, human nature being what it is. But the ones you do get should be interesting and helpful. You do have to realize that certain ethnic groups are less likely to answer such questions. They may be suspicious. Realizing this, you can allow for low returns from certain parts of your territory. You might consider some sort of incentive for return—but I think that this would cause more trouble than it is worth.

3. Another method of determining home addresses of customers is to do interviewing outside the store, or in the shopping mall if you are a part of such a place. Here you can use people from a local research firm, or perhaps hire people yourself. In any case, you should follow the hints mentioned in the chapter on interviewing. These researchers can find where people live; they also can ask other questions, such as the degree of satisfaction with the merchandise and service received; where else these respondents shop; at what stores in this mall do they shop regularly; how regularly, etc.

4. Another device is to take license numbers from cars parked in a shopping mall. Here, as with the interviewing mentioned above, it is vital to

space the work over a period of time in order to get the Saturday shopper, the Monday shopper, working people, etc. Some states are reluctant to give out information about who owns cars. Other states will do so. You will have to find out what the rules are for your state.

To do the best job, it would be good to repeat these performances throughout the year at regular intervals, to catch seasonal shoppers who may come to you in good driving weather, but not in winter. Cost of such interviewing, or of reading license plates, is minor, compared to the possible benefits if the information is acted upon. Additionally, in a mall, the expense can be spread among all the stores, thus amounting to a very small sum for any particular store.

Learn where your customers live—and what to do about it.

Now that I know where the customers live, what do I do about it? If you have plotted your customers on a map—both cash and charge—and indicated by some code which are the regular, loyal customers, and which are only occasional visitors, you are in a position to find out a great deal about these people. Now is the time to turn to some of the Department of Commerce publications described in Chapter 4. City statistics, tract statistics, and block statistics may be available to you. You are in a position to learn a great deal about average income, number of children, size of families, and much more. What a wonderful guide you suddenly have. An accurate description of the lives of people that you do *not* have as customers, but would like.

What do my customers really think of my store? Ignorance in this matter definitely does not lead to bliss. I think it can be taken on faith that every store should have some peculiar attraction of its very own. An independent (and high-priced) grocery may succeed because of the personality of the proprietor and because customers know that the store "has almost anything you want." A policy of quality goods, higher-than-average prices, excellent inventory of specialty goods on hand, and a proprietor who is well liked pays off in a successful store. A store I know is only a half mile from an excellent, clean, well-stocked unit of a chain, but one that unfortunately seems to have few customers. The local store has personality; the other does not. The one store fits its home town perfectly. The other has a "national" personality which is comparatively cold and uninviting.

Other competing stores are within easy driving distance. How could you discover their position in the eyes of potential customers?

A telephone survey conducted by some local research firm is a possibility. The identity of the sponsor can be hidden, and questions may be asked about the strengths and weaknesses of the important stores in the minds of an adequate sample of those who live in the trading area.

Another possibility would be mall interviewing. Again, a sample of people could be picked over a period of days and hours so that a good representation of all types of customers could be talked with. Now we are going further than just finding where people live. As mentioned in the chapter on interviewing, it is advisable for those who are approaching strangers to wear some sort of identification: either a button, a little lapel sign, or even some distinctive jacket.

The types of questions must fit the peculiar circumstances of the area. But in both the telephone and the personal interviews, customers can be asked what is their *favorite* store, and why. What is their next favorite, etc. They can also be asked for negative comments on each store in which they indicate they have shopped recently. Respondents can be invited to comment on the parking situation for each store, the friendliness of the salespeople or check-out-counter workers. Breadth of inventory is a topic. Pricing policies, brands carried, all such matters can be subjects for inquiry. Personal interviews can be a little longer than telephone interviews. Once a respondent has been stopped, the researcher can usually hold him or her for a sufficient time to learn a great many things.

It would be advisable to work out the questions ahead of time, of course. But it is also advisable to do some practice interviews and then revise the questions and the procedure, if necessary.

Rarely do noncompeting stores work together in a fact-finding mission, and I do not know why. Costs can be shared between a group of stores which have the same general problems and purposes. It probably takes more leadership than most merchants have been willing to give; it can be hoped that the retailer reading this chapter will assume that role.

Unfortunately, mail questionnaires are likely to have a very low return percentage for this kind of work. The best method of all is probably the personal interview at the shopping site itself. Next best would be a telephone survey, but this would run into some opposition, and might create more ill will than the local retailers want to incur.

There will have to be careful supervision of all interviewers at frequent intervals. They should be hired for the purpose—not local people who may know too many customers. Shoppers cannot be interviewed properly if they are carrying large bags of groceries. And the interviewers must be closely watched to determine that they are not simply interviewing the nice-looking, well-dressed people.

At the same time as your research people are asking the above questions, they can learn something about where the people read store advertising. "What grocery ad do you remember reading last?" "Do you remember anything that was advertised?" "Can you remember the price that was advertised for that item?" These sorts of questions can be asked for most types of stores that do any advertising at all. By combining answers about what ads people last saw, you can begin to get some definitive notion of which advertising medium is doing the best job. The reason for asking the respondents to name a specific ad is to avoid general answers which may or may not be factual. Both questions can be asked, if you wish. "Where do you generally expect to see grocery advertisements?" and "What grocery ad do you remember seeing last, and where was it (newspaper or TV, etc.)?"

Respondents can also be asked what brought them to this shopping area today. Was there a specific item, or items, that they wanted? Were they successful in obtaining what they wanted? If not, why not? Where else will they go if they were not successful?

Remarks about surly cashiers should lead to immediate training programs in courtesy.

Since the interviewees cannot be held indefinitely, it is necessary to include only those vital questions which can lead to action. There is a good question about continuing advertising in a medium which no one mentions as having seen. A great many remarks about surly cashiers should lead to an immediate training program in courtesy. If a large number of people say they were unsuccessful in finding what they wanted (and some say that they can "never find anything in that store"), the need for a good look at stocking policies is quite apparent.

Other Types of Research

Group interviews have already been discussed. They might seem a bit formidable for one store (except the large department stores which were discussed in Chapter 7), but group sessions can be undertaken on a cooperative basis by several noncompeting stores. See Chapter 7 for details—but briefly, it is quite easy to find a group of club members, a sorority, a church group, and so on, in almost any town, that would be happy to talk about its attitudes toward your stores, in return for a little extra money in the treasury. Or even free gifts from your stores. Such sessions, on a continuing basis, could provide a sort of early warning system to let you know of impending trouble. Traffic and parking is getting worse and shoppers may be beginning to avoid your area because they cannot find a place to stop. Or the new shopping center in the next town is beginning to eat into your trade more than you know. And so on.

In-store interviews have the advantage of having the respondent right on the premises. He is there because he wanted to be, so I suppose he is a little biased in favor of your store. But there are things that can be learned at a front door exit interview. Did he get what he came for? Is he happy with the treatment he got? And so on. Some sort of randomness can be practiced, taking every fifth person, or something of the sort. Once again, the interviewer should be cautioned not to avoid anyone—you really want a good random sample of your customers. And people will generally be honest in their answers if they are led to believe that that is what is *really* wanted.

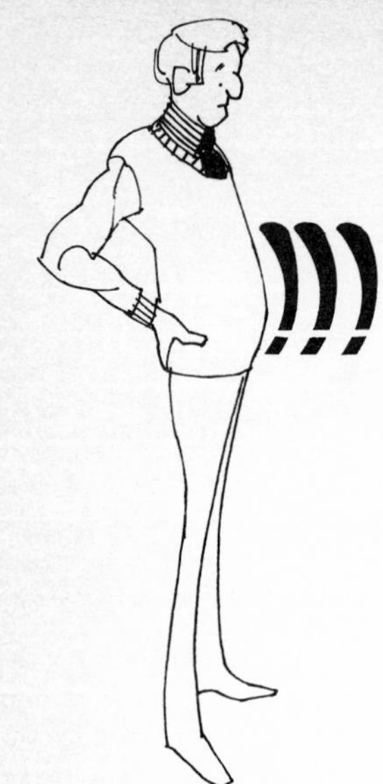

Sometimes the "gut feeling" of management can be incorrect.

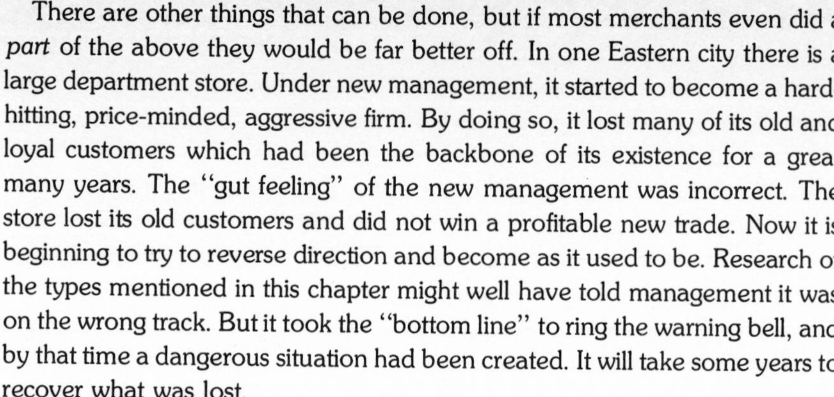

There are other things that can be done, but if most merchants even did a *part* of the above they would be far better off. In one Eastern city there is a large department store. Under new management, it started to become a hard-hitting, price-minded, aggressive firm. By doing so, it lost many of its old and loyal customers which had been the backbone of its existence for a great many years. The "gut feeling" of the new management was incorrect. The store lost its old customers and did not win a profitable new trade. Now it is beginning to try to reverse direction and become as it used to be. Research of the types mentioned in this chapter might well have told management it was on the wrong track. But it took the "bottom line" to ring the warning bell, and by that time a dangerous situation had been created. It will take some years to recover what was lost.

So—small merchant—do not think you are alone. The whole retail trade needs better and more marketing research. Computers and gut feelings cannot substitute for factual knowledge of the market. And for good, solid planning.

Site Selection

This section of the chapter is addressed to (1) those who feel they should move, after conducting research in their present markets, (2) those who want to start a new store, and (3) those who want to start a branch operation. The principles are the same. I am going to try to cover the various questions that should be given consideration, topic by topic.

Site selection is at best a pseudoscience. Specialist firms exist and are used by those who can afford them. For the most part, such firms offer a great deal of experience, but have no greater information than is available to you with a little effort. I cannot give you the experience, but I can suggest some of the problems that need consideration.

Site selection is at best a pseudoscience.

Customer traffic versus rent This is a balance that must be made in terms of the kind of store. The worst mistake of all is to seek low rents when you really need a great deal of customer traffic. With very few exceptions, low rents for a storeroom mean fewer people going by, fewer people being attracted to the area. You cannot sell something to nobody.

Some kinds of retail establishments can thrive in out-of-the-way places. Good shops, selling high-quality antiques or home furnishings, may give up a major traffic location for the sake of more room. They know that other factors will be sufficient draw.

But for every such store, there are ten bookstores, for example, that start business in a location that is entirely wrong, apparently in the belief that culture and the love of knowledge will attract enough trade to the "wrong side of the street" or a back location away from the major retail trade.

This can be suicide, as many a bookstore and cardshop have found to their sorrow. A healthy rent may be the cheapest thing of all to pay, because it is perfectly logical that rent should only be viewed as a percentage of sales. A rent of several thousand dollars a month can be perfectly acceptable if it amounts to only 5 or 6 percent of sales. A rent of several hundred dollars a month is completely unacceptable if it amounts to 20 percent of sales. The big question is customer traffic.

Patterns of auto movement and public transportation are something that you must study yourself. Of course, the first thing to do is to study the map of the city to see where the major arteries are. Where are the wealthier suburbs? Where do these people come to shop? How do they get to where they want to go? Your own knowledge of your own city will be a big help.

But there are other things that you can do. You can get help in traffic movements from the state highway department and from the city highway people. Traffic flow at different hours of the day will give you some clue about when you can expect shoppers and how many will be going by, or stopping.

The state and city highway departments, the state and city planners, whatever they call themselves where you live, can also give you some idea of future plans. If a new highway is scheduled to bypass the location you are looking at, you had better know about it in advance. New streets, new parking garages, new parking regulations—all these things are important, and all are more or less available from public planning authorities.

What sales per month do you need to survive? What percentage of the customer traffic can be converted into sales in your store? There is no scientific way of answering these questions, but you do have to make an estimate if you are to choose a location wisely.

Customer traffic in light of the kind of people you want If you are starting a new store, or thinking about moving from your present store, your possible choices of location are limited. Even if there is the possibility of building a new structure, you still have to face zoning regulations. In other words, the places you can go are more scarce than you might like.

I assume that you have some experience in the *kind* of store you are planning. You know something about hardware, or about shoes, etc. Enough to be able to make some judgment concerning the kinds of people that will be needed as customers if you are to be successful. Your own judgment, therefore, will eliminate many of the locations available.

There are so many factors to be considered, this chapter cannot begin to cover them all. Shopping centers of various sizes and ages are in your town, but not all will have vacancies of the size you need. These centers may have done some good basic site research but not necessarily enough for your own store. Smaller shopping areas are in the better suburbs (the word "better" implies no moral measurement—it simply means more money is there), and these will or will not have a space that you would consider.

You will prefer a place within reasonable traveling distance of your own home. And probably within reasonable traveling distance of people you know, the kind of people with whom you get along best. So once again you have eliminated more possible spots.

So, if you are picking a spot for a new store, or preparing yourself for a move, the fact is that the number of possible places that are worth further consideration is rather severely limited.

Some of the judgments that you have made during the elimination process are irrational in the sense that they cannot be based upon wholly reasonable results from unbiased research. These irrational reasons include the choice of a spot not too far from your home and your friends.

It would be good now to do some of the things talked about in the beginning of this chapter. Write your own plan for the *kind* of store you want. For the kind of policy you believe you are best suited to follow successfully. For that type of store, then, you can do a little accounting in advance. From your own experience, or from associations, sometimes from wholesalers, you can get average or typical figures for rent, employee cost, heat and light, etc., as a percentage of sales. What do you expect to take out of the store, if you are the prospective owner? Or what will the manager have to have, if you are considering a possible new branch? It is worth the time to make out a list of minimums that will have to be met if this new store is to succeed.

To find out if you have the needed customer traffic of the right quality, there is the research method of noting the license plate numbers of patrons.

Will sufficient customer traffic be available at these new locations? And will it be the right kind of traffic for the person you are and for the store you want to operate? These are very basic questions that clearly are not asked often enough, or even at all in many cases, judging from the number of empty stores that are so present.

How will you find the answer to whether you have the needed customer traffic of the right quality? Once again you can go back to the research methods discussed earlier: noting license plates of people who are patronizing nearby stores, conducting interviews, setting up a few group interview sessions. The interviews and the license plates will give you a good idea where the shoppers live. And census data can tell you what kind of people these are. Do they seem to be of sufficient affluence to patronize your store and its kind of merchandise? What are the ways of life that these people have chosen? Are they sports-minded? cultural-minded? All sorts of knowledge will be available from one or more of these research methods and from secondary data.

It is vital to make the best decision possible, also, on what the business trend will be at each possible site. Much of the answer will come from state and city planning departments, and from opinions of the people that are interviewed. Visual inspection of the shopping area is just as necessary as more formal research. Even an inexperienced eye can see evidence of decay, or changing ethnic groups; possibly even of a trend away from the use of structures as homes to their use as small businesses. Law offices may be replacing family dwellings.

Summary

None of the above is difficult. All can be done by any retailer who makes up his mind to take this trouble. The government departments are ready and willing to help. Group and individual interviewing can be organized. City maps are almost always available, even for the smallest of towns. Customer plotting can be done on these, as well as indications of those roads where major automobile traffic flows. If you have determined which neighborhoods you wish to appeal to, the map can help in the determination of whether it is feasible for these people to reach your proposed locations. It is all so simple that I cannot help wondering again why so few stores ever bother. And certainly they do not; it is a rare store indeed that has even made any effort to research its own charge customers. Almost always the refrain is, "We certainly should know more, and I guess we should do it, . . . one of these days." Why not *now?*

ELEVEN

What You Need to Know about Sampling

The do-it-yourself researcher for whom this book was written need not feel apologetic before the more "scientific" professionals. Both groups are doing their jobs; both are necessary in the modern business world.

The basic principles of sampling have not changed much over the years, but the practices have grown considerably. To a significant extent this growth has become possible through the development of computers which can do calculations in minutes that used to take hours, or were impossible.

As has been true for many years, there are two major approaches to sampling procedure: probability samples, and nonprobability samples. It is very likely that the "quick and dirty" studies discussed in these chapters will be done by nonprobability methods.

This does not mean that the results are too incorrect to be useful, or that good business decisions cannot be based upon their findings. It simply means that the sampling methods do not allow the calculation of probabilities that the findings are indeed correct within a certain known range of error. The standard error and confidence limits and other statistical measurements which are likely to appear in large (particularly consumer) studies cannot be determined.

A probability sample, for example, will allow a statement that the arithmetic average of the total population under study is within a certain number of points of the arithmetic average of the sample. Normally, in most probability samples the confidence level of 95 is selected. Therefore, it becomes possible to say that, in 95 chances out of 100, the true average of the population in this particular study would lie between a certain number of points on each side of the figure calculated in the sample. The user of the study, therefore, knows what his chances are of being right if he uses the figures reported to him by the researcher. The user of the study should be able to say what accuracy he needs. As his demand for accuracy (a lessening of the probable error on both sides of the sample result) increases, the size of the sample will increase—possibly beyond what is commercially feasible.

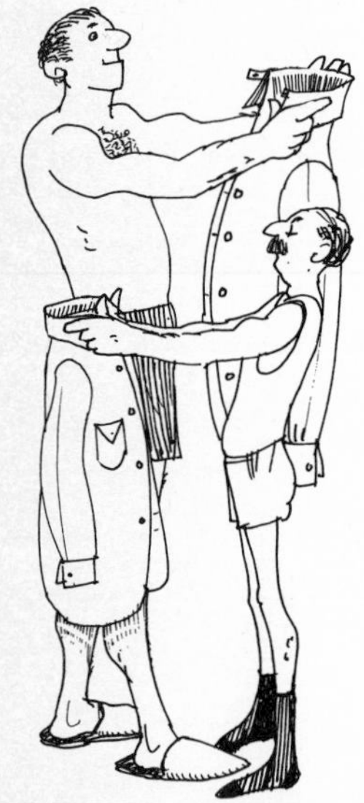

In between the few size 20s and 12s lie the greatest number of average size 15s.

The mathematics of probability sampling are based on the assumption that the values being studied for a population (sometimes called the "universe") are spread approximately in the shape of what is called a "normal curve." Many human and nonhuman characteristics are spread around the arithmetic average in a curve that, when plotted on a graph, resembles a bell. A few extremely large men wear a size 19 or 20 shirt collar. On the other end, a few small men wear a size 12 or 13. In between lie all the rest, with the greatest number somewhere around 15. A few minutes of thought will convince you that a great many natural facts of nature will follow such a normal curve. It is true of everything from hat size to the brainpower that lies under the hats. Given such a characteristic to study, the researcher can, by properly planning his work and the sampling process to be used, calculate the probability that his study has found the correct numbers within certain known limits of error. If nothing has gone wrong with the sampling process itself, and no bias or clerical mistakes have interfered, he can report his figures and results along with the "chances" that these answers are correct.

Obviously, any businessperson would prefer knowing these odds. They certainly would make his decision less "chancy."

But, in practice, in most small studies of the sort discussed in this book, probability sampling is very likely to be slow, costly, and cumbersome. Moreover, the number of people to be interviewed, or to receive questionnaires, is generally so small as to make true random sampling unnecessary, or literally impossible. At any rate, it is unneeded in many cases.

For example, a structured sample is unneeded when we are trying to determine certain operating practices in an industry where not over twenty or thirty men make all the decisions which are being studied. Or, for our present purposes, in a shopping center study, where we do not know in advance the area people are coming from, how many come regularly, or what kind of people they are. In this case, for a do-it-yourself study, all that is necessary is to do enough interviews—asking the right questions; spreading the interviews over the week or the month; making contact with an agreed-upon quota of men and women, old and young, etc., to achieve stability of results.

What Is a Sample, for the Purposes of This Book?

Sometimes it is the "universe" Especially in industrial research, no selection process may be needed at all. *All* the people who have anything to do with the matter at hand are communicated with in some fashion or other.

There are things to be mindful of. If you see every person except one—and that one happens to buy 50 percent of whatever it is that you are studying—your research may not reveal anything like the truth for the whole industry. The one person who refused to see you may well be a maverick, doing things in a different way than his fellow practitioners. He may work for a company with such a large share of its own market that he is able to buy in a different way, perhaps directly instead of through a distributor. Or the company may be big enough to take advantage of its own packing and shipping methods. A sample of this industry that did not include this maverick would be a poor and inaccurate sample. Conditions vary so much from study to study, and industry to industry, that the only thing possible is to warn against situations

Sometimes a sample is the "universe."

like this. Most of the time your own knowledge and good judgment will tell you if you have missed any of the "biggies."

As a matter of judgment in your sampling, you may want to leave out the other coast.

Sometimes a large part of the universe, but not all As a matter of judgment on your part, you may leave out the opposite coast, or some geographic area of the country. Not enough of the people you want to question are in this area. Or preliminary inquiries indicate that their practices are not significantly different than those in more fruitful research areas. You see a universe of *part* of the country, with all indications that the rest of the country is sufficiently similar.

Sometimes quotas of persons representing different groups A retailer, or a group of retailers, or even a manufacturer, may wish to obtain consumer opinions, and do so as close as possible to the actual points of sale. Retailers may wish to find where their customers are actually coming from. It would be helpful for them to know what are the "gripes" that their customers have.

With some careful planning, it will be possible to issue instructions to interviewers, requiring a certain percentage of completed interviews to be with men, another percentage with women, others with old and young, families and single shoppers, and so on. These quotas will be largely a matter of judgment and observation. Once agreed upon, it will be necessary to supervise the interviewers very carefully to make sure that these quotas are being observed honestly and without bias.

There are things that *must* be worried about. Have we stationed our interviewers, or license plate recorders, at *every* entrance, so that we are not missing groups that come from particular areas? And are we doing our interviewing, or recording, on all days of the week, including all hours of the day and evening? We must think, in some areas, when paydays exist for our customers. And whether any special wave of customers occurs, such as customers arriving immediately after receiving their Social Security checks on the third of the month. And so on.

There are things that must be worried about.

Our sample here, then, must really cover all possible surges of customer traffic. Certain quotas can be assigned for various hours of the day and days of the week—even for each of the entrances and exits to the parking areas. It would be wise to do some warm-up interviewing, or license plate counting, to make sure that the "bugs" are out of the procedure, and also to discover to what extent the special waves of shoppers occur at different times. Your quotas of interviews may have to be altered a bit.

You may wish to determine something of the validity of your sample. Steadiness of results is one way. There will come a time when you can clearly and accurately forecast what each new day's findings will be. No further interviewing seems to be necessary.

Another validation can be made by comparing your results with statistics that are available about your city from the Department of Commerce;

specifically, the figures available for blocks and for census tracts. A few questions may be put into the questionnaire just for this purpose. If area figures for family size, income, education, marital status, and so on agree reasonably with your findings, you cannot be completely sure, but you can be much *more* sure that you have discovered an important fact: Certain kinds of customers are not coming to your shopping area. Further research may be required to verify this and to discover why such a circumstance exists. If your interview findings are steady, but do not agree with known social characteristics of your area, you may have found a real weakness in the merchandising of the shopping area.

A selection of telephone numbers Telephone surveys are best made by professional practitioners. The women (usually) who do this work know, much better than you ever will, how to get the most out of an interview, and how to cut down on refusals. Usually cost will determine how many telephone interviews can be made. Often it is a compromise. The interviewing firm will tell you what they consider an adequate sample, based on their own long experience. You will say how much you have to spend, and a compromise is reached on what cities will be covered and how many calls in each.

Telephone interviews have their faults, as has been previously discussed. Some people will refuse. Others have unlisted telephones. There are problems of calling outside the city proper, and how far. In many cities, a call to the suburbs is a toll call. Yet, for many products, the suburbs are where the buyers live. You must assume the cost of the tolls, or be satisfied with an inadequate representation of buyers.

Telephone samples must include the hours when buyers are at home. Often this means evening calls. Even calls aimed at women must frequently be made in the evening because of the large proportion of working wives, especially in the young, accumulating age group.

Use of tables to determine sample size The use of printed tables to determine sample size is probably more common than most market researchers care to admit. Even though the research that follows is not really done on a probability basis. Devices that look like slide rules are in common circulation. By manipulating these, it is possible to find what size samples are necessary to determine facts within certain reliabilities. Confidence levels are usually 95 out of 100. The size of the population is necessary to know (or estimate). The use of such tables is possibly better than pure guess, but it must be emphasized again that they are devised for probability studies where respondents are chosen at random or by some means that ensures a known probability of each member of the universe being chosen.

A good use for these tables (slightly unethical, perhaps) is to convince others in the company of the necessity of a large enough sample. There are still too many executives who believe that the only real way to find the "right"

All nice folks may not want your boat.

answer is to call Old Joe in Minneapolis. His judgment is taken as gospel because he has been around the industry for so long. One biased older man's word is taken to represent what a million young buyers are likely to do. Putting it that way makes it sound ridiculous—and it is.

Arguing for a large enough sample protects you against prejudices of executives. Being human, they have patterns of thought. They water ski, boat, play golf, fish, and somehow are able to persuade themselves that everyone does these things. Many companies which thought that everyone would accept a prefabricated house have unhappily learned better. And many companies which believed in the great future of the boating industry. Certainly there are a host of people in boats, but that does not mean that all these nice folks want *your* boat. In all honesty, anything that can prevent great financial mistakes due to prejudice and lack of knowledge is a good thing for the company. Including slide rules.

What Are the Rules for a Good Nonprobability Sample?

1. It must be as representative as possible. In a shopping center interview study, for example, the interviewers must make every effort to question a cross section of the population of people who come to this center. Quotas will help.

It is very difficult in interviews around stores to set up any schedule of interviewing every *x*th person. People come in batches, unfortunately, und there really is no way to determine who is that *x*th person. The quota system is much easier to handle.

One mistake to avoid in a consumer interview study is to count both husband and wife as separate interviews. One or the other is certain to dominate the responses, and only one truly effective interview has been obtained.

Interviewers are often likely to talk only to "nice" people.

2. Bias is more pervasive than most of us realize, or recognize. Unless closely supervised, interviewers are very likely to talk only to "nice" people. How they define nice is a function of their own set of biases.

Bias of the interviewer can be present in all forms of research discussed in this book. People—even the best of researchers—tend to hear what they expect to hear, or want to hear. Most of the time this is not deliberate, or even recognized by the interviewer himself. Even in group interviews, the researcher may unconsciously be leading the group toward some conclusion that he or she either expects or hopes for. These attitudes are very hard to control and require constant effort.

3. Incomplete or even deliberately falsified answers may be given by respondents in bad weather, or in any situation where the person being

interviewed is in a hurry and simply wants to get rid of the interviewer as rapidly as possible. Part of the training of interviewers must be to weigh the validity of such interviews and discard those which appear useless. Again, judgment enters the picture, and some further degree of randomness is lost. One example in my own experience was the woman whose only reply to me was "none of your damn business." This is an interview to be remembered, but hardly added anything worthwhile to my knowledge. The woman even modified the word "damn" with the usual preceding appeal to the Deity. At least she was positive in her answer.

Interviewers must learn to weigh the validity of interviews.

4. The questions to be asked, either in a mailing or by personal interview, should cover the needs of the study as completely as possible. It is foolish to miss something important just for the sake of shortening the questioning process. The type of sampling being done cannot be separated from the preparation of questions. What kind of people do we expect to take part in this study? What do they know that we need to know? How can we ask the right questions in the light of who those respondents are? It is well to remember some recently quoted figures to the effect that a shocking percentage of the American population is basically illiterate. People in this group cannot even read a help-wanted advertisement. Another group is only slightly better. A questionnaire, or an interview question, that talks over the head of most of the respondents is not producing a representative sample.

5. Error can be introduced by the order in which questions are asked. Almost anyone would have sense enough not to spend the first part of an interview or of a mail questionnaire asking people about their age and family income. The response might well be the same as the one given to me by the woman mentioned above (I had not asked her anything personal; perhaps she had just come from a fight with her husband). There is a buildup of questions that is possible in any survey. From the easy and obvious to the real "meat" that we want. Once entangled in answering questions, either in an interview or in a mail questionnaire, it is difficult for the respondent to stop. The trick is to develop that entanglement. Without getting cooperation from most of the persons approached, there is no real sample.

Strangely enough, people will indeed give their age brackets, and their family income within brackets, if they have been led along through other topics that interest them. Even in New York City, supposedly full of tough sophisticates, street interviews have been able to get answers to family income questions. And these incomes have been checked with averages from other sources, so that overall correctness seemed assured, although certainly a few people exaggerated.

6. Summarizing this section, a good nonprobability sample must still be as close to a cross section as possible. Judgment enters when quotas defining this cross section are set up. Group interviews, of course, make no pretense of

being representative samples; that is not their purpose. A good sample must be as free from bias as possible. The questions must be so easily understood that answers will truly be responsive. The researcher must be particularly watchful that his own preconceptions and biases do not affect the results of his study. His way of questioning, or even his way of tabulating and analyzing the results, may be affected by bias.

This chapter in this form would certainly never appear in a college text-book. Probability sampling has been given short shrift. Even nonprobability sampling could have been dealt with in more detail. However, one learns most by doing. These hints and suggestions are enough to get you started. Your own good brains will supply the rest as you go along.

TWELVE

How to Write a Report That Will Get Action

You and I have come a long way together in this book. I hope that you have gained a new insight into what you can do yourself. Whether by mail questionnaire, telephone survey, group interviews, in-office interviews, or point-of-sale interviews, you know now that there is a large amount of solid fact finding that does not necessarily need the help of a professional researcher. The principal aim of these chapters was to convince you that you *can* do this job, and to give you some practical advice on how to go about it.

If the book has succeeded in this aim, then you have decided to make a start on research into one or more of your own problems. If you are new at research, you will take special pride in your first job. This is particularly so when your findings and recommendations are put into a report that causes action to be taken. It is a rare company where the person who does the research is also the sole reader of the report and the sole person to act upon it. In most instances, others have to be convinced. Even if these others are your subordinates, you know in your own heart that they must believe in the correctness of your methods, the facts that have been found, and the actions that you urge as a result of these facts.

A good report, therefore, is almost always necessary. In most cases it will go to persons higher in the company organization, and can either hurt you or help you, depending upon how good your presentation is.

How to Analyze and Evaluate Your Data

It is necessary, before beginning to write any report at all, to take a clear and objective look at what you have found.

Another look at the problem Now is the time to go back to the beginning of your planning and take a fresh, new look at the problem and how it was stated. What were the major questions, and the minor ones? Does it appear that the gathered facts will satisfy the problems, and answer the questions? Patently, there is no point in writing a report about a study that has not done its job.

However, if you have supervised the study carefully while it was in progress, the chances are that you have, indeed, satisfied all the major possible doubts. But, before putting a word on paper, it is good to do a little meditating about the meaning of what you have found. (In this case, the word "meditating" does not imply a blank mind.)

One caution: It is extremely doubtful in any study that you will get everything you wish for. There will be some lingering doubts about some of the matters. The big question is answered, but you wish that you had done a

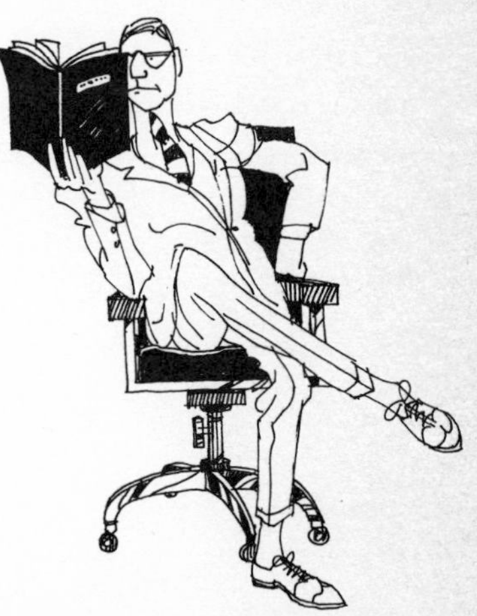

Your report in most cases will go to people higher in the company organization.

little more work on some other phase. This lack of completeness *must* be pointed out in your report, together with reasons why. To try hiding a small omission, by not mentioning it, is to invite uncertainty about the validity of the whole report. It is perfectly satisfactory to describe things left undone, with reasons why, and suggest further research at some future time.

How clear are the results? In a sense, this section is a bit repetitive, having been partly covered in the last section. However, it is important for you to realize how strongly the results of your study lean one way or another. If for the production of a new form of widgets we had an overwhelmingly positive reaction, a clear road for action has unfolded. But if the response was 60 to 40, say, or split about even, further thought would have to be given to the true meaning of the results. Remember, you do not have a probability sample, but your nonprobability sample was well thought out. You have faith that your results are good. If about half the respondents said "yes, go ahead," the recommendation might still be positive, depending upon other factors, such as anticipated volume and profit. Even a lower positive reaction might still result in a recommendation to proceed.

Of course, for other kinds of research, such as group interviewing, there is no real question of going or not going. *How* people think is what we are after, not a signal to do something or not to do it.

If the research needs a clear negative or positive attitude before management can make its decision, and this clear reaction did not come about, further research might be in order. Perhaps a smaller-scale study much like the one you just completed. Does this further research produce the same split in opinions? If so, then that is the way life is, and management will have to make a decision. But, if further research produces different results, then perhaps the whole project was done carelessly and inadequately, and you may have to start all over again.

What alternative actions can be recommended? Now that all the scores are in, what do they mean? What alternative actions can be recommended? Is there a very clear no or yes? Go or not go?

I cannot enter into all the variations that may occur in study results. But let us say that a shopping center study has shown that almost all the center's customers come from a small area. A more affluent group from another area is not patronizing this center. Since you talked only to people who *did* come there for shopping, you have no evidence about those who did *not* come.

Several recommendations are immediately apparent. First, you are now in a position to recommend study of the nonshoppers. This involves further research, more time, and more money.

Second, the findings may show a satisfactory condition. There is enough potential business from the area now being served. Stocking and service policies of all the stores seem to be quite acceptable.

Or, third, the differences between the people of the area being served and the people in an adjacent area not being served seem minimal. A little more advertising effort—perhaps some further easing of parking problems—can win new business.

What I am saying is that very few studies produce clear recommendations for only one course of action. There are alternative actions, or supplemental actions, and all these have to be thought about before the report is written. The final report will have to be quite direct, but you will have to spend some prewriting time going through a "on the one hand, on the other hand" stage of thinking.

Middle management people may find holes in your work.

Can You Benefit from Again Consulting Other Departments?

Most of the time: yes! Go to the people who are going to have to put your recommendations into action. Not top management at this point, if you have a choice. Show these middle management persons what you have, what you think the returns mean, and what action you believe should be recommended. If you have the kind of rapport that you should have with these people, you will benefit from their advice.

You may also feel aggrieved and hurt, since almost certainly some fault will be found with your work. But two points are important. If these people feel that there are some holes in your work, they will be only halfhearted in fulfilling your recommendations. And, second, if they point to missing material, you have a chance to repair your study a bit before writing it for management. Then you will have the rest of the people on your side instead of against you. This may sound like a small point, but it has saved many written studies from oblivion. A small argument now is far better than a large confrontation at a later date, when the full written report is presented to management.

Possible Pitfalls in Writing a Report

Report can be too long No one in business—with *no* exceptions—likes a report that is long and wordy. Avoid this completely.

One fault that is prevalent in young report writers is a tendency toward "fine writing." Probably a result of college training, it must be weeded out and destroyed. Reports are likely to become the kind of themes that used to please the professors. I have been on both sides of this fence. A professor, facing a pile of term reports, subconsciously tends to equate length with quality. Skipping through the massive sentences and the weight of paper, somehow he sees completeness and thoroughness staring him in the face. Not all professors, of course, have this weakness. But young people have told

No one in business likes a report that is too long and wordy.

me about getting good grades through writing reams about "what the professor wanted." Suddenly I saw myself as others probably saw me in former years.

Report can have too many details This is always a problem with a report. Conclusions and recommendations should be backed up with facts. But to load a report with numbers, figures, charts, and tables ad infinitum leads to reader boredom. A judicious mixture is sometimes the answer. Enough important facts in the report itself to lend credence to the findings, with remaining figures kept for an appendix.

This all depends upon the nature of the study and the final report. Often there is no problem at all. Everything can go right into the report. But if there are a great many numbers, there are three possible solutions that I have seen. One is to put the less important, more complex tables in an appendix. Another is to separate these numbers completely, making an A and a B section of the report. A third solution is to keep the backup figures in the office, letting everyone know that they are there for examination by anyone interested. How you decide depends a good deal on the faith that people have in your judgment. If you have been "right" most of the time, they are more likely to accept what you say without wanting to examine your evidence. If you are new, you had better have those figures very handy for the reader.

Failure to come to the point The last thing you want is for your readers to wonder, with considerable exasperation, what on earth you are trying to say. Come to the point. Those are four of the best words in the literature of business writing. You are not producing great and timeless literature. You are communicating a recommendation or finding to some other businessperson who is as harried and rushed as you are. Come to the point. Do not waste his time in attempts to understand what you are saying. An outline of the report, covered in an earlier chapter, will greatly help. However you do it—come to the point.

Putting conclusions and recommendations at the wrong point in the report This is another area of disagreement.

1. Some say that the report should lead toward the conclusion. So, logically, the recommendations should be at the end of the report, just ahead of the appendix. Clearly, this is a reasonable way of doing things. The main trouble is that so many readers of your report will be interested only in the conclusions and recommendations, and do not want to have to take time to look for them.

2. So, another possibility is to start with the major conclusions, followed by the recommendations, all on one or two pages. After that will come the report itself.

3. Still another way is to have a separate and highly condensed report, merely covering the most important questions at issue. A larger report then could go to others who are interested in the details. Those getting the condensed version could be told that the larger version is available to them upon request. Where the conclusions are placed is a matter of the kind of report, the length of the report, and the wishes of those who will read it. More and more, over the years, our own reports tended toward the use of an "executive summary" at the beginning. People came to expect this and it became almost standard in later years. The only real trouble with this method is the fact that many of these executives tend not to read anything else. The main report itself is read only by those lower-echelon folk who have to do something about lesser matters. But even this trouble, if it really is a trouble, is not major. Everything that really is important is put up ahead, and it does not matter a great deal whether top management does or does not read the whole thing.

You need not "pander" to your readers.

Failure to write for the particular persons who must accept and act upon the report Your report should be written directly *to* the people who must act upon it. You know their foibles and weaknesses. You know their prejudices. You know what they really want to hear. Does it not make good sense to take all these very human characteristics into account when speaking to them through your report?

I am not saying to "pander" to your readers. Or to depart in any way from the truth. But there are ways of making the truth more palatable. Let us say that the manager of a division believes that one of his products is something the world has been waiting for. No research was done before the product was introduced, since he was so strongly in favor of it. Now it is not selling well, and your research shows why this is so: It does not do a very good job, and almost no one wants it. In other words, your report must show that the favorite new product of the division head is a real "dog" in the retail stores.

You may have a wild temptation to say it just like that in your report. Eschew such a temptation. Be very gentle to the division head—and lead him very carefully to the point where *he* concludes that the product never will sell. That becomes his own conclusion, and his face has been saved. And maybe you will be "saved," too. Too much directness would be like thumbing your nose at Muhammad Ali. These are not gestures that lead to a bright, new world.

Think, then, of all the people that will be reading your report. What is the best way of breaking the news to Mr. A? How can you best bring help to Mr. B? How can you pacify the highly emotional Mr. C? Be truthful, but also be discreet.

Too much directness would be like thumbing your nose at Muhammad Ali.

Failure to consider legal problems in certain terminology This needs emphasizing. These days, with Uncle Sam watching every business move, it is quite conceivable that some completely innocent statement of a junior executive could wind up in a court of law years later. It can happen that a very young and inexperienced junior executive studies a market and recommends buying a small competitor so that the merged companies can "dominate" the market. The young executive has no authority, and his or her recommendation is ignored and forgotten. But at a much later date, after the Federal Trade Commission has begun proceedings against a merger, the junior executive's note finds its way into the legal records. It was innocent, it was naïve, it was not followed, and it was forgotten; yet it becomes a document used against the company.

Before a study is "published" in any company, and later filed away, it should be scrutinized by someone in the legal office for all the "no-no's" that should not be put into print. Counsel is not interested in the study itself; all he wants to catch are the words that might lead to trouble if later used out of context and in a different situation.

How to Write a Strong Report

Early in the study you wrote, I hope, a tentative outline of what the final report would be like. If you did do this, you will be thankful. The next step will be to take this first outline and add to it. Certainly the intervening days of work have added much to your knowledge; the outline can now be expanded and made complete.

The study should be scrutinized by someone in the legal department for all the "no-no's" that should not be put into print.

The best help is what is sometimes called (I believe) a "sentence outline." Major and subheadings are placed just as they usually are, but the supporting topics are written in the form of phrases or sentences. In a sense, this is a half-report; it could almost be used as it is. Forcing yourself to do this helps to clear the mind regarding just exactly what you have and what you do not have.

The resulting outline would never win you a good grade in college, but it will prove most useful when actual writing of the final report gets under way.

One of the problems with the "fine writing" that was mentioned before is the long sentence. The simple declarative sentence is the best of all for a business report. Short, to the point, it never requires a second reading by anyone.

The thing that must always be remembered in writing a report for business people is their possible difficulty in reading. At a time when the results of college entrance examinations show less and less verbal ability, you really cannot assume that every important reader can, with ease, follow through all the clauses, phrases, and five-syllable words that you might like to use. Business ability is not necessarily correlated with high verbal ability. People who read easily and quickly will not be offended by a simple report. People who read with difficulty will be happy not to be required to work so hard.

After the report is written, it is wise to go through it, breaking up long sentences where possible, substituting short words for long ones, simplifying the mathematical presentations. I suppose what I have been saying again and again in different ways is: Do not make them work so hard. Make your report a joy to read, not a substitute for a sleeping pill.

Make your report a joy to read, not a substitute for a sleeping pill.

One hundred percent accuracy is just a dream. You simply cannot be completely sure that you are right. But an attitude that has sustained me through many moments of doubt can be simply stated: "At this moment, and in this company, you know more than anyone else about this particular problem." You really are the company expert in this matter—no matter how small it may be in the total scheme of company affairs. This attitude of authority will help you later, if a verbal presentation of recommendations is to be made. You never need to apologize to anyone if your research work was well done. And if you are that sure of yourself, others will have more faith in you. Your recommendations are more likely to be approved and acted upon. But be sure that you are as right as you possibly can be. Your research should be pure, unbiased, thorough, complete. Then, and only then, can you hold your head up and be impressive.

Especially when you reach the point of describing the most important findings and recommendations, it is extremely necessary to speak with authority. Short sentences, short words—but with authority. Do not ever forget that people tend to accept your own valuation of yourself. If you believe in what you have done, others will also believe. So say what you have to say with firmness, with authority, with no self-doubts in your voice or between the lines of a report.

Strength can come from anticipating objections and answering them before they arise. It does not take much sagacity to forecast what Joe, or Bob, or Jim will probably say. If you think for a moment, you can almost hear each of them voicing his prejudices, his habitual mode of thought. So it is only wise to have answers for such attitudes before they are brought out publicly. Thinking in advance about such objections will also force your research to be that much better and complete. If a sales manager believes that all new trends start on the West Coast, and you are investigating a "trendy" sort of an item, you know that he will have some criticism if you have neglected the West in your research.

Objections will differ for each company and its personnel. They will differ through the nature of the problem and the study. All that can be said here is that the wise person prepares himself for questions that a moment of thought tells him will arise.

A strong report will bring up alternative actions which might result from the findings. And it will show which is the best alternative, and why.

A strong report will openly discuss its shortcomings. This topic or that was not covered, and here is the reason. Perhaps it was a question of money or time. Perhaps a little beginning research showed that certain topics, geographic areas, or some other matters simply were not important for the purposes of the research. A great element of weakness is introduced when a cover-up is attempted to hide insufficient or poorly done research.

Once in awhile the nature of a study demands thought about the effect of your recommendations upon the competition. If your company does this or that, what counteraction are competitors going to take? This is another example of the need for forethought, some meditation. If we do this, and competition does that, how can we counter his counteraction? If we bring out product X, how soon are we likely to face competition? How many months must elapse before we begin to make a profit? What will happen to the price levels when competition appears?

Or, if the shopping center takes certain steps to attract more trade, what will the shopping center a mile away do about it? Will our actions simply mean that everyone spends more money with no resulting and lasting benefits? Or can we get such a jump on our competition that they can only catch up with great difficulty and expense? This kind of thinking distinguishes a good report from a weak one. At least the recognition of these problems, even if no answer is presently possible, will show that you have done your homework.

Presentation of a Report

Ordinarily a report that has taken a significant bit of time and money deserves more than just being mailed. Your report coming to someone else's desk in the morning will take its place alongside the usual pile of advertising, minor matters of all kinds, and crucial matters that demand instant action. Where will your report stand in this hierarchy?

At the very least, a finished report deserves personal delivery. The first receiver will be your own supervisor, of course. There is nothing worse than for him than to hear from *his* supervisor about a report that he has not yet seen. This is elementary, but such elementary mistakes continue to be made in the human business world. Once your own boss has received the report, and given permission for it to go to others, then a fistful can be taken on a personal delivery tour.

Much better, if at all possible, is an oral presentation of the study. Even if it is small and relatively unimportant to the company as a whole, it can still be presented to a few members of middle management.

An oral presentation can emphasize the importance of the findings and recommendations. It gives people their opportunity to voice objections and questions. And gives you the chance to answer them before they spread like a cancer. Only in the give and take of a meeting can you be reasonably sure that everyone understands exactly what is being said.

A finished report deserves personal delivery.

Insist on an oral presentation if you can, therefore, although a delay of a week or so may be necessary to get everyone in the same room at the same time.

An oral presentation should be accompanied by some imaginative visual material. It should never consist of having the report read out loud. In fact, it is a very good idea not to distribute the written report until the oral presentation has ended. With a report in front of them, many listeners will be looking at the end of the report when you want them to concentrate on how the study was done. Distributing the report in advance also causes some disruption from rattling of paper and turning of leaves. Members of the audience whisper to each other about points that are made, even about points that you have not made as yet, but which they have read at the end of the study.

Here are some suggestions for visual activities in connection with an oral presentation:

A podium is always good—it hides notes, shaking knees, and sweaty palms.

1. Make an outline of the points to be covered, but if at all possible, refrain from preparing anything at all that has to be read out loud. Notes can be used, perhaps on a 3 by 5 card held in your hand. A podium is always good—it hides notes. It may also hide your shaking knees and sweaty palms. However, a podium is not always possible. Your presentation may be in someone's office. But still use notes and not prepared material to be read out loud.

2. Avoid details, so far as possible. The listening group knows that it will get a written report. For the most part your presentation should cover only findings and recommendations—and these should be boiled down to the most important and most interesting.

3. It is always better to have two people present a study, or even three. Any audience will get tired of just one person unless that person is an unusually professional speaker. A change of voices, or a change in manner of speaking, will hold interest longer.

4. Hold any presentation to a maximum of an hour except under the most unusual circumstances. The span of human attention is short. The report can be read later. Your oral job is to interest and convince the listeners. Questions may run the meeting beyond the hour, but this is the option of the group, not of you. Many questions will show interest and success.

5. Without making an obvious thing of it, a good speaker can refer to some members of the audience by name. The more the speaker can involve particular people, the more likely he is of being convincing. "As John Jones said three months ago, we really do not know enough about the X market. Now, John, I think we can say we really know a little more." John is pleased at having his thinking publicly mentioned. "I'm glad that Joe told us about the man in Milwaukee. We really got a lot from him—and he sends his best regards, Joe." This can be carried too far, but a little can help ease the tension in the room, both for your listeners and yourself.

6. There are so many visual aids that it is impossible to mention them all. If time allows, slides can be prepared of some of the charts and tables in the report. Pictures of store displays, or parking difficulties, this sort of thing on slides can make a meeting much more interesting.

If slides are to be used, for the sake of everyone *please* practice ahead of the meeting. All my working life I have had to watch upside-down slides, projectors that were too far away, bulbs that burned out when no replacement was available.

Show your self-confidence in your presentation—you are the expert in this particular subject.

Now that we are talking about practice, let us continue. Any oral presentation should be practiced. It is absolutely stupid to get a group of executives together and then muff your presentation.

There is an almost aggressive spirit that you should develop for an oral presentation. As was said before, at this moment in time, in this company, you are the expert in this particular subject. Self-confidence is built upon such emotional foundations. Whether you have the full board of directors and all the officers in front of you, or just a few of middle management people, you are still *the expert in this problem, in this company, at this time.* It is very important that you remember this and pitch your presentation accordingly. The listeners will respect your self-confidence, and will more readily believe your findings.

Even what some of your listeners may call a "dog and pony show" can have its advantages. Corny as it may be, it can be amusing; the audience can be grateful for the respite in their dull days. And you will win respect for your presentation, partly because you are so plainly right, and partly because you amused your people.

There are various devices easily available in most cities, if your company does not already have them on hand. The projector which shows printed material, pages from the report, and so on, transferred to a film, is one. And, of course, a good slide projector.

There are felt boards which can grasp signs, or other paper objects. Using a felt board, it is possible to build your presentation toward a climax, adding one object after another. These additions and the movement of putting them up for view keeps interest from flagging.

It is not good to remain in one spot during the entire period. Move about, perhaps to the felt board, or to a blackboard to write something. Do not operate your own projection equipment, if you can possibly get out of it. Interest should center upon you and not upon your struggles with mechanical equipment.

Almost any presentation deserves a full-scale dress rehearsal. This would include going over everything you are going to say and cuing the machine operator about what he is to do.

Probably the major fault of most business presentations, such as we are discussing here is their tendency to drag. Keeping the pace up is vital if you are to grasp and hold the attention of your group.

Have you ever noticed, too, how people whom you know very well will change their voice and mannerisms when in front of a group? A much better relationship between speaker and audience will come about if the speaker is perfectly natural. Voices at a meeting take on a monotone characteristic. And this monotone becomes monotonous. For most of us, the best thing we can do is to speak in a perfectly normal way, as though we were talking over last Sunday's golf game.

All these things help to establish rapport with an audience. And without this rapport much of the meaning and importance of what is being said is lost. And following these suggestions is not at all difficult. Anyone can become an interesting speaker. First, of course, the person must have something to say. And you do. Second, some deliberate effort to form a good relationship with the group in front is necessary—and you can do it!

Who Should Get Copies of the Report? Who Should Be Invited to a Presentation?

The only reason these questions are asked here is to force you to think about them in the light of any study you do. Some agreement must be reached in advance.

Those who have a working interest in the study and who will make decisions on the basis of it will get copies and be invited to a presentation. But beyond that, there may be some persons who must be considered. People can be very touchy if they feel overlooked. Some are more likely to be emotional about these things than others. You will need advice.

The matter becomes especially touchy when the contents of the report are at least semiconfidential. The more people who see it, the more chance of a leak. Nevertheless, the head of another section of the company may still feel slighted if he fancies there is some relationship between the report and his own interests—and he is not included. Within reason, it is probably better to err on the side of inviting too many instead of too few.

Summary

This chapter has not talked about the "meat" of your study. It has only been about how to "cook" that meat. Some of the hints and suggestions are so plainly true that I wonder why I have had to sit through dull, boring, and everlasting meetings for so many years. And have had to read equally dull and boresome reports. A dull presentation of an important study is inexcusable, when it can so easily be turned into an interesting, sprightly, amusing, and thoroughly convincing performance. There is nothing wrong with a little laughter. Not jokes filched out of an old jokebook, but laughter that comes from hearing serious things told with just a little unexpected twist. If this chapter can keep anyone in any company from having to yawn and squirm while you make a bad presentation, then it has done its job. What I would like from you, the reader, is a promise that never, never, never will you be guilty of conducting a bad meeting. At least, promise that you will try your very hardest to be interesting.

THIRTEEN

How to Choose an Outside Research Firm, if Necessary

In spite of the devotion of this book to do-it-yourself research, there are times when it is wiser to turn to an outside marketing research firm. Almost certainly, every American and Canadian city of any size will have one or more such firms available. The kinds of firms can be roughly classified:

1. The local one- or two-person companies, which often call themselves names such as Joseph Jones and Associates. But do not let this bit of puffery put you off; many of these small companies are very able practitioners. Moreover, they can give personal attention by the principals that you would find almost impossible to have from a large national consultant.
2. Local companies that specialize in interviewing, either by telephone or by face-to-face work at such places as shopping malls. These companies may also work under contract for one or more large national consultants. Sometimes these local companies amount to little more than a skilled "supervisor" who employs interviewers when needed. But some local companies are equipped to provide facilities for group interviews, including all the paraphernalia (one-way windows, microphones in the ceiling, and so on).
3. Regional and national firms which offer a variety of services, of which marketing research is only one.
4. A host of specialists of one sort or another. These include packaging consultants, advertising consultants who profess to be experts on advertising measurement, personnel advisors who can help with the organization and development of sales forces, and so on.
5. Agencies whose particular speciality is engineering, electronics, etc., but who will do some marketing research on a new product or new process, if asked.

In fact, there are so many kinds of consultants that you may find yourself quite confused in choosing one, should you feel the need. The rest of this chapter will cover: (1) the reasons why an outside expert is sometimes needed and (2) ways of finding the right firm for your needs.

The reasons why some companies go outside for research are too numerous to be covered satisfactorily in one book. One major reason has been the inspiration for this volume: Marketing problems of some importance exist, and no one in the company feels capable of doing the marketing research. The science of research seems to be too esoteric for the ordinary businessperson, so problems are given to outside experts. Our thesis is that such a move often leads to unnecessary expense and wasted time; marketing people can do much marketing research themselves.

Most American and Canadian cities of any size have one or more kinds of research firms available.

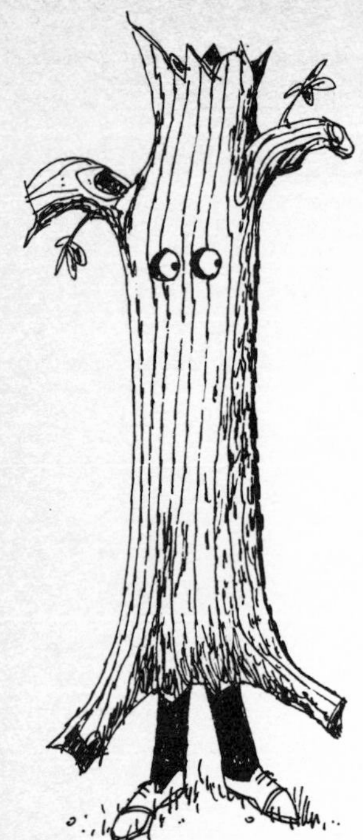

Sometimes there is a valid need for secrecy.

Here, however, are some of the reasons why it is occasionally an intelligent move to hire an outside consultant:

1. If, at the time that the research job needs doing, you have tasks which are far more important for the company. Under such circumstances it would be financially foolish to take your hours and days for this relatively small job, leaving larger decisions hanging. Only you and your supervisor can decide such a matter. Outside expertise may be available at a few thousand dollars. Ordinarily you could do the work less expensively, but this will not be true if it means holding up a project that promises an even greater return to the company. If such a situation exists, then going to an outside firm means actual dollar savings, and should be done. Just do not rationalize; if you can really do the job better and cheaper, then you should. Perhaps you can find the time, if you really try.
2. If there is a valid need for secrecy. The company's name is not to be connected with the research in any way. You are afraid of forewarning competitors of some impending move. Or you honestly think that the company name would bias research results far too much. Or biased results would lead to an untrue rating of your company compared with competition. Sometimes these reasons are valid and the expenditure of thousands of dollars on the outside can be justified.
3. If so much emotional heat has already been raised that few in your company would believe *anything* you found in research. A neutral outside party is needed to calm people down.

One balancing factor that must always be considered before you hire an outside firm is the need to educate these outside people concerning the nature of your company, your problem, and the quality of answers and facts that you need. This will take your time, or the time of someone with enough knowledge to do the teaching chore. Outside researchers must be selected, hired, taught, and supervised. Frequently there must be collaboration during the report-writing phase and the presentation to your management. All this time is money. The time costs must be added to the actual out-of-pocket expense of using the outsider.

There can be no guiding rule or formula. At certain times, weighing all the factors, it will seem wise to go outside for the needed work. Other occasions will require only your own personal efforts. All that I urge is that you be aware of all the costs involved and all the factors mentioned above, before making a decision to do it yourself or hire an outsider.

So much emotional heat may be raised that few in your company would believe anything *you found in research.*

How to Choose an Outside Firm

If, after weighing all these factors, the decision is to employ a professional research and consulting firm, there are ways of protecting yourself from hiring incompetent people.

At the beginning of this chapter there was a rather rough list of kinds of research firms that you can consider. Generally, and obviously, the large nationally known research companies are the most expensive. Although some will do relatively small jobs, this is not really their major interest. Again, circumstances will dictate events. If a large research firm feels that larger and more profitable studies can be expected in the future, and your small problem is an opening wedge, you might get first-class treatment. Without such hope of profit in the future, a large firm may assign a relatively new young employee to your job. The results of this person's work can then depend very much on the quality of your supervision.

Perhaps, for the kind of studies described here, a local firm (or one-person office) would be a better bet. Being close, this local agency may already know something about your company. The teaching job will then take less time. Constant supervision of the efforts will also be easier for you, since you can see the person more often. He may be only a local telephone call away from you.

There is one thing to be very careful about if you do decide to hire a large national firm. It is common for the first contacts to be made by someone with an impressive personality and an equally impressive title. Yes, he will say, we can do the job you want. Almost all the time, at this stage of negotiating, his firm is made to appear able to do any research or consulting job at all. And, no doubt, some of these companies really can do almost anything. But be very careful of such claims; it is much more likely that each company which you contact has a specialty, some one or two kinds of research where it is quite qualified. It has done other kinds of research, but has no particular expertise. If you hire such a company, you may find yourself doing half the work and almost all the thinking.

Moreover, the breezy vice-president disappears and his place is taken by people who are really no better able to do the job than you are. Or less able. Mr. Wonderful only makes his appearance again when it is time to present a shiny, big, wide-margin report, together with his bill. I know that I am being a little unfair to some top-notch consulting firms, but this second-rate treatment happens often enough so that you should be wary and watchful.

Mr. Wonderful, in an outside research firm, sometimes only makes his appearance at the first contact—and then again to present a shiny, big, wide-margin report, together with the bill.

Steps to take in seeking and employing a research firm These will vary according to your choice of "going national" or sticking with a local firm. But the principles are the same.

1. A good start is to get on the phone and talk to marketing people in other companies. They do not need to be in the same line of business—but preferably should be companies that would need similar outside help.

Once again (my old refrain), a thoroughly open and honest approach is the best. You have had little experience with research firms; you would like some suggestions for firms that could do the kind of work you want done.

Naturally you will pick a Southern firm for research in the South.

Describe in general terms the study that is needed: a telephone study, a personal interview study in the industrial field, an interview study in shopping malls, or whatever. Has the person you are talking with had experience in hiring outside firms? What company did a good job? Can these people list two or three good firms, in order of their own preference?

It is not wise to ask if any firm did a *bad* job. They may volunteer this information if they were badly burned recently. It is enough to have two or three suggestions of competent people in the field. If you are able to talk with a half-dozen to a dozen companies that have had experience with research firms, you will begin to get repetition of names. One research company may be named by half your respondents.

One advantage of talking over the telephone is to give the person on the other end of the wire an opportunity to say things that he probably would not put into writing. And, if you have a sharp ear, you can detect the degree of sincerity with which his recommendations are made.

If you believe that you want a local research person to do your work, the same telephoning procedure is in order, but your calls will be within the territory that the person covers. There are companies that confine their research activities to the Midwest for the most part. Others stick to the South. Naturally, if the South is where you want your research to be done, then it would be one of these local Southern companies that you would look for. And your first inquiring calls to other users of research will be in that area. If the people you telephone have had any experience with outside research at all, they almost always will be willing to give you some help.

A good person to ask for in larger firms is the head of the marketing research department. You can find that individual's name in the *Directory of Marketing Services and Membership Roster* of the American Marketing Association.[1] This book is published every few years; the latest edition is 1975. As the title says, some marketing research companies list themselves in a separate section of this roster. No effort is made by the association itself to rate these companies. Research companies are also listed geographically. In neither case is the list complete for the country. For the most part, these are firms that seek to do research on a national basis. Names of the companies and principals are given, together with addresses.

2. Second step, I believe, is to write letters to those research firms which were most frequently and enthusiastically recommended. In all fairness to these companies, make the first letter long enough to describe the nature of the research required and the time deadline. Even for local research people, a letter is better than a phone call. It gives them an opportunity for thought. Local people can be invited to phone you when convenient. Whether the

[1]See Figure 12.

Alphabetical Product Service Listings by Company

Sample—Firm name.
Address.
Phone number.
Persons to contact.
Services available.
Specialty.
Page number of advertisement.

ACKER RETAIL AUDITS, INC.
1185 Avenue of Americas
New York, N.Y. 10036
(212) 757 4213
Henry Brenner, Chm. of Bd.
Jack Acker, Pres.
Raymond Capozzi, V.P.

Specializing in a complete line of in-store research services including trend audits, projectable audits, controlled sales experiments, computerized store matching procedures, distribution studies, product age surveys, national product purchasing system. Fully automated data processing facilities, statistical and design consulting, analysis and report writing. Personalized Service—Problem Oriented.

ACTION MARKETING RESEARCH, INC.
103 Park Avenue
New York, N.Y. 10017
(212) 889 3565
Phyllis Schwartz, Pres.

Quality oriented, providing complete marketing research services, from study design through analysis, or any part thereof. National field coverage with malls in all major markets. We work closely with clients in all aspects of study to ensure actionable results.

ADCOM RESEARCH LTD.
95 Berkeley Street.
Toronto, ON M5A 2W8 CANADA
(416) 869 1912
A.T. Gamble, Pres.
E.R. Lyons, Exec. V.P.
D.R. Longden, Sales Mgr.

Permanent centralized and supervised telephone facilities in 22 cities from Newfoundland to B.C. Over 150 phones. Adcom tests concepts, commercials (DAR's) and the effectiveness of campaigns, also group interviewing, tracking and other ad hoc studies. Adcom operates the most complete, accurate and sophisticated telephone field operation in Canada.

ADMAR RESEARCH COMPANY
300 Park Avenue South
New York, N.Y. 10010
(212) 677 1700
Henry D. Ostberg, Pres.
David M. Braverman, Sr. V.P.
Robert S. Wikowitz, Exec. V.P.
Ruth Y. Weiner, V.P.
Jeffrey Harris, Sr. Proj. Dir.
Seymour Fleischman, Sr. Proj. Dir.

919 N. Michigan Avenue
Chicago, IL 60611
(312) 266 1366
Gail A. Kennedy, V.P.
Stephen R. Grove, V.P.

Admar is a full-service marketing research organization. We have developed several exclusive research techniques, including: PRE/dict, which estimates the trial level of a new product before test marketing; START, a system for measuring the repurchase rate of test brands; and MAX, a method for evaluating the growth potential of new and existing products.
To insure maximum field supervision, the company maintains field offices nationwide. The firm also has extensive research facilities, including its own computer and processing department, central interviewing facilities and audio/visual equipment.
Admar specializes in obtaining actionable information, reporting results in easy-to-read formats and offering unique follow-up procedures.

(see ad page 4)

ARIZONA INSTITUTE FOR RESEARCH
6411 East Brian Kent
Tucson, AZ 85710
(602) 296 6186
Charles Lupu, Ph.D. Pres.
Marian Lupu, V.P.

Field interviewing, management consultants, market research and analysis, consumer panels, surveys and testing. Specialty: Market and Social Research.

ASI/BEHAVIOR SCIENCE CORPORATION
7655 Sunset Boulevard
Los Angeles, CA 90046

FIG. 12 Page from the *Directory of Marketing Services and Membership Roster*, available from the American Marketing Association, 222 S. Riverside Plaza, Chicago, Ill. 60606. *(Courtesy of American Marketing Association.)*

recommended firms are local, regional, or national, you will get responses to your inquiries. Not always do the companies want your business. But a negative attitude is most rare. The odds are great for a positive response. Here is the second step of weeding: Some of the responses will clearly indicate a lack of knowledge of your field, of the kind of problem and how to go about solving it. What they are really saying is that, yes, they want the job, and they expect to learn how to do it as they go along.

Other responses will show a very hardheaded grasp of the problem. It is clear that these people have done this type of work before. Your kind of product is sold in these types of market. We have skilled interviewers who contact such markets constantly. And so on. Lacking specifics, they can give you only a general idea of how the problem might be investigated. But their experience shows through between the lines. If you are fortunate, at this point you have two or three research companies that sound very good to you. Their responses have been sound and complete. They have given you a "ball park" figure for what the research would cost, and the time it would take to complete and have a report in your hands. Local people may call and want to come in with their proposals. By all means let them do so.

3. The third step is to interview the firms which have lasted through these weeding-out procedures. Local people can come to your office. If nonlocal people are not too far away, it is better for you to visit them, just to see what kind of a shop they have, what kind of people work there, and whether there is a real air of success in the atmosphere. These visits can be extremely revealing. The principal can look like a Harvard Business School type, but all his assistants could look like members of a motorcycle club.

The principal can look like a Harvard Business School type, but his assistants look like members of a motorcycle club.

One very important thing for you to settle (and for the research firm to settle) is whether there is compatibility. You simply must be able to get along; the research study cannot be turned into competition to see who will look smarter. And the research firm must be willing to allow you to take some small part in its work. In fact, this is one question that often makes a research person gag a bit, but reveals a good deal about his own feeling of security. If he is perfectly willing to accept my services in a small part of the field work, then I always think he is secure and probably knows what he is doing. If you do ask this, however, make it perfectly clear that you will in no way dictate his findings or his recommendations. That is what you are paying him for, and that is his responsibility.

In the past I have asked if someone in my department might take a small city, or a state, and do a little work under the supervision of the research firm. I cannot say that this was universally pleasing; but the response of the firm was usually quite revealing.

4. And finally, when you have narrowed your list to one or two research companies, it is good to invite each to visit you in your own office. Now is the

time to begin working out final details. What will be the cost? What does this figure include? All travel, rented cars, etc.? Or is this separate? Who will do the actual work? Are the interviewers (if this is the kind of study) really competent for the job, or are they bored persons looking for a few extra dollars? What is the background of all the people who will work on the study? I cannot tell you all the questions to ask, but there is no reason not to bore in, seeking any possible weakness that would later lead to a useless report. Most business people will probably not agree with me on one small point. I never would allow these research companies to buy my lunch, even after one had been chosen. I felt much more in command of the situation if the lunch and drinks (if any) were on me. Otherwise there is some small feeling of obligation—unexpressed perhaps, but still there.

5. When one firm has been chosen, it is advisable to have a written agreement, spelling out in some detail what can be expected, and when. Now is the time to bring up all the little things that may cause trouble later on. Does the research company plan to use tape recorders, and are you against them? Have it out, and reach a decision. Does the research firm plan to use both men and women? If all calls are to be made at coal mines, you may be a male chauvinist pig, and say that this is a man's job. It is surprising how such specifics can arise to haunt you at a later date. The time to lay them right out on the desk is when final agreements are being made.

Even such things as the number of reports, how they are to be bound, the form of the report, and so on are worthy of discussion and agreement. If you know that expensive reports with great wide margins are a "pet peeve" of some of your executives, it would be kind to tell the researchers that fact ahead of time. There are executives that will not believe a report unless it includes the other coast, the South, Ohio, Chicago, or some other place. Everything else being equal, these places can be included, and everyone is happy.

Possible Pitfalls in the Choice and Use of an Outside Firm

In spite of all that was said above, there are ways that things can go wrong. Whether you have hired a one-person or a large national firm, you must not lose sight of the fact that these people are probably strangers to you and to your company. After awhile, it is possible that you can build a regular relationship with one research company, but at the time we are now discussing these people are really outsiders. You may have lunch with them a number of times, have some drinks, make small talk, and even do some kidding and chaffing, but intimate knowledge of each other's work is not yet present. So projects that have begun in the best type of friendly atmosphere may end in distrust and hostility. If this state of affairs should happen, it will be as much your fault as the fault of the firm you have hired.

Recognizing this possibility, I would like to take a few pages of this book to cover some details of a good and continuing working relationship.

One of the worst things you can do is to give an assignment to a company and then leave it entirely alone until close to the deadline date for reporting. By that time it could have gone down the wrong road so far that no possibility exists for return. From the very beginning of a research study assigned to an outside firm, therefore, it is necessary to have contacts at reasonably frequent intervals. It is not an absolute necessity, but often a way of self-discipline to set up a written schedule of meetings and progress reports.

If more than one person has been assigned to your particular research study, it would be good for you to know and talk with each one. This may not be possible because of time and geography, but it is a goal to be aimed at. Certainly the principals should be known. Though your first and major contact person at the research company thoroughly understands your problem, it is quite possible that directions and procedures are changed a bit and watered down as they sift to lower working echelons.

A contract price has certainly been agreed upon at the beginning. Usually this is quoted as a dollar figure, plus or minus a small percentage. But there is always the chance that more money will be needed to guarantee a good job. Neither you nor the firm you employed may have foreseen complications that require further interviews or more traveling. By keeping in frequent contact with the research company, you can be aware of such a situation arising. If no further money is going to be available, the research procedure may have to be changed a little to get as good a study as possible without going over budget. Not an ideal study, no doubt, but one that produces usable results.

Do a little research on your own; otherwise you'll be flying blind.

Whether or not you work directly with the research company, you *should* do a little research of your own. Otherwise you will be flying completely blind when it comes to making a judgment on the quality of work submitted and the validity of the recommendations. The actual interviewers, in an industrial interview study, for example, may have been so busy with their tape recorders and their prepared questions that they missed several extremely important leads. If you have time to do some research yourself, you may easily find matters that should be a part of the professional study.

Suddenly a new way of thinking about the matter unfolds, or some unexpected positive or negative opinions. Even in shopping center interviews this can happen. The parking situation appears to be much more important than you had thought. Or the quality and price level of merchandise being stocked by the several stores shows itself to be the wrong level for the type of trade desired. Your early evidence demonstrates that more emphasis should be put on this factor.

As the research work goes along, since everyone is quite human, there will be misunderstandings. Nerves will jump, and emotions will rise. The research company is more aware of these bumpy roads than you are, and is more ready to cope with them. You will have to discipline yourself, since a good research firm will consider that it was hired for *its* ability. It will not be pleased to work entirely under your direction. It will be happy to accept suggestions—up to a point. But always there is that point beyond which you should not go, if you really want a professional job. This advice applies only if you have hired a complete professional, however. If you have employed a firm which provides basic interviewing services and makes no attempt to analyze the results or make recommendations, you not only may, but will have to, do all the thinking and make all the decisions.

As research proceeds, nerves will jump . . .

How to Recognize Good or Poor Work

If you have done everything recommended in this chapter, including a little of the field research work yourself, then it is unlikely that the final study will be poor. You will have supervised so well, and so frequently, that you know what will be in the final report and know that it is good.

Beyond that, there is a certain feel for completeness and adequacy. You are thoroughly familiar with your own industry, or your own business area, and should be able to tell, just from how the report is written, whether the research firm has dug deeply enough to know what it is talking about. Again, this applies only to commissioned work that includes analysis and recommendations. In such a report, if the stated facts somehow seem out of balance, a feeling of reality does not come through, or there is no "thrill of recognition" as you read the words, then you should worry a little. Before the report is presented to higher management, it will be wise to go back to the beginning and recheck all the procedures. This kind of a result at the end of a field study by a reputable firm is highly unlikely. But be careful; your own reputation also rides on what is recommended to management.

. . . and emotions will rise.

Specific Suggestions about Where to Go for Help

There are two associations that might be able to suggest names of research firms in your area:

Marketing Research Association, Inc.
409 No. Franklin
Chicago, Illinois 60610
(312) 222-0079

American Marketing Association
222 S. Riverside Plaza
Chicago, Illinois 60606
(312) 648-0536

Neither association would be happy to give you only a single name. Both, under proper circumstances, may be able to suggest several companies that are near you and that can presumably do the job that you want done.

Here is a list of competent firms in different areas of the country. By no means is this complete. There are many other companies of equal ability, I am sure. These happen to be groups that I have had experience with, or about which I have heard favorable comments.

California

Wade West Associates, Inc.
13148 Saticoy Street
North Hollywood 91605
(213) 983-1727

Field Research Corp.
234 Front Street
San Francisco 94111

MSI International
3440 West 8th Street
Los Angeles 90005

Stanford Research Institute
333 Ravenswood Avenue
Menlo Park 94025

Colorado

Colorado Market Research Services, Inc.
2149 South Grape
Denver 80222

Connecticut

Karen Associates, Inc.
10 Karen Road
West Hartford 06117

Palshaw Measurement, Inc.
411 Pequot Road
Southport 06490

Trendex, Inc.
15 Riverside Avenue
Westport 06490

Illinois

Market Facts, Inc.
100 South Wacker Drive
Chicago 60606

A. C. Neilsen
2101 Howard Street
Chicago 60645

Elrick and Lavidge, Inc.
10 South Riverside Plaza
Chicago 60606

Bee Angell and Associates, Inc.
233 East Ontario
Chicago 60611

Quality Controlled Services, Inc.
Suite 14, 1500 No. Skokie Blvd.
Northbrook 60062

Indiana

Walker Research, Inc.
2809 East 56th Street
Indianapolis 46220

Kansas

Quality Controlled Services, Inc.

8739 W. 95th Street
Overland Park 66212

(There are "Quality" offices in a number of cities. Locations of these may be obtained at this address.)

Massachusetts

Audits and Surveys, Inc.
450 King Street
Cohasset 02025

Michigan

Ducker Research Inc.
4050 W. Maple Road
Birmingham 48010

Market Opinion Research, Inc.
28 West Adams
Detroit 48226

Minnesota

Molgren Research Associates
6480 Wayzata Blvd.
Minneapolis 55426

Missouri

C.I.S. Market Research
Suite 205 E., Promenade Balcony
8600 Ward Parkway
Kansas City 64114

New Jersey

Clare Brown Associates, Inc.
Garwood Mall
350 South Avenue
Garwood 07027

Erhart-Babic Associates, Inc.
120 Route 9-W
Englewood Cliffs 07632

Opinion Research Corporation
N. Harrison Street
Princeton 08540

Marketing Information Systems, Inc.
530 Main Street
Fort Lee 07024

Gallup and Robinson
Research Park
Princeton 08540

New York

Richard Manville Research, Inc.
211 East 43rd Street
New York 10017

Cole Y. Bender CBA Research
369 Lexington Avenue
New York 10017

Callahan Research Associates
31 East 28th Street
New York 10016

North Carolina

W. H. Long Marketing, Inc.

122 Keeling Rd. East
Greensboro 27410

Ohio

Burke Marketing Research, Inc.
1529 Madison Road
Cincinnati 45206

Great Lakes Marketing Associates
4334 West Central
Toledo 43615

Texas

Southwest Research, Inc.
Suite 126, 1750 Regal Row
Dallas 75235

Ontario, Canada

Southam Marketing Research Services
1450 Don Mills Road
Don Mills, Ontario M3B 2X7

Even Maine, where industrial activity is low, has a number of research firms with interviewers available.

Some of the above have staffs available for actual interviewing. Others plan and carry out research projects, employing one or more interviewing firms for the actual field work. The trouble with giving *any* names is that there are so many good firms that are left out for lack of space. In Illinois alone, for example, there are well over fifty firms that are in the marketing research business, mostly in Chicago. Even Maine, where industrial activity is low, has a number of research firms with interviewing people available.

So the best thing to do is consult the Yellow Pages, or get in touch with the Marketing Research Association or the American Marketing Association. From these sources you can at least get a list of names that can eventually be weeded down to a final choice.

Summary

For the relatively small problems faced with such frequency by the readers of this book, employing a professional research firm will be a rare event. In that sense, this chapter has been superfluous. But it will happen now and again that work does have to be put out. Great mistakes can be made, large amounts of money can be wasted, if the choosing, hiring, and supervising of the outside firm is not well done. For the most part, a poor job from a professional firm can be blamed on the company employing it. Unfortunately, however, many research firms are too likely to claim too much. They want a constant flow of jobs coming in, and are prone to overrate their own abilities. So it is up to you, if it comes about that you need outside help, to take extreme care before you sign a contract. If you hire a good firm which specializes in one marketing field, but would like to spread out a little by doing a different type of work, then the burden of proof is entirely on you when you tell management that this is the firm you want.

Good luck!

FOURTEEN

Company "Politics": How to Get Your Research Taken Seriously

If the president of a corporation takes note of a gathering storm on the horizon, somehow that storm seems to be much more serious and important than a mail boy's observation of the same phenomenon. A statement of belief or of fact cannot be separated from the speaker. The president's belief is more believable, the facts he uses seem more factual—just because of his long period of success and because he has clearly been right more often than wrong, or he would not be president.

This is an oversimplified illustration of an important matter: It is not enough for you to do good research, or have good research done. And it is not enough to produce a well-written report and presentation. Your own personality, your own record of success, and the validity of your past recommendations will all be in the room where you are describing your findings.

The words "company politics" are used more often (although probably not *practiced* more often) among middle-management and lower-management people. The expression is often pejorative, implying something not quite aboveboard. Something that would probably not be done by upstanding, honest citizens.

This is nonsense, of course. Not because dirty tricks are never practiced in companies, as well as in national political parties, but because really *dirty* tricks are so scarce.

People who do not advance in a company are likely to use that great mental aspirin tablet called "rationalizing." And people whose recommendations are viewed with suspicion, even though backed by marketing research, often ease their pain with the same remedy. The fact is, of course, that those who succeed, those whose recommendations are most likely to be accepted, are people who have built up a belief in themselves. What they have done, they have done well. What they have recommended has usually turned out to be right.

And when they see a storm coming up in the west, somehow the clouds look darker and more threatening.

The cases where the president's son is "promoted" from the factory to a vice-presidency after two weeks of training are rare. No firm is full of holy do-gooders who love all their brothers; rather, it is a fight all the way for the person who wants to go to a top position.

But a great part of this fight is being right most of the time. It is doing a little bit better in every job than anyone really expected. So that a person of this caliber comes to mind immediately when a vacancy occurs in a higher position.

This sounds almost too goody-goody, I know. Exceptions in any company are obvious, but, in general, the statement is true that the best people do get

People who do not advance are likely to use that great mental aspirin tablet called "rationalization."

ahead. They are not necessarily lovable, charming folks. You may suspect that their mothers kept the neighbors awake by barking all night. But you have to give them one thing: They have a reputation of hard and good work, and of being right.

It is necessary to say these things because you have to assess yourself and how you stand with others, in the planning of a study, in the thoroughness of its execution, and in its presentation.

If you have determined, as I hope, that marketing research will be used more often in your work, you will have to give serious thought to your own image and how to improve it. How can you most easily bring people around to your way of thinking? How can you make your research reports more likely to be accepted and acted upon? What people think of you has a lot to do with the answer.

So I will not apologize for putting this chapter into a book on marketing research. If there are steps that you can take that will make your recommendations more acceptable to management, you should begin taking these steps immediately. The combination of personal and mental characteristics that leads to success has never been defined or measured properly. So, even though you may do all the things talked about in this chapter, unhappily we cannot guarantee the presidency for you. All that can be said is that good steps of preparation will help the acceptance of your research. And if you build up a history—either through research or just natural ability—of successful recommendations and actions, your chances of promotion will certainly be enhanced.

But primarily look on the following suggestions as ways to help make sure that your marketing research is taken seriously—and acted upon if possible.

You may win a halo in Heaven for going down with a lost cause—but not in modern business.

First, as I probably said a dozen times during the writing of this book, it is good to get others involved. A research job backed by a team is much more likely to be accepted than is a one-person job. It is much more likely to be done well and thoroughly, and your presentation is just as likely to be taken seriously and followed. All these things are what you want, so do not hesitate to ask advice. Give in gracefully if some of your planning is shown to be wrong. Seek advice on what the various findings can mean. Giving up a bit of your own precious "rightness" can ultimately benefit your cause.

If you are convinced that your research is correct and you have lined up a little team of backers in advance, it is smart to be firm in your presentation. Lacking other evidence, people tend to take you at your own valuation. A record of bad recommendations and poor success will require twice as much evidence, twice as much effort in your presentation. Only you know where you stand in your own organization. I must assume here that the research was done carefully and thoroughly; all you need now is to convince others of this fact.

You may win a brighter halo in Heaven for going down with a lost cause.

No halo is passed out in modern business for taking part in glorious failure. Research cannot save a product, or a marketing action that is obviously incorrect. There are many instances where it is not sensible to become associated with a project. And research should not even be considered when final failure looms. At some point, impossible of description here, nothing can save a situation. Not research, or even prayer. Sometimes the product or project is not yet buried, but for all practical purposes it has died. This is no place for you or your research. Field work can only confirm what is transparently true: that someone is the possessor of a "dog." And the dog can be a bad product, a bad idea, a poorly located store or shopping center. There are times when you will be smart to do what a friend of mine recently did when he bought a new car. It was a real, honest, brightly colored lemon. So he traded it after seven months, took his licking, and now has the car he wants. He did not need to study his situation for months and months to know what he had in his garage: a great, big lemon-on-wheels.

Too much humor will make you seem a mental lightweight.

Humor has its place in life, even business life. But too much humor will make you seem a mental lightweight. Your research project—and *you*—must be taken seriously. My suggestion would be to be very careful about the use of humor at any place in marketing research. Indeed, even your job and your chances of promotion can be seriously endangered by allowing yourself to become too much of a likeable joker. The research you do is designed to make money for the company, or to keep it from losing money. This is a serious matter, and you will be strengthened by treating it so.

The research that you do should be very much the way you do your own job: always a little better than people had expected. More facts, better evidence, wise conclusions, workable recommendations. This is the stuff of which success is built.

"Using" others has a bad sound. But gratefully and gracefully allowing other people to help you is only a different way of doing the same thing. Without the help and good will of other people, the job of selling research, or of getting ahead, is much more difficult. No one can make it entirely on his own—even if he owns the company. The need for teamwork in doing research, or in doing the regular work of the day, is so obvious that one wonders why it is so difficult for many people to cooperate.

A young person and an older person make a winning combination.

Part of any person's job in any company is the requirement of training a successor. Many are the people who have lost out on promotion possibilities because they had not prepared their own replacements. Research is a fine training opportunity—in fact one of the best ways through which young people can get management's "point of view." If at all possible, then, use an up-and-coming young man or woman to do some of the research and to back you up in the presentation. A young person and an older person together make a winning combination. Not necessarily May and September. Perhaps May and July would be more accurate. But in any case, there is a difference in age that can be used for a number of good reasons. Aside from the training aspects of research, an attractive youngster can add a helpful bit of showmanship to the final presentation.

To be avoided assiduously is the temptation to make research sound mysterious. Here is a place where a little knowledge can truly be a dangerous thing. Actually, as you know by now, there is nothing mysterious about any research that you will be doing. Get everyone into the act; ask for suggestions about the questionnaire or the interviewing procedures. Ask for suggestions from others with more experience about how a presentation can best be made. Get everyone rooting for your success in this particular research program. And then again and again in the future. Until no one expects anything *but* success for you. In that way you can do a good job for the company and for yourself—a nice combination of purposes.

All these things are true, even if you are connected with a store in a shopping mall and are merely conducting some customer factfinding. You still have to present the study to someone, and your success, or lack of it, will go on your record in the minds of other people.

At the risk of being considered an old fuddy-duddy by my readers, I venture courageously into the question of dress. It is my personal opinion that the man or woman who confidently expects success *dresses* that way. I am not advocating the return of the "sincere" grey flannel double-breasted suit. Or the equally sincere little black business dress for women. (With fashions going in circles, by the time this is in print these things may be back again.) I do think that the man or woman who wishes to impress others will dress conservatively to "look" successful. In fashion advertising, I suppose this would be called the "successful look." In the presentation of a research report, appearance plays a factor, whether you think it right or not. If the research and the report are accepted, then you want to be accepted with it, so that people who matter will begin to think of you as promotable material. There are exceptions, naturally. Some men or women are so very good at their jobs that they can come to work in tennis shoes and still get ahead. But most of us are not so fortunate, and must pay some attention to the effect we make upon others.

The man or woman that confidently expects success dresses that way.

I have sometimes observed that the man who suddenly sports a beard, and comes to work in bright jackets and slacks, is unconsciously announcing that he has given up hope of further advancement. This is not true of the young man who has just been hired from college. But I think there is truth in it for the man who has been around for awhile and suddenly blossoms like a field of lilies. In your research, in your presentation, and in your job, therefore, my own inclination is to urge you to look like you expect the next step up the ladder—and soon.

You may not really expect to step on up the ladder. Subconsciously you may not even *want* to do so. Most of us are not really joking when we say that we would like the salary of the president, but could not stand his life. There is a special place alongside angels for the man or woman who can recognize his or her limitations, and be content with a place on the lower rungs. But even so, for the sake of the job and the research, it is just good common sense to be serious, to look serious, and to lend a personal importance to the study.

Summary

Let me extend a welcome to those who have stayed with me through the book. It is my most sincere hope that you have decided to try some marketing research of your own. As a man who heads a large professional research firm (and who wishes to remain anonymous for obvious reasons) said to me the other day, marketing research can only get to be more and more expensive in the future. The small jobs that used to be done to help decide small problems just cannot be done except on a do-it-yourself basis. He recognizes that this book does not compete with him. Larger jobs that require expert knowledge will more likely come his way if more marketing people have come to accept the discipline of research. So I close with his blessing; we will all be better off if more business decisions are based upon the science of factfinding. You can do your part.

Index